AN INTRODUCTION
TO THE HISTORY
OF PRINTING TYPES

An Introduction to

THE
HISTORY
OF PRINTING
TYPES

*An Illustrated Summary
of the Main Stages in the Development
of Type Design from 1440
up to the Present Day
An Aid to Type Face Identification*

BY GEOFFREY DOWDING

THE BRITISH LIBRARY
&
OAK KNOLL PRESS

First published 1961
by Wace & Company Ltd

This edition published 1998
jointly by The British Library
96 Euston Road
St Pancras
London NW1
UK
and Oak Knoll Press
414 Delaware Street
New Castle
DE 19720
USA

by kind permission of Wace UK Ltd

ISBN 0 7123 4577 9 (UK cased edition)
ISBN 0 7123 4563 9 (UK paperback edition)
ISBN 1 884718 43 4 (US cased edition)
ISBN 1 884718 44 2 (US paperback edition)

Library of Congress Cataloging-in-Publication Data
Dowding, Geoffrey, 1911–
    An introduction to the history of printing types : an illustrated
summary of the main stages in the development of type design from
1440 up to the present day : an aid to type face identification / by
Geoffrey Dowding.
        p.   cm.
    Originally published: Clerkenwell [London]: Wace, c1961. With new
foreword.
    Includes bibliographical references (p.   ) and index.
    ISBN 0-7123-4563-9 (British Library : pbk.). — ISBN 1-884718-43-4
(Oak Knoll Press : hard). — ISBN 1-884718-44-2 (Oak Knoll Press :
pbk.)
    1. Type and type-founding—History.   I. Title.
Z250.A2D6   1997
686.2'21—dc21   97-43152
                                                                          CIP

British Library Cataloguing in Publication Data
A CIP record is available from The British Library

Printed in England by Wace Specialist Print
Burgess (Abingdon)

He had pitched, as I have said, against the bulwarks

I met Geoffrey Dowding once. He was checking a page proof. He fin-ished by scribbling at the bottom, 'Straighten up'. The printer I was with said, 'But Geoffrey, you didn't check that, how do you know it's not straight?' 'Never is, is it?' GD replied.

With today's film output, casually locked-up formes of type are not one of our worries, and on the whole one need not shed many tears for the demise of letterpress printing. And, in contrast to today's CD-Roms, metal type required a lot of storage space. Nonetheless Wace, like the other big trade typesetting firms of the 50s and 60s, held an enormous range, both as matrices for hot metal composition and as metal fonts for hand-set display. They produced a cabinet of type sheets showing the full alphabet, with its italic and bold, and including figures and ligatures, of every type and every size held. Four or usually seven lines of text (taken from *Treasure Island*) were also shown set solid and leaded, in all sizes from 6pt to 14pt. Each sheet was 9½×14½ inches. The full range of Baskerville, for instance, required six of these. Periodically augmented by new additions, the complete cabinet was given free to regular customers. To such users, re-reading that imagin-atively chosen extract from *Treasure Island* summons up a vanished era.

A look at those specimen sheets usefully reminds us how subtly or, sometimes, how extensively, the design of metal types was modified in different sizes in order to look the same. Although we have learnt to live with it—meanwhile availing ourselves of the many advantages of digi-tal filmsetting—the use of one master for all sizes is one of the more re-grettable developments of the last 25-30 years. It comes second only to the badly-handled adaptation of many PostScript types, a large number perpetrated by producers who should know better. The meticulous Dowding would, with one good heave, have tumbled them overboard.

This book, originally published in 1961, shows metal types. But it is a history book, and history does not change. (Well, not much.) Over the years, I have found its admirably concise arrangement immensely use-ful. Since much of the material comes from what was then the British Museum, and is now The British Library, it is fitting that the Library has re-issued it, and made it available to a new and wider public.

ALAN BARTRAM

10 ABCDEFGHIJKLMNOPQRSTUVWXYZ&ÆŒ
abcdefghijklmnopqrstuvwxyzæœfffifflffifflffl£1234567890.,;:-?!'"()

He had pitched, as I have said, against the bulwarks, where he lay like some horrible, ungainly sort of puppet; life-sized, in-deed, but how different from life's colour or life's comeliness! In that position, I could easily have my way with him; and as the habit of tragical adventures had worn off almost all my terror for the dead, I took him by the waist as if he had been a sack of bran, and, with one good heave, tumbled him overboard.

He had pitched, as I have said, against the bulwarks, where he lay like some horrible, ungainly sort of puppet; life-sized, in-deed, but how different from life's colour or life's comeliness! In that position, I could easily have my way with him; and as the habit of tragical adventures had worn off almost all my terror for the dead, I took him by the waist as if he had been a sack of bran, and, with one good heave, tumbled him overboard.

THREE POINT LEADED

TO
ALFRED FORBES JOHNSON
HISTORIAN
OF PRINTED BOOKS
WHOSE HELP MADE THIS
WORK POSSIBLE

Acknowledgements

I am indebted, above all, to Mr A. F. Johnson of the British Museum for his help with this book, particularly for reading and correcting the text, for assistance with the choice of illustrations, and for counsel at all times so readily and freely given.

Likewise my grateful thanks are due to Sir Sydney Carlyle Cockerell for wise advice on a number of things connected with the contents of this book, for his encouragement, and for his help in choosing from his library the Venetian MS an example from which is shown on page 20.

Dr B. Frans Enschedé was kind enough to send me the material for the examples on pages 74, 119, 120, 152 and 153 and to settle a number of queries on the decorated types of Jacques and Matthais Rosart. The safes of the Caslon Letter Foundry revealed some of their treasures to me. For the illustrations on pages 141, 151, 159, 164, 165, 166, 168, 172, 174, 178, 182, 184, 194 & 196 and for the type from which the heading on page 97 was reproduced I am obliged to Sir Francis Stephenson, Mr James B. Blake and Mr Charles Stephenson, each of whom have given most generously of their time, assistance and advice.

I am also indebted to Professor A. Ruppel, Director of the Gutenberg Museum, Mainz, for sending me the illustration shown on page 4, to M. Arnoult of the Imprimerie Nationale for so generously making available many examples of the work of the celebrated French type-cutters of the seventeenth, eighteenth and nineteenth centuries and for giving me permission to reproduce those shown on pages 67, 78, 88, 89 & 90.

I would like to thank the Trustees of the British Museum for permitting me to reproduce the illustrations on pages 6, 9, 10, 11, 13, 15, 16, 23, 25, 27, 28, 30, 33, 34, 35, 36, 37, 38, 39, 40, 44, 46, 48, 49, 50, 52, 54, 56, 57, 58, 60, 66, 69, 70, 71, 72, 77, 79, 80, 81, 82, 86, 93, 95, 108, 112, 114, 116, 118, 121, 122, 123, 124, 126, 128, 135, 136, 137, 139, 144, 146, 149, 154, 162 and 173; and also to acknowledge the help given to me by Mr George Painter, and the staff of the North Library; by Mr D. H. Turner, Assistant Keeper of the Department of Manuscripts and members of the staff of that Department, and by the staff of the Print Room.

It gives me pleasure to thank Mr James Mosley for making it possible for me to examine quietly a number of books in the St Bride Foundation Printing Library and also for making some of these precious volumes available for photography(see illustrations on pages 62,68,83,92,94,96, 125,130,132,133,142,150,151,156,158,160,170,176,180,182,186,188, 190 & 192); Mr A.W.Wheen and the staff of the Library of the Victoria and Albert Museum for help and for permission to print the illustration on page 42; Mr Edward K. Timings of the Public Record Office for most helpful assistance (the example on page 138 is reproduced by permission of the Controller of H.M. Stationery Office and is Crown Copyright); and also Mr V.C. Elliot of The Mediaeval Academy of America for allowing me to show the example on page 18 from Professor Rand's book; and Mrs Irene Wellington for generously allowing me to reproduce the only writing sheet she produced for her students.

Others to whom I am grateful for help or counsel are Mr B. S. Cron, Ann and Paul Dowding, Monsieur G. Chardon of Deberny & Peignot, Dr James Eckman of Rochester, Minnesota, Priscilla Johnston, Mr Jan van der Ploeg of the American Type Founders Co, Mr Walter Soldan, Mrs K.Wightwick, the authorities at Quedlinberg for the search made for an MS in the Carolingian hand, and to the Monotype Corporation for the setting on page 100 and for the special sorts appearing in the text of this book.

My brother Howard's constant help in all the stages of the production of this book has been invaluable; & I am again indebted to my publishers, and in particular to their Managing Director, Mr Edward Sykes, for the complete freedom he has given me in producing this book and for his forbearance once again in the matter of production time.

And for a third time it gives me great pleasure to thank Mr E. J. Goddard whose keyboard operators & compositors have maintained in this book the high standards evidenced in the settings of the first two volumes in this series. Such standards of composition could not have been achieved without his unremitting surveillance. My warm thanks are

Acknowledgements

also due to the Taurus Press for printing difficult material so splendidly.

I would also like to thank Mr B. E. Freeman for the excellence of his photography; my friend Peter Gates for giving me the original of the title-page reproduced on pages 84 and 85; my old friend S. who has so often helped me in ways unknown to him; & finally, Ruth, for willing help in the exacting task of reading the proofs.

Comme quelqu'un pourrait dire de moi que
j'ai seulement fait ici un amas de fleurs étrangères,
n'y ayant fourni du mien que le filet à les lier.

Montaigne. *Essais*, III.xii

The next step in the study of type is to learn
to recognize the various forms or 'tribes' of type
and the subtle differentiations between varieties
of the same general form of type-face. These
differences are very slight; often to the casual
observer no differences appear. There is no way
to learn to recognize them except by training
the eye.   D. B. Updike
Printing Types, Their History, Forms, and Use, 1937

Of every class of type there are many forms, but
one or two forms only that are the best. We can
learn what these best forms are by knowing what
early handwriting and early type was, and what early
printers meant to do. Only when we understand
their problem can we justly judge how well they
solved it. To see what the manuscripts were that
they tried to reproduce in type is a step to this
knowledge; to see how forms produced by a pen
were changed when rendered in metal is another.
A third step is the realization of the influence of
history, nationality, scholarship, and custom upon
type-forms. We must also have a comprehension of
the evolution of economic problems—how cheaper
books were demanded, how that want was met,
and what its effect was on types and their use. The
ability to recognize all this can be arrived at only
by that historical perspective and that training of
the eye which is gained by study and observation.
ibid.

But any one may arrive at sound conclusions as
to types, if he knows thoroughly the history of
type-forms, has an eye sensitive to their variations,
and has familiarized himself with the ways in which
they have been employed by masters of typography.
ibid.

Preface

This book is intended simply as an introduction to a subject which has already been well documented by D. B. Updike, A. F. Johnson, Stanley Morison, Paul Beaujon, Harry Carter, James Wardrop and others. It has been written to help those students who have not as yet had an opportunity to study the work of these authors with any thoroughness, if indeed at all: or, having both opportunity and inclination, yet feel dismayed at the immensity of the subject—covering as it does so many countries and compassing a period of over five hundred years. From that point it may only be a short step to questioning the need to delve into the history of printing types at all: to regard it as a field remote from present day needs & the task of earning a living, in fact, one best left to scholars—to the historians of printed books and ephemera—some of whom they realize may already have devoted a lifetime to such research.

Yet without some knowledge of the history of type faces—of the historical, personal, economic, industrial, & other factors which determined the development of types in certain ways at certain times—& without some familiarity with the ways in which the great printer-publishers of the past have used those types, we cannot hope to be able to identify type faces, to choose them intelligently, to mix them with assurance, or to produce with them work having that quality of *inevitability* which the late Mr Bruce Rogers said always marked successful typography.

In this *Introduction* types have been grouped and the groups appear in chronological order. Each group of faces is prefaced with a brief historical note, the material for which in most instances I am entirely indebted to the historians cited above. Following these historical notes, and confined to the book faces, are notes on the characteristics of the types in the particular groups, written in the hope that they will help to facilitate the identification of individual specimens. For these analyses I am especially indebted to Mr A. F. Johnson of the Department of Printed Books, British Museum, and also to Mr W. Turner Berry, until recently Librarian of the St Bride Foundation Printing Library.

Preface

The illustrations are, subject to the groupings, to the availability of particular examples, & to the exigencies of make-up, arranged chronologically also. They are printed, within photographic limits, in facsimile, size precluding such a course only rarely. Although the decision to print in facsimile meant that page margins would have to be sacrificed & only part of a page could be shown on quite a number of occasions these courses seemed preferable to reducing the size of a very large number of the specimens considerably. The method of reproduction, line engraving, leaves much to be desired. We rejected fine screen halftone because it would have meant, with the make-up envisaged, printing the complete book on coated paper. Collotype, the ideal process, was precluded on the score of cost. Lithography, the next choice, & preferable to both line engraving or halftone, was not available at the Press when this book was printed.

The number in brackets following the title of an illustration refers to the page on which a descriptive note on that example appears, while the number in brackets at the end of each descriptive note is that of the page on which the illustration referred to will be found. The text of this book has been deliberately condensed: the notes on the illustrations will enlarge and reinforce it.

Within each group will be found a short list of contemporary examples where these have been cut. That some of the types named are no longer available, that is, are not being cast—either through lack of demand or because the foundries which produced them have ceased to exist or have been taken over by other foundries—does not invalidate them in the least as examples: founders' or printers' specimens or other reproductions of these 'lost' faces are available to the student for reference.

From the very large range of alphabetic type specimens issued in recent years by trade typesetting houses, by typefounders, & by printers, readers may build up their own collections for the purposes of identification and of study.

G.D

February 1961

Contents

PART I
THE BOOK TYPES

PART II
THE DISPLAY TYPES

Contents

List of Illustrations

xvii

Introduction

The text has not only been made deliberately brief but we have tried not to bestrew it with too many names or dates. Only a few of the most famous typefounders, printers & publishers are mentioned in this book: and only some of the most important dates in the five hundred year period in which types have evolved from the first gothic or black-letter faces. The bones of the matter are here. It is for the student to clothe them appropriately by reading the authors already cited in the *Preface*, among others, and by studying as many specimens of old and contemporary types as possible.

There has never been anything sudden or spectacular in this long process of evolution. Many forces have been at work. Tradition, economics, new scientific discoveries, changes in techniques—both of paper-making and of printing—and in the fashions of the day, have all played their part in the evolution of printing types.

Roughly we may divide types into two groups: those that are used in books for continuous reading and those best reserved for the production of ephemera. The examples in this book are so divided, but from an examination of them it will be seen that anything like clear-cut divisions in the groupings are virtually impossible, so many and so subtle are the variations in type designs.

The subject of type classification, the attempt to group or sort into different categories types sharing similar traits in relation to their design, has for some years been occupying the attention of various bodies & individuals. It is a large & complex one because of (1) the large number of faces extant—estimated as as many as five thousand (2) the number of type foundries operating in this country, Europe & the USA. The term 'type foundries' of course includes the makers of type composing and casting machinery (3) the fact that plagiarism has flourished in this field since the beginning.

Many of the flood of type faces which have been produced during the last thirty or forty years are fairly exact renderings of earlier classic designs such as Garamond or Bodoni. Versions of these two, for example have been cut by foundries in this country, in Europe & in America each with the particular foundry's variations from Garamond's or Bodoni's original designs. The clamour for more and more display faces by the printers & designers of ephemera has resulted in a whole range of weights and widths being cut for many of the faces originally designed as types for bookwork.

A *sine qua non* of any system of type face classification is that the types accepted should conform to reasonably decent standards of letter design. The work of the would-be reformers of our present system of nomenclature would be immeasurably simplified if they began with a firm resolve to ignore the scores of faces which are patent distortions of good letter forms. No useful purpose is served by attempting to assign to particular categories types like Kino, Parsons, Belwe, Hobo and Royal Lining, to name but a few of a large class. Not only would the task of the classifiers be lightened if they ignored the badly designed type faces still available for hand & machine composition but students of typography, to whom the ramifications of type face nomenclature are sufficiently confusing without the addition of worthless material, would not be led to believe—because they have seen some of these 'designs' included in suggested systems of classification—that there must be something of intrinsic worth in these productions of the nineteenth & early twentieth century and in other more recent travesties of the roman alphabet.

Of the suggested systems of classification much has been written of that devised by M. Maximilien Vox first published in Paris in 1954. In it all types are classified under nine (originally ten) heads. We shall not outline M. Vox's scheme here for descriptions & criticisms have already appeared in various journals, the names of which will be found among a list of suggested systems for the classification of type faces published since 1921 in Berry, Johnson and Jaspert's *Encyclopædia of Typefaces* 1958. In an excellent review, NEW APPROACHES TO THE CLASSIFICATION OF TYPEFACES by Mr James Mosley, Librarian of the St Bride Foundation Printing Library, published in *The British Printer* March 1960, students will find much interesting material for study.

Introduction

There is no doubt that our typefounders, our printers, & some writers on typography are regrettably largely responsible for the present confusions in the naming of type faces despite the fact that works on this subject have been available since the early 1930's. To mention but two there were Mr A. F. Johnson's series of articles in *Paper & Print*, A GUIDE TO PRESENT-DAY TYPES, and his book *Type Designs*, first published in 1934. Many printers have not even adhered to the names given to the types by their founders. Instead they have invented completely new ones in some cases or even more inaccurate ones. Examples of such misleading changes will be found in this writer's plea for a rational terminology which appeared in *Typographica* No 4, published in 1951. That article was responsible for the series of meetings arranged by the British Standards Institution on this subject. The work of this BSI Committee is still in progress.

In this book we have adhered to Mr Johnson's classification of type designs almost entirely, for two reasons. First, to those who have made any study of typography the terms gothic, Venetian, old face, transitional, modern, Old Style, twentieth-century, shaded, egyptian, & so on are names with which they are perfectly familiar: each presents a clear mental picture of a particular design of letter. Certainly to a layman the term *modern* in relation to a type face would mean a design which had a contemporary flavour. But to typographers it has one well-defined meaning only: a type face with vertical stress, great contrast between thick & thin strokes, hairline serifs and so on. Does it really matter then that the term is meaningless outside the field of typography—that it was used originally to describe a face which was quite unlike the old faces with their oblique stress, gradual modelling and bracketed serifs which had been in use for nearly three hundred years before the first fully-fledged 'modern' face appeared?

Second, all the classics or authoritative works on the history of type faces to which this work is intended as an introduction, and many other works on typography, have used our present familiar terminology. It is most unlikely that any of these works would be reprinted to make them accord with a system which, though formulated, had as yet secured no measure of general approval. We must also remember that students of typography in the various schools of this country have for years been familiarized with our present terminology in the publicity material of the founders and the makers of type composing and casting machinery. An example is the widely distributed leaflet *What's that Type face?*

It is, of course, no part of the typographer's job to be able to recognize and name at sight any specimen of type face placed before him. Such is an impossible task and would only be demanded by one ignorant of the subject. In actual practice one can name only those faces that one knows really well. But what the typographer must be able to do reasonably quickly is to place any face into its appropriate category or group, thus narrowing the field in which a search has to be made and to that extent simplifying identification.

This book has been published to familiarize students with the various categories or groups of printing types. We hope that it will also introduce them to wide reading in a fascinating subject.

THE BOOK TYPES

PART ONE

THE BOOK TYPES

I

The earliest printed books were produced from wooden blocks on which both the pictures and the text were cut. The printed pages were glued back to back & a collection of such leaves was bound together to form what we know as a block-book. These xylographic, or woodcut block-books date from early in the fifteenth century(*circa* 1420).

Such a laborious method of producing books undoubtedly spurred on the inventor or inventors in their search for an easier method of reproducing texts and thus of superseding the scribes. The Chinese were printing from movable metal types in the eleventh century but there is no connection between its invention in the East, and its appearance in Europe approximately four centuries later. Hundreds of works have been written with the aim of unravelling the mystery which surrounds the birth of the art in Europe yet none can name the inventor, nor the place or time of its invention. Despite the uncertainties of scholars some writers state categorically that the goldsmith Johann Gutenberg was its inventor & that Mainz, his birthplace, the home of its invention. But the rudiments of the art were known before he began his experiments. Gutenberg's genius lay, if not in inventing, then in perfecting the hand-mould in which types could be cast by the hundred in the course of a day thus making possible the production of books in quantities and at speeds undreamt of before his time.

It must be understood that the earliest printers were of necessity their own typefounders also—the two arts were not separated until about the year 1530.

3

preceptis a pharaone instituit li
beratos: totidem hic epistolis a
dyaboli et ydolatrie sutute edoce
acquisitos · Nam et duas tabu
las lapideas: duox testametox
figura habuisse viri eruditissim
tradiderut · Epłam sane que ad
hebreos scribit quidam pauli no
esse contendut: eo qp no sit ei no
mine tytulata · et ppter smonis
stiliqz distanciam: Sed aut barna
te iuxta tercullianu · aut luce iu
xta quosdam: uel certe clemetis
discipli apłox · et epi romane ee
post apłos ordinati · Quibz ita re
spondendu est · Si pptea pauli no
erit · qp eius no habz nome: ergo
nec alterius erit: qa nulli noie
tytulatur · Qd si absurdum est:
ipius magis esse credenda est · qui
tanto doctrine sue fulget eloquio ·
Sed qu apud hebreox ecclesias
quasi destructor legis falsa suspi
cione habebat: uoluit tacito no
mine de figuris legis et ueritate
xpi reddere racione: ne odiu no
minis fronte plati · utilitate ex
duder lechionis · Non est sane nu

2. *From a manuscript written at Mainz, circa 1440* [211]

Gothic

The invention of printing from movable types in Europe dates from about 1440. The originators of the new art naturally took as models for their types the formal manuscript hands of the day which were at that time predominantly in a letter known to us now as gothic or black-letter. Gothic was the derisive name given by the Renaissance humanists to the compressed, angular, and heavy style of writing used at that time for formal texts all over Europe. To them it *was* barbarous.

Printing from movable types put the professional copyists out of business but the books printed in these earliest of all types had spaces left for initials, marginal decorations and line finishings, for it was the wish of the printers that their work might be taken for that of the scribes: the pages were completed by illuminators. One of the most magnificent books to be set in black-letter type was the Gutenberg or 42-line Bible printed at Mainz *circa* 1455.

This historical note, although correctly placed chronologically, is nevertheless only included here for the sake of completeness. Black-letter types were originally widely used in Europe as text types, i.e. as types for continuous reading (especially in church service books) but now their use for text matter survives only in Germany, and even there they are gradually being ousted by the roman letter. Elsewhere, that is outside Germany, the use of black-letter is confined to display sizes in ecclesiastical and legal work. Forms of it also survive in ephemeral printing, for example, in newspaper title pieces.

Black-letter types have been divided into four main groups (1) Text-uras (2) Fere-humanisticas or Gotico-antiquas (3) Rotundas or Round-

quam apostoli pbauerunt. De nouo
nunc loquor testamento qd grecu esse
nō dubiū est:excepto apostolo matheo
qui primus in iudea euangelium xp̄i
hebraicis litteris edidit . Hoc certe cū
in nostro sermone discordat·et diuer=
sos riuulor̗ tramites ducit: uno de
fonte querendus est. Pretermitto eos
codices q̄s a luciano et esycio nuncu=
patores paucor̗ hominū asserit puer=
sa cōtentio: quibus utiq̗ nec in ueteri
instrumēto post septuaginta interpre=
tes emendare quid licuit·nec in nouo
profuit emendasse: cum multar̗ gen=
tium linguis scriptura āte translata
doceat falsa esse que addita sunt. Igi=
tur hec p̄sens p̄faciuncula pollicetur
quatuor tantū euangelia·quor̗ ordo
est iste · matheus · marcus · lucas·io=
hānes · codicum grecor̗ emendata col=
latione sed ueterū:que ne multū a lecti=
onis latine cōsuetudine discreparent
ita calamo imperauim9: ut hijs tan=
tum que sensum uidebantur mutare
correctis · reliqua manere paterent ut
fuerāt . Canones quoq̗ quos eusebi=
us cesariensis episcopus allexādrinū
secut9 ammoniū in dece numeros or=

3. *42-line Bible, Mainz, circa 1455* [211]

Texts (4) The vernacular types or Bastardas. In Germany this last group has been subdivided into (a) Schwabacher, (b) The Upper-Rhine type, (c) The Wittenberg letter, and (d) Fraktur.[1]

Now that interest in the black-letter group of type faces is mainly historical the characteristics of the earliest of the texturas only will be described here. We have, however, for the sake of completeness, included illustrations and brief descriptions of the other formal gothic types and of the four Bastardas.

Throughout this book the numbers in square brackets immediately following the title lines under illustrations refer to the pages on which short descriptive notes will be found.

Characteristics of the Texturas

The Texturas, the earliest and most formal of the black-letter faces are upright, angular and heavy letters. Curved strokes hardly occur in the lower-case but are evident in the capitals. The ascenders and descenders are short, strokes finishing on the line, e.g. h, i, m, end in diamond shaped, or pointed feet, and not with serifs as we know them. There were, of course, considerable variations in the design of types in this group, some being more condensed, some more open than others, for example. The heads and feet are more pointed in some texturas than in others, and the colour, or degree of blackness, varies markedly. In the other forms of black-letter the angularities of Textura were softened. Curves, for example, are a feature of the Rotundas, as the name suggests.

[1] A. F. Johnson. THE CLASSIFICATION OF GOTHIC TYPES. *The Library*. Vol IX. No 4. March 1929.

e audiuimus eū loquentē discipulis suis·ꝗ vidim̄
um ascendentē in cœlum.Q̊ si tacuerimus·pctm ha
ꝺuerimus,Exurgentesꝗ principes p legem dñi adiu
cauerūt eos ne ampliꝰ annūciarent bc verba·dantes
is pecuniā·ꝗ ꝺenūciantes·ne starent i itĺm.Congre
gatisꝗ omibꝰ iutais fecerūt lamentatōꝛ magnaꝛ di
entes.Q̊ signū est factum in israbel.Anna autē ꝗ
Cayphas ꝯsolantes eos·dixerunt;Nunqꝺ custodibꝰ
credendū est·ꝗ angelus dñi reuoluit lapicm·Forsan
discipuli aꝰ instruxerūt eos·ꝺonantes eis pecuniam·
ꝺt tollerent cœpus iꞡu,Non ē credendū alienigenis·
ꝗm a noꝫ accepta pecunia sic ꝺocuimꝰ eos sic dixerūt,
Exurgens nichodemus,Recte loquami filij israbel·
ꝺos audistis omia que locuti sunt tres viri·iurantes
n lege ꝺomi· ꝗ dicentes,Vidimus iꞡm loquentē cū
discipulis suis· ꝗ ascendentem i cœlū· ꝗ scriptura ꝺocet
ꝺos·ꝗ beatus helias assumptus est. Et interrogatꝰ be
ꝛeus a filijs ꝓphetaꝛ vbi est pater noster belias·Di
itꝗ assumptꝰ est·ꝗ dixerūt filij ꝓꞡaꝛ·forsitan spūs
ius rapuit eum·ꝗ punit eum in montibꝰ israbel·sed
ligamus viros nobiscum·ꝗ circūuenientes montes
israbel· forsitan inuenimus eum , Et ambulauit be
ꝛeus cū illis tribꝰ diebꝰ·ꝗ non inuenerūt eum, Itaꝗ
audite me filij israbel· ꝗ mittamus viros in montibꝰ
israbel·ne forte spūs rapuerit iꞡm·ꝗ forsitan inuenie
nus penitentiam,Et placuit ħmo omi ꝓꝓo·ꝗ missis
ꝺiris·qurentes non inuenerūt·ꝗ reuersi sunt·ꝗ dixert,
Circumeuntes non inpenimus hiesum·sed ioseph in
iuitate sua arimathia est,Quo audito gauisi sunt
ꝓincipes sacerdotum·ꝗ glorificauerunt deum·quia in
ientus ē ioseph quem incluserant·factoꝗ ꝯcilio·quo
ꝺdine vocarent ioseph· scripserunt ad eū thenocarte
ꝺicentes·pax tecū·ꝗ vibꝰ q̃ tecū sūt·Scimꝰ ꝗ peccauiꝰ

mihi ad tutamentum ment
et corporis·et ad anime med
lam percipiendam·Qui cu
deo p̄re et sp̄ū sancto viuis
regnas deus·   Quando co
pus christi accipit in manus
cat Panem celestem accip
et nomen domini inuocab
Et dicat ter Domine nō su
dignus vt intres sub tectu
meum·sed tantum dic ver
et sanabitur anima mea· C
sumit dicat Corpus dom
nostri iesu christi sit mihi ad
medium sempiternum in v

Esar in orbe decus:doctorū
gloria vatum
Dux tribuis meritis pre/
mia digna suis
Cinge precor viridi mereor
si forte corona.
Tempora: ptingat lau/
rea sancta comas
Tūc ego pro tanto semper
tibi munere vinctus
Cantabo laudes dum mihi vita tuas
Dū mihi vita manet tollā super astra nepotes
Cesaris ethereos:inclita facta canens.

Ode Monocolos Tetrametros Choriā bicos Conradi Celtis ad diuinū Fride ricum paranetice et palinodice:

Cesar magnificis laudibus inclitus
Rex regum dominus maxime principum
Si quis prisca tuis tempora seculis
Vel conferre velit regna prioribus
Que vel sub rudibus cepta phenicibus
Seu que docta tulit grecia milite
Aut que romuleis parta quiritibus
Non te crede queunt vincere gloria:
Sit quis tirio vellere nobilis
Arabs et varijs diues odoribus
Sabeo relegens balsama stipite
Non fortem poterit vincere Cesarem:
Qui carpit lapides fluminis aurei
Hiberus tepidis solibus obditus

6. *The gothic Bastardas (a) Schwabacher* [213]

II

vernuwet Inde desse tzyt helt dye
hylge kyrch vā dē Aduēt bys kers
dach tzo · wāt dā so leest men ysay
am den prophetē der vā dysser ver
nuwynge clerlych sprycht Dye
tzyt der versoenynge · ys dye tzyt
da twyr durch xpūs versonet wor
den · ynd dysse tzyt helt dye heylige
kyrch vā payschē bys pynstē · wat
dan leest mē Apocalipsis · dat ys
dat boych ō verhoelenheyt dat vol
komlich sprycht vā der versoenū
ge Dye tzyt der pylgremaciē ys
die tzyt des leuēs · da wyr synt pyl
grym yn altzyt in strydē · ynd dese
tzyt helt dye hylge kyrch acht dach
na pinxtē bys tzo dē Aduēt · want
dā leest mē ō konyngē boiche daer
men yn leest vā mēnigerhādē stry
dē · yn dye machabeusche · daer onse
geystliche stryt myt wyrt betzeichet
Mer die tzyt dy da is vā kyrstdach
bys septuagesima · eyn deyl ys be/
grepen vnder der tzyt der versoc/
nynge ynde dye ys van vreuden ·
als vā kyrstach bys tzo dem achtē
dach na dē druytzehē dach · ynd eyn
deyl is begrepē vnder ō tzyt der pyl
gremagiē · dat ys vāder octaue vā
druytzē dache tzo der septuagesima
Ind die vier verwādelynge vā dys
sen tzydē machmē nemē na dē vier
deile van dē iair · so datmē dē wyn
ter reche off schicke by dē eirstē · ynd
den lentzē tzo dē anderē · den somer
tzo dē derdē · yn dye herfst tzo dē viet
den Tzo dē anderē, mail so mach
men sy rechē gegen dye vier tzyden
vā dem daghē · soe dat mē dye nacht
reche tzo dē eirsten · den morghēn tzo
dem anderen · dē middach tzo dem
dyrdē · dye vesper tzyt tzo dē vierdē ·
wāt all was dat dye dwalyng eer

Als dye tzyt
des leuēs wy
rt in vierē ge
deilt · als in
die tzit ō dwa
linge ynd in
dye tzyt ō we
derropynge
off der vernu
wynge ynd in dye tzyt der soenyn/
ge ynd der pilgrym gie Dye tzyt
der dwalynge ys vā Adā tzyt dae
he van gode dwaeld durch dye sun
den · docrēde tzo moyses tzo · ynd de
se tzyt helt dye kyrche vā septuage/
sima bys paschē · Glosa Septuage
sima ys als men leecht Alleluya
voer vastauent · want dan so leest
men dat begynsel vāder bybel daer
beschreuē ys der eirster vader dwa/
lynge · Dye tzyt der wederroe/
pynge off der vernuwinge begynd
van moyses yn duerde bys dat crif
tus gheboren was In wylcher tzyt
dye mynschē worden tzo dem gbelo
ue gheroefen durch die prophetē yn

7. *The gothic Bastardas (b) Upper-Rhine type* [214]

13

...ch vormals. In czweyen meinen schrifften. Die ich aus meiner eren not/
...hab ausgehen lassen/angeczeigt.wy der hochgeborn furst herr Heinrich
...og czu Sachssen ꝛc. Uff gehaltem tag czu Molhawsen/mir in rucken vn
...huldt.das ich vnwarheit solle geret vnd damit wider mein pflicht gehan
...habē.hat czumessen lassen.wie ich dargegē mein entschuldung getan/auch
...nd ander vnrechten beswerung halben.so mir vō gemeltem hertzog Hein
...n manigfeltiglich begegent/den vffrichtigstē wegk ordenlichs rechten czu
...suchen vorgenomenn. Hab ich hertzog Heinrich montags nach Letare
...stuerschinnen/mit czweien meiner frunde Hugoldt vnnd Wolffgang von
...itz/sampt einem offenbaren schreiber/mein offen brieff geschickt/des in
...hirnach volget.   Dem hochgebornen furstē vn hern.hern Heinrichen
...oge czu Sachssen ꝛc. Thue ich Heinrich von Sleinitz obermarschal/mit
...n meinem offenbrue ersuchen. Nachdem ewer furstliche wird/mich mit
...ten vn schrifften/an mein Eren vnd gelympff/wider recht vn alle billickeit
...ichseldig beswert/damit in mergklichen schaden gedrungen. Darumb ich
...ewern furstlichen wirden willens bin/ordenlichs rechten czugebrauchen.
...wegen ich ewer furstliche wirde.mit diesem offen brieff vermanhne. Das
...furstliche wirde.als furst des heiligen reichs. Lauts Romischer keyser
...Maiestat/vn des heiligen reichs ordnūg czu Worms vfgericht. mir ewer
...ichen wirde Rete.verorden vnd benennē/vor welchen ich mein forderung
...ꝛge/nach vormogen der recht/vnd berurter ordnung/gegen vn wider ewer
...iche wird/thun vn verfuren magk.nsit Protestacion. Ap mir diese ersuch
...nd forderung/aus crafft bemelter ordnung ader sunst von recht/in ander
...ader mas tzuthun geburt/das ich solichs hirmit wil gethan/vnd an mey
...rechtigkeit/clag vnd forderung nichtes verseumet ader begeben habenn.
...hrieben vnder meinem petzschir am Montag nach Letare.Anno ꝛc.xv.c.
...o.   In welchem brieff ich hertzog Heinrich ermant/mir lauts Keyser
...Ma.vnd des heiligen reichs ordnung/vor seiner furstlichen wirdē Retē
...czupflegen/in czuuersicht es worde seinen furstlichen wirden/mecher gelie
...sesasten hassigen willen/mit rechtlicher ordnung/dan durch vnbewerliche
.../gegen mir czuuorfuren. Vnd so keyserliche ordnung/einem yedern Chur
...fursten vnd farstmessigem vflegt/vfs clegers ansuchen/bynnen Monats
...dem cleger/vnuorpflicht czu widerclag ein rechts tag czuernennenn. Ime
...n anwaldt vnd der selben beystādt/czu vn von solchem rechts tage/sicher
...rey geleit czugeben. Solchs alles hertzog Heinrich/bis an einen tag/vier
...en lang enthalden. Vnd nach solcher verlauffenner czeit. Hat sein furst
...wird obgemelte vō Miltitz schrifftlich/wy hirnach volget czu sich erfordert
...Lieben getrewen.Wir begern.das ir Montags schirsten/czu frwer tage
...hie czu Freybergk/bey vns erscheinet/wollē wir euch fugsts abeschledts/
...meinung eroffen. Heben czu Freybergk Sonabents in der heiligē Oster
...en.Anno dñi ꝛc.decimo.   Die vō Miltitz.sampt dem offenbaren schrei
...in vnuorczugklich erschynen/in czuuersicht.geburlichen vorbeschiedt czu
...nen.Oy doch nicht/anders dā ein offene schrifft/lauts nachuolgēder mey
...erlanget.   Heinrich von Sleynitz.auff dein schreiben/vns durch Hu
... vnd Wolffen von Miltitz vberschickt/saltu wissen/was wir erheischūg
... vnwarheit vnnd leichtuertigen hendele/von dir gesagt/dir czuentpotten

Dem Erberen vnnd wolgeachten Herrn Wilibald Pirckeymer/ K
serlicher maiestat raht etc. meinem gönstigen lieben Herrn/
vnd großer sprießlichen freund/ Empewt ich
Albrecht Dürer meyn willig dinst.

Jewol ich Gönstiger Herr vnd freund nit zweyfel sich werden etlich dis
fürnem̄ zu straffen vnderstehn/darumb das ich als ein vngelerter/ kleins
standts/vnd mit wenig kunst begabt/schreiben vn̄ leren thar/das/so ich sel
gelernt hab/oder von yemand anders vnderwisen bin worden/Nochdan̄
weil ihr mir zu merem mal angehalten/ auch zum teil gedrungen habt/ das ich dise n
bücher an tag geb/hab ich mich vil ehe in die geuerd der nachred geben wölle/daß euch
bit versagen/Wiewol ich hoff/mir werd nymands/der mit tugenden vn̄ verstand be
ist/zu argem außlegen/das ich das so ich mit hohem fleyß/steter mühe vnd arbeit/auc
mit kleiner verseumung zeytlicher hab/so miltiglich/vn̄ zu gemeinem nutz aller kun
an das liecht kommen laß/sonder meniglich werd mein gütwilligkeit vnd geneigte v
loben/vnd den im allerbesten verstehen. Dieweil ich nun in keinen zweyffel setz/ ich n
allen kunstliebhabenden/vnd denen so zu leren begird haben/hierin ein gefallen thün/
ich dem neyd/so nichts vngestraft lest/seinen gewönlichen gang lassen/ vn̄ antworter
gar vil leichter sey ein ding zu tadeln/dann selbs zuerfinden/vnd ist wol nit an/wo di
cher der alten/so von den kunsten des malens geschriben haben noch vor augen were
möcht mir dis mein vorhaben als vermeint ich ein bessers zufinden zu arg außgelegt
den.Dieweil aber solche bucher durch leng der zeyt gantz verloren sind worden/so kar
mit keiner billigkeit verwisen werden/ob ich/wie auch die alten gethan haben/meinn
nung vnd erfindung schrifftlich aus lasse gehn/damit auch anderen verstendigen der
chen züthün vrsach gegeben werd/vnd vnser nachkommen haben/ das sy meren vnd
ren mögen/damit die kunst der malerey mit der zeit wider zu jrer volkommenheit re
vnd kommen mög. Doch ist nymand gezwungen diser meiner lehr/ als sey die gantz
komen an allen orten nachzugehn/dann die menschlich natur hat noch nit also abgen
das ein ander nit auch etwas bessers erfinden möge/derhalb mag sich ein yeglicher
meiner vnderrichtung/so lang ime geliebt/oder er ein bessers erfindet/gebrauchen/ w
mag er wol darfur achten/dise lehr sey nit ime sonder anderen/so die anzunemen beg
beschriben.Dan es mus gar ein spröder verstand sein der ime nit trawet auch etwas
ters zuerfinden/sonder lige allwegen auff der alten ban/volgt allein anderen nach /
vndersteht sich nichten weitter nach zudencken/Derhalb geburt einem yeglichen ver
digen also einem anderen nachzubolgē/das er nit verzweyfel/ das er mit der zeyt au
bessers erfinden mög/dann so das geschicht/darff es keine zweyffel/das dise kunst m
zeit wider wie vor alter/jr volkommenheit erlangen mög, dann offenbar ist/das die
schen maler mit jrer hand vnd brauch der farben nit wenig geschickt sind / wiewol s
her an der kunst der messung/auch Perspectiua vnd anderem dergleichen mangel g
haben/Darumb wol zu hoffen/wo sy die auch erlangen/ vn̄ also den brauch vn̄ kunst
einander vberkommen/sie werden mit der zeit keiner anderen Nation den preis vor
lassen / Aber ohn rechte proportion kan ye kein bild volkommen sein/ ob es auch so f
als das ymer möglich ist/gemache wirdet/wiewol ohn not alle vnd zuvor gar klein
nach der mas zu machen/dann solchs zuuil muhe wurd brauchen/ So man aber der

A ij

9. *The gothic Bastardas (d) Fraktur* [214]

Some contemporary gothic or black-letter types

Ancient Black (Stephenson Blake), Caslon Old Black (originally
Caslon and now Stephenson Blake), Cloister Black (American
Type Founders), Goudy Text (Monotype). Monotype offer various
Schwabachers and Frakturs but naturally the German founders
show the greatest range of gothic faces.

et conuiuium illius exponit · et homi
nummorum esse origonis illius prae
claros quibus a monitis iuuant et
quam celeriter in locis illius fata
proueniant ·

III Ubi dicit quod tunc alexandria in
ter episcopos et monachos inutilia
certamina ɜ erabantur ne
qui origenis libros legeret ·

IIII Ubi bethleem oppidum petiit cuius
loci ecclesiam sci hieronimus regebat
et ubi monachorum uel clericorum an
mos uel conuersationis exponet
et quod die noctuq: aut legebat
aliquit semper aut scribebat ·

V Ubi dicit in aegypto multa esse
monasteria ubi prima uirtus

10. *Caroline minuscule* [217]

Roman
VENETIAN

German printers spread the new art all over Europe in a little over a generation, the sack of the city of Mainz in 1462 accelerating the process. Of this disaster Mr Updike says that it 'influenced the spread of typography, for it wiped out commerce there, and the consequent lack of money led printers, who were established in a kind of industrial group, to scatter widely. This accounts for the German names we find among the earliest printers in other countries throughout Europe.'[1]

Many of these printers went to Italy, the country which in the previous century had witnessed the birth of the Renaissance—that 'fructifying of the human mind through contact with the classical world of Greece and Rome.' The Renaissance humanists, in transcribing the works of classical authors had rejected the gothic hand and copied the script in which many of these works were written out—a clear, regular hand perfected some centuries earlier in the reign of Charlemagne (b.743—d.814) and known to us as the Caroline minuscule—a style of writing which we have no difficulty in recognizing as the forbear of our upper- & lower-case today. The scribes modified this hand, making it even more beautiful. Thus it is understandable why this neo-caroline minuscule had, by the time the first printers arrived from the North, to some extent ousted the gothic script in Italy.

When Conrad Sweynheym & Arnold Pannartz set up the first printing press in Italy at the Benedictine Monastery at Subiaco near Rome

[1] In *Printing Types, Their History, Forms, and Use*. Harvard University Press, Cambridge (Mass.) Vol I. Second Edition 1937.

ableg, consilio: dimittat ipse solus rex, absolutu a q pecunia a
demnet: pecunia n reddat. Huic hoiem iudicum nuo hebim? hic alt
am senatoria iudex obtinebit: hic de capite libero iudicabit: hui
lis tabella comittet? qua n modo cera: uerq a sanguine si uisu er
Quid n horq se negat fecisse: illud vs vnu q necesse e pec. accepis:
iste negat? At eques R. q Soparru defendit: qui omibus eius cofil
interfuit. Q. Minutius iuratus dicit pec. datam: iuratus dicit Ti
dixisse maiorem ab accusatoribus pec. dari. dicent hoc Siculi om
Alutenses: dicet et ptextatus Sopatri filius: qui ab isto homic cu
te inocentissio pecuniaq: patria priuatus e. verq si de pecunia a
nu facere n possem: illud negare posses aut nuc negabis te consili
fo uiris primarus qui i consilio. C. sacerdotis fuerat: tibiq: ce sol
tis de re iudicata iudicasse: teq: cu que C. sacerdos adhibito con
nita absoluisse: cunde remoto consilio ca incognita absoluisse e
hoc confessus eris q in foro palam Syracusis ioit acq: oculis puir
negato sane si uoles pec. accepisse. reperies credo aliquem q cum he
gesta sut uideat: qrat q tu occulte geris: aut q dubitet uerq malit
an tuis defensoribus credere. Dixi iam antea me n oia istius q i
essent enuaturq: sed electurq q maxime excellerent. Accipite n
eius facinus nobile: et multis locis sepe comemoratu: et ciusmoi
oia maleficia inesse uideant. Attenditur n diligenter: iuenietur
natum a cupiditate: auctu p stuprq: crudelitate pfectu acq: c
Sthenius e is q nobis assidet. Thermitanus antea multis ppt f
tem summaq: nobilitatem: nuc ppt suam calamitati acq: isti
iniuriam omnibus notus: huius hospitio Verres cu eet usus: et
n modo solu Thermis sepenuo fuisse: sed et hitasse, domo e
lit: que paulomagis aim cuiuspiam aut oculos possent comoue
nius ab adolescentia: paulo studiosius hoc copat suppellectil
gantior et delicia et chorinthia: tabulas pictas et argenti
puit Thermitani hois facultates ferebat satis que cu eet i Asi
studiose uti dixi compabat: no ta sue delectatois causa: q ad i
aduentusq: morq hoim suorq amicorq acq: hospitii: q postea q i

11. *Humanistic or neo-caroline hand, Venice, circa 1476* [217]

the first type they cut was used to print Cicero's *De Oratore* (1465). Mr Morison, in a paper in which he asks 'What then is to be said of the generally accepted statement that (this) Subiaco fount is not a "pure roman"?' reaches the conclusion that it 'is entitled to rank as the first humanistic or roman type'[1].

After two years work at Subiaco Sweynheym and Pannartz moved, in 1467, to Rome where they employed a second fount which though less regular and pleasing than the Subiaco type, was much lighter and can be considered as a further, definite step in the direction of roman as we are familiar with it today. The partnership of these two printers continued at Rome for six years during which time they printed about fifty books.

But Venice, not Rome, became the most important printing centre in Italy, and it was in that city that two brothers, John and Wendelin da Spira cut a roman type, first used in 1469, which Mr Updike says 'today appears roman to us.'[2] In the previous year another foreigner settled in Venice—the Frenchman Nicolas Jenson. Two years later he had produced his first roman type based on the finest humanistic manuscripts of the day—a great advance on the types of his contemporaries. The characteristics of Jenson's fount were, says Mr Updike, 'its readability, its mellowness of form, and the evenness of colour in mass.'[3]

In the decade before his death at Venice in 1480 Jenson printed over 150 books. He was famous both as a letter-cutter and printer, and as a publisher. His types have been widely reproduced in our own day and the style is known as *Venetian.*

Characteristics of Venetian romans

STRESS OR SHADING
Oblique or biassed, i.e. thickest parts of curved forms approximately North-East/South-West.

[1]EARLY HUMANISTIC SCRIPT AND THE FIRST ROMAN TYPE. Stanley Morison. *The Library.* Fourth Series. Vol XXIV. Nos 1, 2. June/September 1943.
[2]In *Printing Types, Their History, Forms, and Use.*
[3]*ibid.*

MODELLING, OR GRADATION FROM THICK TO THIN STROKES
Gradual.
SERIFS (FEET)
Bracketed, heavy, and sometimes slablike. Often cupped.
OTHER DISTINGUISHING FEATURES
The letters are in general wide, and strong in colour: this is so in the capitals especially. The lower-case e has a diagonal bar, (that is, a tilted bar rising towards the right).

moyfes: Ipe i noniffimis diebus circúcidet dñs cor ueftrũ ad domĩnũ deũ
uũ amandũ.Itẽ ihefus naue fucceffor eius.Et dixit dñs ad ihefum:fac tibi
ultellos petrínos mimis acutos et fede et circúcide fecúdo filios ifrael:fecũ
dam circúcifionẽ futurã effe dixit:nõ carnis ficut fuit þma:qua etiã nũc iu
dei utunt:fed cordis ac fpíritus quã tradidit xpus q fuit uerus ihefus: Nõ
i ,ppheta fic ait.Et dixit ihefus ad me:fed ad ihefum ut oftenderet qd nõ
de eo loqueret fed de xpo ad quẽ tunc deus loquebat:xpi eni figurã gere
at ille ihefus:q quom þmũ aufes uocaret moifes figurã pfentiens iuffit eũ
hefum uocari:ut dux militiẹ delectus effet aduerfus amalech qui oppug
abant filios ifrahel:et aduerfariũ debellaret p nois figuram:et populũ in
errã ,pmifliois induceret.Et iccirco etiã moifi fucceffit:ut oftenderet nouã
gem p xpm ihefum datã ueteri legi fucceffurã quẹ data p moifen fuit.Nã
la carnis cireúcifio caret utiq; rõne:qa fi deus uellet fic a þncipio formaf
t hoiem ut þputiũ nõ haberet:fed huius fecũdẹ circumcifiomis figura erat
gnificãs nudandũ effe pectus ideft aperto & fimplici corde oportere nos
iuere quomã pars illa corporis quẹ circúcidit habet quandã fimilitudĩne
ordis et eft pudẽda. Et ob hãc caufam deus nudari eã iuffit ut hoc argu
iento nos admoneret ne iuolutũ pectus haberemus:ideft neqd pudendũ
icimus intra confciẽtiẹ fecreta uelemus.Hẹc eft cordis circúcifio de qua ,p
hete loquunt quã deus a carne mortali ad aiam tranftulit quẹ fola mãfura
t.Volens eni túitẹ ac faluti nrẹ ,p ẹterna fua pietate confulere:poenitentiã
obis i illa circúcifione ,ppofuit:ut fi cor nudauerimus:ideft fi peccata cõ
fi:fatis deo fecerimus ueniã confequamur:quẹ cõtumacibus et admiffa
a cẹlantibus denegat ab eo qui nõ faciẽ ficut homo fed intima et archana
ctoris intuet:Eodẽ etiã fpectat carnis fuille iterdictio a qua cũ deus ab
nere iuffit id potiffimũ uoluit itelligi ut fe a peccatis atq; imunditiis ab
nerẽt.Eft eni lutulentũ hoc aimal et immũdum:nec unq; cẹlũ afpicit:fed i
rra toto corpore ,piectũ et ore:uentri femper pabulo feruit:nec ullũ aliũ
niuit þftare ufum poteft:ficut cẹterẹ animátes:quẹ uel fedendi uehicu
uel in culnbus agroẓ iuuant:uel plauftra collo trahunt:uel onera tergo
tant:uel idumẽtis:exuuiis fuis exhibent:uel copia lactis exuberãt:uel
todiẽdis domibus iuigilant:Interdixit ergo ne porcína carne uterent
eft ne uitã porcorũ imitaret q ad fola mortẽ nutriunt:ne uentri ac uo
ꝺtatibus feruiétes:ad faciendã iuftitiã inutiles effent ac morte afficerẽt.
ne fe fedis libidínibus imergerẽt ficut fus:quẹ fe ceno igurgitat:uel ne
renis feruiãt fimulachris ac fe luto ĩnqnent:luto eni fe oblimiũt qui deos

ceps dicere inſtitui : quantum ſatis eſſe uiſum eſt diſputauimus.hunc
que hbrum aliquando claudamus.

NTEQVAM DE INSTITVTIONE hominis
dicam: ubi duarum ciuitatum quátum ad rationalium
mortaliumque genus attinet apparebit exortus : ſicut
ſuperiore libro apparuiſſe in angelis iam uideť: prius
mihi quędam de ipſis angelis uideo eſſe dicenda:qbus
demonſtreť quantú a nobis poteſt :ꝗm nó incóueniés
neque incongrua dicatur eſſe hominibus angeliſque
ſocietas:ut non quattuor:duę ſcilic& angeloꝝ totidéꝗ
ninum : ſed duę potius ciuitates hoc eſt ſocietates merito eſſe dicanť:una
onis altera in malis non ſolum angelis ueꝝ etiam hominibus conſtitutę.
gelorum bonorum & malorum inter ſe contrarios appetitus : nó naturis
ıcipiıſꝗ diuerſis:cum deus omnium ſubſtantiaꝝ bonus auctor & códitor
ſꝗ creauerit:ſed uoluntatibus & cupiditatibus extitiſſe dubitare fas non
dum alii conſtantes in communi onınibus bono quod ipſe illis deus eſt:
ıe in eius ęternitate:ueritate: caritate perſiſtunt . Alii ſua poteſtate potius
ǝtati:uelut ſuum bonum ſibiipſi eſſent : a ſuperiore communi omnium
ıco bono ad ꝓpria defluxerunt.et habentes elationis faſtú ꝓ excellétiſſima
ıitate:uanitatis aſtutiam pro certiſſima ueritate:ſtudia partiú ꝓ indiuidua
ate: ſuperbi fallaces inuidi effecti ſunt. Beatitudinis igitur illorum cauſa
dhęrere deo.quocirca ıſtoꝝ miſerıꝗ cauſa ex cótrario eſt ıtelligęda:quod eſt
dhęrere deo.Quamobrem ſi cú quęriť quare illı beati ſint: recte reſpódeť
adhęrent deo. Et cum quęritur cur ıſtı ſunt miſeri:recte reſpondeť :quia
adhęrent deo . Non eſt creaturę rationalıs uel intellectualis bonum quo
a ſit:niſi deus.Ita quamuıs nó omnıs beata poſſit eſſe creatura:neꝗ enim
munus adipiſcuntur aut capıút fere:ligna:ſaxa:& ſi quid huiuſmodi eſt:
men quę poteſt non ex ſeipſa poteſt:quia ex nıhilo creata eſt:ſed ex illo a
creata eſt.Hoc enim adepto beata eſt:quo amiſſo miſera eſt.Ille uero qui
alıo ſed ſeipſo beatus eſt : ideo miſer non poteſt eſſe : quia non ſe poteſt
tere.Dicimus itaque immutabile bonum nó eſſe niſi unum uerú deum
ım .ea uero quę fecit bona quidem eſſe ꝗ ab illo ueruntamen mutabilia:
ɔn de illo ſed de nihilo facta ſunt.Quanquá ergo ſumma non ſint ꝗbus
ɔeus maius bonum:magna ſunt tamen ea mutabilıa bona: quae adhęrere
ınt ut beata ſint immutabili boɴo . ꝗ uſqueadeo bonum eſt eorum : ut
illo miſera neceſſe eſſe ſit . Nec ıdeo caetera in hac creaturae uniuerſitate
ıora ſunt:quia miſera eſſe nó poſſunt:neꝗ enim membra cętera corporis
rı ıdeo dicendum eſt oculis eſſe meliora:quia cęca eſſe nó poſſunt. Sicut

25

14. *Nicolas Jenson's roman, Venice 1470, on right* [

nſequentia depēdent:ſummā propriamqʒ nobis affert fœlicitatem:
ius quaſi caput religio eſt:nō illa gentilis quæ falſa et ficta errorisqʒ
ena nomen emētita eſt:ſed hæc noſtra quæ ipſarum rerum ueritate
pellationem adinuenit:quam animi ad unum ſolum et uerum deū
mam ſtabilemqʒ conuerſionem & uitam quæ mādatis eius pagatur
e aſſerimus:qua quidem ex uita amicicia etiam inter deum et hoīes
ſtituitur:amiciciam uero beatitudo illa ultima & fœliciſſimus finis
nſequitur:quī a ſuperioribus depend&: inde gubernatur:ac rurſus
peruenturus eſt. Quid igitur hac inter deum et homines amicicia
:lius nobis atqʒ beatius excogitari poteſt? Nōne uitæ:lucis:ueritatis
norumqʒ omniū ipſe fons atqʒ largitor eſt? Annon ipſe ut cuncta &
t & uiuant cauſam in ſe ipſo complectitur?qua ergo re indigebit q
̄ amiciciā adeptus eſt?qui reɤ omniū creatorē caritate ſibi cōiūxit?
i patrem atqʒ tutorem illum ſibi aſcripſit? Non poſſumus profecto
ere quin omnia quæ ad animam :quæ ad corpus:queqʒ ad externa
:tineant optimē beatiſſimeqʒ is poſſideat:qui caritate proximus deo
tus:beatiſſimā eius amiciciā exacta exquiſitaqʒ religione cōſecutus
.Hanc ergo ſalutarem hominum ad deum conuerſionē atqʒ aīciciā
omnipotenti dēo miſſus deus uerbum quaſi lucis īfinitæ ſplendor
ictis annūciat.Non hinc aut aliunde:ſed undiqʒ cunctis ex gētibus
deum uerum:græcos ſimul et barbaros omnem ſexū: omnē ætatē:
ites et pauperes:ſapientes et contra:liberos ac ſeruos magna uoce
iocat:hortaturqʒ omni ſtudio ac cura hoc donū ſuſcipiamus.Nam
iti eiuſdem naturæ atqʒ ſubſtantiæ nos omnes creauit: ſic rurſum
̄nitionem et caritatē ſuam æqualiter omnibus propoſuit qui grām
s ex toto animo cōplectuntur et colunt. Hanc dei erga nos caritatē
riſtus qui ipīus dei patris uerbum eſt ipſe quoqʒ deus:nō reſpiciēs
peccata hominum:ſed ſe ipſū eis recōcilians uniuerſo ſicut diuina
lamat ſcriptura orbi annunciat.Venit nanqʒ ait & ānunciauit pacē
̄ qui longe ſūt et pacem illis qui prope ſunt : quæ olim hebræi di-
itus docti prædicabant.Quidam enim eoɤ clamāt:recordabuntur
euertentur ad dominum omnes fines terre:& adorabunt coram eo
nes patriæ gentiū:quia domini eſt regnū terre et ipſe dominabitur
:tiū: et rurſus:dicite īgētibus qa dominus regnáuit: et enī firmauit
em terræ qui non cōmouebitur. Alius:conſpicuus erit dominus in
is:et cōteret penitus deos omnes gētium terræ:adorabuntqʒ ipſum
ʒuli ex loco ſuo:hæc ex priſcis tēporibus dicta diuinis oraculis:nūc
nos ſaluatoris noſtri Ieſu chriſti prædicatione peruenerūt: ſic præ-

27

greffu fuftinuere hoftes quoad machina ex grauitate cõfracta
eft ut Ifidis ꝓdigio ignis ab ea emiffus uideret. Qua ex re Mi-
thridates defperata pugna exercitum deduxit a rhodo. Ad pa-
tareos deinde copias agens facrum Latone nemus in cõficien-
dis machinis concidere aggreffus eft. Veꝝ fomnio perterritus
luco abftinuit : & Pelopidam qui cum lycijs bellũ gereret ducem ftatuens Archelaum pręmifit i gręciam qui uniuerfa uel
gratia uel metu fibi afcifceret. Ipfe cum cęteris ducibus temu-
lentus & uino madens aut delectus faciebat aut arma ptracta-
bat & cum Stratonicia oblectabat muliere & ius in eos qui uel
infidias fibi intuliffent aut noui aliquid moliti effent aut omnino romanoꝝ partibus fauiffent proferebat.In his itaꜩ uerfa-
batur rex . In grecia uero hęc deinceps fecuta funt . Archelaus
magno cõmeatu & exercitu claffem mouens delum ab athenienfibus deficientẽ aliaꜩ loca ui ac potentia redegit i ditionẽ
uiginti millibus hominũ his i locis neci traditis quoꝝ plurimi
itali fuere.Loca pręterea athenienfibus attribuit:aliaꜩ huiuf-
modi arroganter admodũ exercens & Mithridatẽ utplurimũ
extollens ad amicitiã compulit . Pecunias uero & facra p Ari-
ftonem athenienfem ac pecuniaꝝ cuftodes ufꜩ ad duũ milliũ
numeꝝ pręmifit e delo:quibus ufus Arifton tyrannidẽ patrię
intulit: Ex athenienfibus hos ftatim interficiens ueluti romia-
norũ fecutos partes:alios ad Mithridatẽ ire iubens.Et hic quidem epicuri edoctus difciplinis.Sed nec ꝓfecto folus ifte athe-
nienfiũ:neꜩ Critias etiam ante hunc:& quicunꜩ cum Critia
philofophię una dedere operã tyranni extiterũt . Sed in italia
& Pythagoras & in reliqua grecia qui fepte fapiętes dicebant
& qui negocia fibi defumpfere potentia ufi funt & tyrannide
crudelius ꝑletũꜩ ignaris litterarum fic ut de alijs philofophis
dubiũ fit ac fufpitiofũ an ꝓpter uirtutẽ aut paupertatẽ potius
& inhabilitatẽ rerũ gerendarũ folamen quoddã fapientiã fibi
effecerint cum plurimi ignorantes nũc & egeni aut neceffitate

15. *One of Erhard Ratdolt's romans, Venice 1477* [218]

Some contemporary Venetian romans

Centaur (Monotype), designed by Mr Bruce Rogers, has
been described as a modernized Venetian, Cloister (American
Type Founders & Monotype), Eusebius, originally called Nicolas
Jenson (Ludlow), Venezia (Linotype).

hominum negligentia deperierint : nos
enim ;dum Romae eſſemus;unam ,quae
in ima ripa ſpeculi eſt Dianae Aricinae,
pro miraculo uidimus. Sed nihil eſt pro
fecto (mihi crede) , nihil eſt fili (ut ego
ſemper dicere ſoleo) ; quod effici ab homine cura , diligentiáq; non poſſit: nos
enim (ut de me ipſo loquar) ;quibus tamen ; ex quo hanc uillam exaedificaui-
mus, iam inde ánte, q̃ tu es natus, conſu
mere hic nondum etiam licuit triginta in
tegros dies; neq; quando licebit ſcio , cū-
piam certe ſemper, et peroptabo ; uides
q̃ multos tibi poſuerim? ordines pulcher
rimarum arborum uel noſtratium , uel
aduenarum:q̃ ſi etiam Platanos habuiſ-
ſem ; nunq̃ illae me uiuo periiſſent; et ha
beres tu quidem nunc,quo melius inuita
re poſſes Faunum tuum ; et ille , quo li-
bentius accedere. B. F. Vellem equi
dem mi páter:ſed(quando id effici nó po
teſt)oblecta te populis tuis:tum etiam (ſi

B

16. *'The origin of all old-faces'* [220]

Roman
OLD FACE

No new type face approaching that of Jenson appeared until almost the close of the century. In 1495 Aldus Manutius, a scholar interested in the editing of greek texts set up a press in Venice, and issued in that year a tract by the Renaissance humanist Pietro Bembo printed in a variation of the roman letter, which was in a comparatively short time to supersede Jenson's. In this type we have, says Mr Stanley Morison 'the origin of all old-faces'[1] though he remarks that it represents only a 'first-state'. It is marred, among other things by over-large capitals and by poor cutting. But in its final and perfected form it is a face of great beauty: the capitals are smaller and both these and the lower-case are lighter. The cutting is greatly improved. Our illustration on page 33 is from the beautiful Aldine book in which it was first used, the famous *Hypnerotomachia Poliphili* by Francesco Colonna published by Aldus in 1499. A year later, Aldus, who has been named as the greatest of all the Venetian printer-publishers, designed, with the help of his typecutter, the first italic type face. We shall return to this famous type shortly under the section on italics.

Aldus's fame rests in part on his scholarship: his texts were correct and his books were widely distributed throughout Europe. Not only were his texts copied in all the important printing centres but the types in which they were set were copied also. Thus French printers were soon employing their variations of the Aldine roman. One of the first and most famous typecutters to use Aldus's letter as a model was the

[1] In *Type Designs of the Past and Present.* The Fleuron Ltd. London 1926.

celebrated Parisian Claude Garamond. His beautiful founts had a wide distribution. They were used at Antwerp by Christopher Plantin, and in a comparatively short time appeared in Venice and Florence! Eventually the Aldine roman influenced the design of types in this country through Dutch versions cut by Christoffel van Dijck and others. 'By the end of the (sixteenth) century' says Mr A. F. Johnson 'the Garamond roman had become the standard European type.'[1] Our William Caslon I (1692-1766) has been called 'the first really competent engraver & caster of types in this country'[2] and the last perfector of the old-face design.

Characteristics of old-face romans

STRESS OR SHADING
Oblique or biassed, i.e. thickest parts of curved forms approximately North-East/South-West.

MODELLING, OR GRADATION FROM THICK TO THIN STROKES
Gradual but more pronounced than in the Venetians.

SERIFS (FEET)
Bracketed, but no longer slab and therefore lighter than in the Venetians.

OTHER DISTINGUISHING FEATURES
The capitals are often lower than the ascending lower-case letters and are in general narrower than those of the Venetians. Many of the lower-case letters are also narrower than those of the Venetians. The lower-case e has a horizontal bar.

[1] In *Type Designs: their History and Development*. Grafton & Co. London 1934.
[2] A. F. Johnson in *Type Designs*.

RECEPTO AFFABILMENTE ET DALLE PIE
tofe Nymphe fúmamente afficurato, & tutto dalle blan
diuole puelle cófortato, & gli infugati fpiriti nó medio-
cre recentati, Altutto che effe coniecturare ualeua grato,
& piacerfi, uolétera prompto exhibendome, licentemé-
te familiare & deditiffimo me expofi. Et perche haueão
Alabaftri diapafmatici, & uafculi fmigmatici doro & di petre fine, & lucé
i fpeculi, & aurei difcerniculi nelle fue delicate mano, & candidi uelami
di feta plicati, & balneare interule offerentime portitore, recufabonde
ni differon. Che il fuo acceffo ad quefto loco era perche ueniuano al ba-
no. Et immediate fubiunxeron. Volemo che cum nui tu uengni. Ilqua
e cofti dinanti e, oue funde una fontana, non tu quella uedefti? Io riueré
emente rifpofi, Venuftiffime Nymphe. Si in me mille & uarie lingue fi
itrouafferon, io acconciamente non faperei rendere le demerite gratie, &
engratiare tanta domeftica benignitate, imperoche opportuniffimamé
e uiuificato me hauete Dunque non acceptare tale gratiofo & Nympha
e inuitatorio, ruftica uiltate fi reputarebe. Et per táto cum uui piu præfto
ne fœlice æxiftimeria effendo feruo, che altronde dominare. Il pche quá-
o coniecturare poffo inquiline & contubernale fiate di omni dilecto &
ero bene. Douete fapere chio uidi la mirauegliofa fòntana & cum folerte
enfo fpeculata, piu præclara opera che ad gliochii mei unque fe repræfen
affe cófeffo & affermo. Et tanto lanimo mio folerte occupai illecto circa
li qlla itentaméte riguardátila, & igluuiamente beuendo, la graue & diur
la mia fete falubreméte extinguendo, che piu oltra expiare nó andai.

Refpofe una lepidula placidaméte dicendo. Da mi la mano. Hora fi
u fofpite & il bene uenuto. Nui al præfente fiamo cinque fociale comite
ome il uedi, Et io me chiamo' Aphea. Et quefta che porta li buxuli & gli
ianchiffimi linteamini, e nominata Offreffia. Et queftaltra che dil fplen
lente fpeculo (delitie noftre) e gerula, Oraffia e il fuo nome. Coftei che te-
ie la fonora lyra, e dicta Achoe. Quefta ultima, che quefto uafo di pretio
iffimo liquore baiula, ha nome Geuffia. Et andiamo compare ad quefte
emperate Therme, ad oblectamento & dilecto. Dique breuemente anco
a tu (poi che la propitia fortuna tua quiui e caduta) uenirai cum nui læta

17. *Roman employed by Aldus in 1499* [220]

c   iiii

E

RATE Stephano da Siena priore:ben che indegno c̄
ordine de sancta Maria de gratia del ordine dela C̄
tosa appresso a Pauia:saluta in nome de quello che
uera salute il uenerádo religioso:& da lui amato de f̄
cero core Fra Thomaso de Antonio da Siena del or
ne deli Predicatori nel conuento de scō Ioáni & P.
lo in Venetia.ho receputo la ūa lettera cō desiderio:& lectola tuta cō ʒ
tentione,per la quale me rechiedite:& p̄gate:che uoglia dare uera info
matione alla charita ūa í publica forma deli facti:& costumi:& uirtu
&doctrina dela famosa sanctitate dela beata uergine Catharina da Sier
cō laquale io hebbi gratia dhauere familiarita:mentre che uixe. seconc
dicite:& maximamente per cagione de una querela facta nel Palazo c
Vescouo a Venetia circa la celebratione dela festa senza fare commem
ratione de essa uergine.Per che sono molti che nó uogliono credere c
siano uere le uirtu che de essa ueraméte se p̄dicano.Per cōfessare aptam
te la uerita ne io ne neuno de mia generatione cognobbe essa uergine:
alcuno de suo sangue fina alanno del Saluatore nr̄o mille trecento sett:
sei o circa:ne ancora a q̄llo tempo desideraua cognoscerla como hon
annegato nele tempestati & fortune dela uita presente:ma la bonta eter̄
la quale non uole che perisca alcuno:dispose liberare lanima mia d:
guance del inferno. In quello tempo adunq; accadette che hauessin
inimicitia senza nostro defecto con gente assai piu potente de noi.In l
le essendose exercitati & affatichati molti citadini deli primi per fare
pace:mai pottetero hauere speranza alcuna de bona uolúta & di pace
quelli nostri inimici. Allhora la decta uergine era nominata per tut.
Thoscana:& laudata cō grandissime laude de uirtute da grandissimo ʒ
mero de persone.Et se diceuano opere marauigliose de essa.Per la.qu
cosa me so decto che se io la pregasse de q̄sta cosa:che senza dubio me f
rebbe facta la pace:p che haueua facte molte cose simile.Io me consigl
có uno uicino gétil homo:il quale lógo tépo haueua hauuto inimici
& poi haueua facto pace & era familiare de essa uergine sacra:Il quale í
teso il mio decto respose:habi p certo che nó trouerai p̄sona in questa
ta piu apta de essa in fare tale pace subiungendo non perlongare piu :
io te accompagnaro.Adunque la uisitassimo & essa me uitte non cor
uergine uergognosa secondo io me credeua:ma con suiscerata charita
mo se hauesse ueduto uno suo fratello carnale che fosse retornato da lo
gissimi paesi:de che io molto me marauigliai.Et attendendo io alla c
catia dele sancte parole soi:con le quali non solamente me induxe ad
fessarme & a uiuere uirtuosamente:ma ancora me spinse & constren

* ii

Ad lectorem linguæ

GALLICAE STVDIOSVM.

L Ibros Galeni de vfu partium corporis humani quum ad Græcum exem
plar magna cura præcipuóque ftudio non modo recognouiffem , fed
propemodū nouos reddidiffem, vigi
liis, curis, labore fractus, materiá difquifiui, in qua
ingenii vires longiore ftudio & grauiore feffas re-
crearem , atque reficerem . Cui ọtio nulla mihi
aptior feges vifa eft hac ipfa fermonis Gallici in-
uentione ſimul ac traditione. Quas res duas dum
añxie parturio , animi contentione non minori
opus mihi effe experior, tantæ molis erat linguæ
Gallicæ rationem inuenire,& in canones coniice-
re. Victa verò tandem operis difficultate, velut in
portum quendam quietiffimum appulfus mihi
ipfe videor , dum mei laboris fructum non me-
diocrem fore video, ex magna etiam doctorú ex-
pectatione.
Abfoluta igitur vtcunque inftituti mei parte priori,
quam Ifagωgen in Gallicum fermonem paraui,
operæpretium me facturum putaui, fi eam in có-
munem omnium aut vtilitatem aut iucúditatem

a.iiii.

19. *Possible Garamond romans, Paris 1531* [220]

Aldine roman, 1500, on left [220]

vne froidure intolerable qu'il fa-
loit fouffrir l'efpace de cinq iours,
& que par deux iours ne trouue-
rions eau quelconque. Tous ces
perilz & incõueniés ne peurent en
rien refroidir ny amortir le har-
dy courage du gouuerneur, ne le
deftourner de fa haute entrepri-
fe. Si deloge au premier iour fui-
uy de fa bonne trouppe bien en-
talentée de ne fuir peines ne tra-
uaux quelconques pour le ferui-
ce de l'imperialle maiefté. Sept
gés de pied fe trouuerent en toute
la cõpagnie que la paour des fuf-
dittes incommoditez & miferes
feit tirer arriere & reprendre l'ad-
droiffe de noftre fort: les autres
tout deliberez tirerent iufques en
vn lieu diftant de deux lieues de
celuy auquel quatre iours aupar-
auant le capitaine Hernand Pi-
C

20. *A possible Garamond roman, Paris 1545* [220]

Le second traicté de

L'ASTROLABE, COMPRE-

nant l'vſaige des dimenſions Geometric-
ques,par l'eſchelle altimetre deſcripte
au dos d'iceluy inſtrumēt,diĉte au-
tremēt,Quarré Geometricqne.

APRES auoir iuſques icy ſuffi
ſammēt declaré l'vſaige de l'A
ſtrolabe, en tant que touche la
ſpeculation coſmographicque,
reſte deduire l'vſaige de leſchelle altimetre
miſe & deſcripte au dos dudiĉt aſtrolabe.
Icelle eſchelle a deux coſtez egaulx,eleuez
perpendiculairement l'vn ſur l'autre qua-
dran d'iceluy dos ſoubz l'horizon, dont
la partie de deſſoubz, croiſſant la ligne
de minuiĉt, ſ'appelle vmbre, ou eſchelle
droiĉte,q eſt faiĉte des corps eleuez droi-
ĉtemēt ſur la terre, comme eſt vne tour, &
aultre choſe ſemblable : Et l'autre qui de-

t ij

21. *Garamond roman and italic, Paris 1545* [220]

37

SERENISS. PRINCIPI

D. MATTHIAE

ARCHIDVCI AVSTRIÆ,

DVCI BVRGVNDIAE, &c.

IMPERATOR. F. FR.Q.

BELGICÆ PROREGI.

Hoc facrum quinquelingue
Bibliorū opus, quod ad ftabilien-
dum Ecclefiæ ftatum, controuer-

diuulgari iufsit, iuuitque;

Quódque Dei in primis, & clarifs. Theolo-
gorum ope, immenfo fúmptu & labore fuo,
Chriftophorus Plantinus feliciter typis fuis
vulgauit;ita vt Sanctifs. D.N. Pontificis, Regum, Principumque, & penè vniuerfi orbis
iudicio, tanti operis comprobata dignitas fit:

IDEM CHRISTOPH. PLANTINVS
ARCHITYPOGRAPHVS REGIVS
Celfit. fuæ perpetuus cliens
D. D.

22. *Roman types used by Christopher Plantin* [221]

Letter-Founder, in Ironmonger-Row, Old

DOUBLE PICA ROMAN.

Quousque tandem abutere, Catilina, patientia nostra? quamdiu nos etiam furor iste tuus eludet? quem ad finem sese effrenata jac-
ABCDEFGHJIKLMNOP

Double Pica Italick.

Quousque tandem abutere, Catilina, patientia nostra? quamdiu nos etiam furor iste tuus eludet? quem ad finem sese effrenata jac-
ABCDEFGHFJIKLMNO

GREAT PRIMER ROMAN.

Quousque tandem abutêre, Catilina, patientia nostra? quamdiu nos etiam furor iste tuus eludet? quem ad finem sc-
se effrenata jactabit audacia? nihilne te nocturnum præsidium palatii, nihil urbis vigiliæ, nihil timor populi, nihil con-
ABCDEFGHIJKLMNOPQRS

Great Primer Italick.

Quousque tandem abutêre, Catilina, patientia nostra? quamdiu nos etiam furor iste tuus eludet? quem ad finem sese effrenata jactabit audacia? nihilne te nocturnum præsidium palatii, nihil urbis vigiliæ, nihil timor populi, nihil con-
ABCDEFGHIJKLMNOPQR

Some contemporary old-face romans

Bembo (Monotype), Caslon (Caslon, now Stephenson Blake),
Estienne and Granjon (Linotype), Imprint, Poliphilus and Van Dijck
(Monotype).

Cadde graue a se steſso il padre antico
Lacero il petto. et pien di morte il uolto :
Et diſse, ahi sordo et di pieta nemico
Deſtin predace et reo. deſtin ingiuſto,
Deſtino a impouerirmi in tutto uolto ;
Perche piu toſto me non hai disciolto
Da queſto graue mio tenace incarco
Piu che non lece, et piu ch'io non uorrei.
Dando a lui gli anni miei,
Che del suo leue inanzi tèmpo hai scarco ?
Laſso alhor poteu'io morir felice :
Hor uiuo sol per dar al mondo eſsempio
Quant'è'l peggio far qui piu lungo indugio ;
S'huom de perdere in breue il suo refugio
Dolce, et poi rimaner a pena et scempio.
O uecchiezza oſtinata et infelice
A che mi serbi anchor nuda radice ;
Sel tronco in cui fioriua la mia ſpeme
È secco, et gelo eterno il cigne et preme.
Qual pianser gia le triſte et pie sorelle ;
Cui le treccie in sul Po tenera fronde,
Et l'altre membra un duro legno auolse ;
Tal con li scogli et con l'aure et con l'onde
Miſera, et còn le genti et con le ſtelle
Del tuo ratto fuggir la tua si dolse.
Per duol Timauo indietro si riuolse ;
Et uider Manto i boschi et le campagne
Errar con gli occhi rugiadosi et molli.
Hadria le riue e i colli

24. *Humanistic cursive hand* [222]

42

The Italics

At this point in these introductory notes we must interrupt the story of the roman letter in order to record that of an offspring. We have seen whence the Italian humanists derived the models for their beautiful scripts—the neo-caroline hands—and how these humanistic scripts were used by the printers as models for their types. When these formal hands were written quickly the speed reacted on the shapes of the letters. The changes may be summarized thus: the letters were compressed, the round letters like 'o', for example, became elliptical (*o*), there was a tendency to ligaturing, or joining of adjacent letters, letter shapes were simplified, and in addition there was a tendency for these hands to incline towards the right, though this characteristic is by no means typical—some are upright and some lean backwards. In this development of writing—the cursive or chancery hands (so-named from their employment in the Papal Chancery)—we have the birth of what we are now accustomed to call our italic types.

Mr A. F. Johnson has divided italic types into four principal groups (a) The Aldine (b) the Vicentino group (c) the group which is the contemporary of old-face roman, and (d) the modernized italics.[1]

THE ALDINE ITALICS

Not only was Aldus a scholar, a printer, and a publisher but he was also a first-class business man. Economic and not aesthetic motives dictated his design of the new type form. Wishing to print editions of the classics in small compass and appreciating the space-saving possibilities

[1] In *Type Designs: their History and Development.*

43

N ec sum adeo informis, nuper me in littore uidi,
C um placidum uentis staret mare. non ego Daphnin
I udice te metuam, si nunquam fallat imago.
O tantum libeat mecum tibi sordida rura,
A tq; humileis habitare casas, & figere ceruos,
O edorum'q; gregem uiridi compellere hib:sco.
M ecum una in syluis imitabere Pana canendo.
P an primus calamos cæra coniungere plures
I nstituit, Pan curat oues, ouium'q; magistros.
N ec te pœniteat calamo triuisse labellum.
H æc eadem ut sciret, quid non faciebat, Amyntas?
E st mihi disparibus septem compacta cicutis
F istula, Damœtas dono mihi quam dedit olim,
E t dixit moriens, te nunc habet ista secundum.
D ixit Damœtas, inuidit stultus Amyntas.
P ræterea duo nec tuta mihi ualle reperti
C apreoli, sparsis etiam nunc pellibus albo,
B ina die siccant ouis ubera, quos tibi seruo.
I am pridem à me illos abducere Thestylis orat.
E t faciet · quoniam sordent tibi munera nostra.
H uc ades o formose puer. tibi lilia plenis
E cce ferunt nymphæ calathis, tibi candida Nais
P allentes uiolas, et summa papauera carpens,
N arcissum, et florem iungit bene olentis anethi,
T um casia, at q; alijs intexens suauibus herbis,
M ollia luteola pingit uacinia caltha.
I pse ego cana legam tenera lanugine mala,
C astaneas'q; nuces, mea quas Amaryllis amabat.
A ddam cærea pruna, et honos erit huic quoq; pomo.
E t uos o lauri carpam & te proxima myrte,

a iiii

25. *The first italic type, 1500 [222]*

44

of a type based on the Chancery hand he had the first of all italic types cut in the year 1500. In the following year he issued his first cheap 8vo volumes (page size of the Virgil approximately 6″ × 3½″) set in the new letter. The popularity of these small books ensured a wide distribution for the new cursive & it was widely copied throughout Europe, versions of it eventually finding their way to England. 'With the Aldine italic,' wrote Mr Updike '*originality of idea* in type-forms ceases.'[1]

Characteristics of the Aldine italic

With the chancery cursive hands the Renaissance scribes used roman capitals. Naturally Aldus followed them when he designed his italic type. Unfortunately he also followed the scribes in ligaturing or tying many characters and largely because of this his type has been described by Mr Johnson as having the characteristics of a 'hasty script.'[2] Aldus tried to make his new type imitate handwriting but only succeeded in complicating the compositor's work: over sixty ligatured letters have been counted in some of his books! It is as well that no contractions were cut for use with this type.

The Aldine italic is a slightly sloped letter. The *b, d, h, k* and *l*, are seriffed at the ascender line only and the *p* and *q* are seriffed at the descender line only. In the latter this serif is a noticeably strong cross-stroke. The shape & treatment of these serifs varies considerably in chancery types.

The roman capitals are shorter than the ascending letters: even the dot over the i is higher than the capitals. Sloping capitals for use with italic lower-case were not generally introduced until about 1550.

THE VICENTINO ITALICS

The wide distribution and popularity of the Aldine italics were not sufficient to secure them to posterity—except in an historical sense. They failed because of the weaknesses inherent in their design. 'Italic,' wrote Mr Updike, 'became a workable type for the printer only when

[1] In *Printing Types, Their History, Forms, and Use.* Vol I.
[2] In *Type Designs: their History and Development.*

45

Auendoti io deſcritto, Studioſo Lettor mio, l'anno paſſato uno libretto da imparar ſcriuere littera Cancellareſca, la quale, a mio iudicio, tiene il primo loco, mi parea integramente non hauerti ſatisfatto , ſe ancho non ti dimoſtraua il modo di acconciarti la penna, coſa in tal exercitio molto neceſſaria, E pero in queſto mio ſecondo librecino, nel quale anchora a ſatisfatione de molti, ho poſto alcune uarie ſorti de littere (come tu uederai) ti ho uoluto deſcriuere al piu breue et chiaro modo che io ho poſſuto come tu habbi a temperarti detta penna.

Dele uarie ſorti de littere poi, che in queſto Trattatello trouerai, ſe io ti uoleſſi ad una per una deſcriuere tutte le ſue ragioni, ſaria troppo longo proceſſo; Ma tu hauendo uolunta de' imparare', ti terrai inanzi queſti exempietti, et sforcerati imitarſi quanto poterai, che in ogni modo ſeguendo quelli, ſenon in tutto, almeno in gran parte' te adiuterano conſeguire quella ſorte' di littera, che' piu in eſſo ti dilettera'. Piglialo adunque, et con felici auſpicii ti exercita, che a chi uuo le conſeguire' una uirtu niente glie' difficile'.

26. *The earliest of the formal chancery italics, 1523* [222]

precisely that characteristic was discarded which made it most Aldine, i.e. imitation of a cursive hand.'[1]

The second group of italic types was also based on the chancery hand but on a more formal variety practised by the writing masters of the sixteenth century. Arrighi,[2] one of the most brilliant of these masters had settled in Rome where he was employed at the Papal Chancery in writing out apostolic briefs. He published, while still in papal employ, his first writing manual in 1522. It was printed from wood blocks. In Venice, in the following year, Arrighi published a continuation also printed from wood blocks, in which appeared a page of text matter printed from type—'the earliest of the formal chancery italics.'[3]

In 1524 he turned printer but unlike Aldus, a printer interested only in the production of fine limited editions. He designed several versions of the formal chancery cursives. Their superiority as types both in design and practicality compared with the italics of Aldus, and the handsome books he printed—together with those printed in his type by Antonio Blado, 'the greatest printer at Rome in the sixteenth century'[4] —made it inevitable that those of Aldus would be ousted and that the new italic would be widely copied throughout Europe.

Characteristics of the Vicentino italics

'Cursiveness and not inclination is the characteristic of chancery, but generations of printers have been so accustomed to the inclined italic that they have come to believe that the word means sloping.'[5]

The letters are narrow, slightly inclined and are separately formed. In Arrighi's early founts the ascenders have rounded terminals (called calligraphic ascenders) in place of serifs but in his later founts serifs replace these. The ascenders & descenders are of generous length. Roman capitals, shorter than the ascending letters, were used but Arrighi was the first to design and use swash capitals also. The bodies of most of his

[1] In *Printing Types, Their History, Forms, and Use*. Vol I.
[2] Lodovico degli Arrighi da Vicenza—hence the name 'Vicentino' for this second group of italic types.
[3][4][5] A. F. Johnson in *Type Designs: their History and Development.*

types are approximately 16 point and the format of his books generally quartos. 'Economy of space (in his types) was not considered in their design'[1] says Mr Johnson. Two forms of *g* are used, often in the same piece of setting, one of which has been called the calligraphic *g*. Diamond shaped full points are another feature of Arrighi's founts.

[1] A. F. Johnson in *Type Designs: their History and Development*.

CORYCIANORVM · LIB · II ·
HYMNI ·

Franc · F ranchinus Consentinus ·
Effigies , vultusq̃ Deum de marmore vidi ,
T ergeminos vir culte , tibi quos ante repertos
S ansonia est experta manus , statuitq̃ per artem.
V idi , altumiq̃ decus pulchra sub imagine seruant,
& laudum tibi magna tenent monimenta, perennes
D um pater in pontum Tiberinus deuehet vndas ,
S tabit dumiq̃ lapis Tarpeius , maxima semper
R elligionis erunt signa , et pietatis honores ·
An forte in saxo veras imitante figuras
I nfanti aridet Latona , Auroráq̃ Phœbo?
N um Venus , et nudus puer , exultaíq̃ Dione ?
N ugæ abeant,non ops,non Vesta,et veiouis,en hic
E st lapis , effinxit quondam quæ Græcia mendax.
Ecce hoʃpes natæ in gremio quantum Anna nepoti
L eniter arridet , gestit puero Anna nepoti ,
Q ui mare,qui terras, quiq̃ æthera,nubila,cœlum,
C ondidit , et forma perfecta condidit orbem ,
N atus et ipʃe Deo quum sit cum patre,nec unquam

Z

27. *Vicentino's first italic* [222]

N atiuam eripiunt formam indignantibus ipsis,

I nuitasque iubent alienos sumere uultus .

H aud magis imprudens mihi erit, et luminis expers

Q ui puero ingentes habitus det ferre gigantis,

Q uàm si quis stabula alta, lares appellet equinos,

A ut crines magnæ genitricis gramina dicat .

P ræstiterit uero faciem, spolia et sua cuique

L inquere, et interdum propriis rem prodere uerbis,

I ndiciisque suis, ea sint modo digna Camœnis .

R es etiam poteris rebus conferre uicissim,

N ominibusque ambas uerisque, suisque uocare .

Q uod faciens, fuge uerborum dispendia, paucisque

I ncludas numeris, unde illa simillima imago

D ucitur, et breuiter confer. ne forte priorum

O blitus sermonum alio traducere mentem,

I nque alia ex aliis uideare exordia labi .

I amque age uerborum qui sit delectus habendus,

Q uæ ratio, nam nec sunt omnia uersibus apta .

O mnia nec pariter tibi sunt uno ordine habenda .

V ersibus ipsa etiam diuisa, et carmina quantum

E iiii

28. *Vicentino's second italic* [222]

F   49

perſeueraſſe con animo di volere pur' ferire col taglio, di man-
dritto, o di riuerſo: Queſto potrebbe riparar' di croce, et ſpinge-
re cõ la punta verſo lui, ouero riparar' di coperta uenẽdo in Prima, & ſpinger' di ſotto, & di ſopra ſecondo le forze ſue: et ſe
pur' in quel tempo il detto auerſario tentaſſe pur d'offenderlo
con detti colpi di taglio dal mezzo in giu' : Queſto andarebbe
contra eſſo ſpingendo ſubito per hauer minor' colpo da lui, et per
farli maggior la riſpoſta. Sono diuerſe altre vie ancora per in
trar per forza d'arme, perche ritrouandoſi vno pur ne la mede-
ſima Terza Guardia larga, & contraſtando à mezza ſpada
col nemico, quando cercaſſe intrarli per forza di fore ſopra la
ſpada per darli nel petto, ritornarebbe di quella Terza ne la Se
conda ſtretta, & ſubito paſſato il ſuo colpo, di nouo ſpingerebbe
verſo di lui, firmandoſi in Terza, ouero Quarta larghe: Et ſe il
detto nemico accompagnando il pie ſiniſtro appreſſo il deſtro, et
tutto in vn tratto caualcaſſe con la ſua ſpada quella di queſt' altro, entrãdo di fore per forza, Queſto ritornarebbe ſubito come
di ſopra in Seconda ſtretta, ſpingendo vn' altra volta contra di
lui, & firmandoſi in vna de le medeſime Guardie Terza, o
Quarta. Ma ſe pur voleſſe far proua con la ſua Terza di met
ter' la punta de la ſua ſpada ſopra quella di queſt' altro, paſſan-
do in quel punto col pie manco innanzi verſo la parte deſtra con
traria, tentãdo nel medeſimo tempo, ſenza firmarſi, d'entrar' per
forza, & ferirlo de la ſua Seconda, o di Terza al quanto alta:
dico s'ei foſſe minore, o piu debole di queſto altro, che Queſto
ſenza creſcer' il paſſo come di ſopra, li voltarebbe ſubito la pun

D

29. *Formal chancery italic, Antonio Blado, 1553* [223]

Some contemporary chancery italics

Arrighi, Bembo, Bembo Condensed and Blado (Monotype),
Cancelleresca Bastarda (Enschedé), Lutetia (Enschedé and Monotype),
Romanée (Enschedé), Spectrum (Enschedé and Monotype).

Infigne ingenuis fuit olim bulla puellis:
  Quum non sis, bullam cur capis, ingenuus?
Scortea fume igitur : quadrant mage fcortea: prolē
  Libertinorum fic decorato tuam.

In quendam.

A me quæris, amet num te tua Fuluia: habeto,
  Si te non odit Fuluia, forfan amat.

Aenigma in filiam Inachi.

Dic, precor, Oedipodes, fit quænam fœmina cŏiux,
  Cui pater eft coniux, nec pater ipfius eft.
Affatur dominum, dominumᵹ affarier ufquam
  Vix potis eft: audit uerba, nec audit herus.

In Geraldum Gallum.

Hærebam, Galli cognomen fi alitis effet,
  Aufpicio, an cafu, docte Geralde tuum.
Præuidere hominis uirtutem fata futuram,
  Hac certo cunctis alite confpicuam.
Huic etenim debet, quicquid Romana triumphi
  Barbarici uicto duxit ab hofte manus.
Impulit hæc Latios fafces , incedere turmas
  Cenfuit, aut cœptos eft remorata gradus.
Solaᵹ fydereos uolucrum crebro afpicit axes:
  Confcia fublimis fit quoque (crede) dei.
Non hærendum igitur, quin omnis curia ab acri
                              h 2   *Pendeat*

---

30. *The Basle italic, Lyons 1537* [223]

THE GROUP OF ITALICS WHICH IS
THE CONTEMPORARY OF OLD-FACE ROMAN

The sixteenth century has been called 'the age of italics.'[1] In Italy, the home of its invention, probably more books were set in italic than in roman during that period.

Until 1524 the new sloping lower-case characters were accompanied by roman capitals, but from that time on attempts were made to design capitals which would accord, in inclination, with the lower-case. Arrighi employed upright capitals with his italics but was the first to design and use a variant with them—swash capitals. By the middle of the century sloped capitals were becoming the norm in italic founts.

In the example on p. 52 is shown the italic which Mr Johnson says inaugurated the old-face group of italics[2] and which he calls the Basle italic after its place of origin. It will be seen that the lower-case of this letter slopes considerably while the upper-case is a collection of letters —it can scarcely be called an alphabet—of very greatly differing degrees of slope. Despite this pecularity it became an extremely popular letter, being used in Germany, France, Italy, and in this country. This style of italic was firmly established by the French type cutters, the most notable of whom was Robert Granjon. In our country 'from John Day to William Caslon, all designers were content to follow continental models.'[3]

For a considerable time italic was regarded as a type in its own right, or in other words, as a face distinct from roman. Gradually however italic came to be employed not for complete books but 'for preliminary matter, citation, and emphasis'[4] only. At the end of the sixteenth century, writes Mr Johnson '. . . books set entirely in italic, especially books of verse, were still common. But there was already one indication that the cursives were becoming the servant of roman; they were being cast on the same body as the romans.'[5] And while some printers & founders continued to show romans & italics quite separately on their

[1][2][3][5] A. F. Johnson. *Type Designs: their History and Development.*
[4] Stanley Morison. *Type Designs of the Past and Present.*

H ac olea ramum dextra, pacemq̃ reuinctam
D efert, ac vigili cura iubet omnia ferues.
S unt fluuij Hungariæ feptem tua fceptra verentes,
Q ui fibi prouideas orant, curfuq̃ perenni
R ite monent curarum molem incumbere Regis
N unc humeris, te follicitum debere caducis
P artibus objicere ex animo, faluamq̃ tueri.
H ac vult, ac petit arma gerens, nec læta puella.
P arte alia eft domitrix Virtus, leo duxq̃ ferarum
C andidus hunc Boëmi fubmittunt Maxmiliane,
I mperio, fortem ingeminant, dominumq̃ falutant,
S ed breuibus repetam fpes quæ patriã tenet ægram.
D epofita ac toties miferè concuffa refurget
P annonia, exitijq̃ modum te Rege futurum
S perat, conftitues Bizantij firma trophæa.
D efinet impietas, te Cæfare purus iniquè
P ofthabitusq̃ Deûm cultus, probitasq̃ redibit.
D iffugient nimbi, fublatis nubibus aèr
I n medio cunctis fplendefcet, te feret vnum
I n terris Regem populus, compage foluta
C orporis, ad Superûm fedes, ftellasq̃ reuifes,
O rnabisq̃ aliquod fidus, propriumq̃ dicabis.
I am tu Magnorum decus, & Rex maxime Regum,
P aucula quæ mitto placida fimul accipe fronte,
Q uoq̃ fauore foles nimium cumulato clientem
S ambucum: meritò tanti qui incenfus amore
P rincipis, hæc offert domino non digna potenti.
S ed mitem noui, facilem expertusq̃ fubinde,
O ro, clementi afpicias munufcula vultu,
Q uæ lufi nuper, poftponens feria nugis:
G andaui in clara generofis ciuibus vrbe,
H ofpitio celebri, feceffu & femper amico.

A 5   *Sufcipe*

31. *A Granjon old-face italic, 1566* [223]

specimen sheets, others, e.g. the Egenolff-Berner foundry of Frankfurt showed each example of roman followed by one of italic on the same body in its famous specimen of 1592.

Characteristics of italics in this group

'By old-face italic we mean the kind of letter of a marked inclination in both upper-case and lower-case which was usual in European typography from about 1540 down to the time of Caslon. It is the italic which accompanies the old-face roman, although it originated somewhat later and was not at first designed as a companion letter.'[1]

These cursives were of 'a decided slope and with an inclined but irregular upper-case. Irregularity of the angle of inclination in both upper- and lower-case, was a general characteristic. Most of the letters, in the initial and final strokes, continued the cursive quality of the hands after which they were originally designed.'[2]

Some contemporary old-face italics

Caslon (Caslon, now Stephenson Blake), Janson (Stempel), Van Dijck (Monotype).

*   *   *

A description of the fourth main grouping of italic faces—the modernized italics—will be left until later. The group will then be in its correct place chronologically and will thus not confuse students who may, as yet, have heard little or nothing of the transitional or modern faces—and may wonder how the latter have developed from the designs of Garamond and Caslon.

[1] [2] A. F. Johnson. *Type Designs: their History and Development.*

PROLEGOMENA IN SOLINUM.

Um ad has primùm Exercitationes descendi elaborandas, id operæ pretium putasse, unumque hoc spectasse fateor, ut eorum, quæ in Plinium olim adnotaveram, specimen aliquod in medium darem, ac veluti gustum proponerem; sepositis tantisper, quas in mente ac manibus habebam in varia Tertulliani opera, in Eliberini Concilii canones, atque universam priscæ Ecclesiæ ritualem historiam Commentationibus. Atque is erat tum mearum rerum status & ratio, ut mutatâ in totum sorte pristinâ vitæ, sic ferentibus fatis, secessu ruris ad tempus electo, animo, ut decuit, remissiore, ac laxius feriante nihil curis gravioribus loci dare possem, utpote qui vix levibus his ac ludicris studiis par essem. In illo tamen otio rusticano quando illa quæ meditabar agere non vacabat, tam malè mihi esse nolui pati, ut ista saltem curare non liceret, quæ me ab beluco, veternoque, cui desidia mea tum maximè patebat, vindicarent. Ceterum cùm illa cogitatio inquietum animum exerceret, tam vastam eam atque infinitam concipere non libuit, ut Plinium totum, qualis quantusque est, in partem hanc curæ studiique reciperem, cui labori nec vires unius hominis quantumlibet diligentis suppetere, nec vitam quantumvis longævi sufficere posse rebar.

ex inmani corpore refectam felectamque sumere, circa quam opera nostra evitesceret, eo tempore optimum ducebam. Nec tamen etiam fine dubitatione hic mihi res abiit, dum disputo mecum quam potissimum sumere deberem. Nunc impetum ceperam tractatum de gemmis suscipere illustrandum; nunc libros qui arbores persequuntur, vel eos qui herbas disquirunt, examinandos. Aliquando avebam eum qui totius operis primus est atque indicem continet, quid singulis libris ceteris contineatur ostendentem, restituere multis partibus mutilum, mendosumque: aliquando illum qui sequitur exoriare, quo ratio universitatis atque mensura explicatur, & quidquid in mundo eximium ac visendum spectatur. Interdum ad sequentes quatuor properabam animadvertendos, qui terrarum situs per partes exponunt & τὰ παραφερόμενα describunt. Modo etiam septimum solum qui de natura hominis agit, & multa gerit consideratione digna, cupiebam recognoscere. Inter hos estus fluctuanti distractoque, & modo his modo illis acquiescenti, fors nescio que Solinum obtulit, quem auctorem pene puer olim cum variis collatum scriptis exemplaribus diligenter emendaveram. Hoc homine reperto non diutius posthac querendum judicavi, qua ex parte mihi Plinius arripiendus esset, unde inciperem, ubi desinerem, quo usque denique & quomodo in illo magno mari velificarem. Ducem hunc capere ac sequi statim placuit, quem auctorem nemo nescit, nihil omnino habere, quod non ex Plinio hauserit. Ex omnibus enim Plinii libris quodcumque potuit, converrit, & in suam istud compendium congessit. Quamvis autem ex professo sola geographica compilavit, & in epitomen redegerit, atque in hanc partem fere inclinatior fit materies, que locorum situm ac commemorationem persequitur, servata ubique orbis distinctione quam Plinius adhibuit: idem tamen quidquid est arborum, gemmarum, animaliumque exoticorum variis regionibus nascentium, id omne soller-

32. Old-face italic of Cristoffel van Dijck, 1689 [223]

57

La crainte de l'Eternel eſt le chef de ſcience: mais les fols meſpriſent ſapiéce & inſtruction. Mon fils, eſcoute l'inſtruction de ton pere, & ne delaiſſe point l'enſeignemēt de ta mere.

Car ils feront graces enfilees enſemble à ton chef, & carquans à ton col. Mon fils, ſi les pecheurs te veulent attraire, ne t'y accorde point.

33. Jean Jannon, Sedan 1621 [224]

The Intermediate[1] or Transitional romans

It will be remembered that by the end of the sixteenth century Claude Garamond's roman had become the standard European type, and for 200 years after his death, in 1561, his types continued to be used throughout Europe. But by the end of the sixteenth century there had been a marked falling off in the standards of printing both in Italy & in France, and in the following century although 'there were considerable changes in the formula for book production...in the history of the development of type-forms the century is almost a blank.'[2]

In France, it was not until Louis XIII established his Royal Printing House in 1640 that a greater interest in printing standards was evoked. Although at first Garamond faces were employed by the Royal Press, two years after its foundation a work by Cardinal Richelieu, its director, was set in new types designed by Jean Jannon of Sedan—types, until 1926, wrongly ascribed to Claude Garamond. But no really significant deviation from the old-face design was made until the year 1692 when Louis XIV ordered a new series of types for the exclusive use of the Royal Printing House. A commission appointed by the Academy of Sciences considered the matter. In a lengthy report it recommended a roman alphabet constructed on a mathematical basis. But Philippe

[1]This term was preferred by J. H. Mason to the more widely used *transitional*.
[2]A. F. Johnson. *Type Designs: their History and Development.*

CE qui a le plus contribué à porter la Peinture & la Sculpture au haut point de perfection, où nous les voyons aujourd'huy en France, c'est la protection dont le Roy les a honorées, & les gratifications fréquentes que Sa Majesté a refpanduës fur ceux qui les cultivoient. Il fonda à Paris une Académie, qu'il compofa des Peintres & des Sculpteurs les plus habiles, & voulut que ce fuft une Efcole publique, où l'on inftruiroit les jeunes gens, qui auroient du genie pour ces deux Arts. Il eftablit des Profeffeurs, ordonna des prix afin d'exciter l'émulation, & n'épargna rien pour un eftabliffement fi utile. Sa magnificence ne fe borna pas là; il inftitua en mefme temps à Rome, une pareille Académie, où les Eléves, qui ont remporté le prix de Peinture ou de Sculpture à Paris, vont fe perfectionner, & font entretenus aux defpens de Sa Majefté, qui fournit jufqu'aux frais de leur voyage.

C'eft le fujet de cette Médaille. On voit deux Génies; l'un s'exerce à peindre, & a prés de luy un chevalet, fur lequel eft un Tableau; l'autre travaille à un Bufte, & a prés de luy le Torfe, fameux fragment de l'antique. Dans l'éloignement paroift un bout du Colifée, refte magnifique d'Amphithéatre dans Rome. La Légende, SCHOLÆ AUGUSTÆ, fignifie, *Efcoles Royales.* L'Exergue, ACADEMIA REGIA PICTURÆ ET SCULPTURÆ, LUTETIÆ ET ROMÆ INSTITUTA. M. DC. LXVII. veut ire *Académie Royale de Peinture & de Sculpture,*

34. *The 'Romain du Roi', Paris 1702* [224]

Grandjean, who cut the punches did not bind himself by the Commission's findings nor tie himself precisely to the designs accompanying the report, but wisely followed, to some extent at least, the dictates of his own eye.

By 1702 the first sizes of the new type (romain du roi) were ready. Our example from the book in which they were first used shows the distinct change in the character of the design as compared with the old-faces of Aldus and Garamond. There is a certain stiffness in the design and sharpness in the cutting. This is because the shading is approaching the vertical and the modelling, or difference between the thick strokes and the thin strokes, is more pronounced. 'The modern face is implicit in this design' but the 'technique (of printing) was not yet sufficiently advanced to allow of the true modern face.'[1]

Grandjean's design was naturally copied by other typefounders, and old face, which had been used on the Continent for the previous 200 years was, in France, superseded by the new letter.

Grandjean's 'work was continued by Jean Alexandre (his friend and pupil) and finally completed by Louis Luce'[2] (Alexandre's son-in-law). Luce was the third of the royal typecutters and also worked on his own account. The romans shown in his specimen of 1771 are remarkable for their *condensation*. Both Luce and Fournier le jeune 'derived their taste for condensed romans from Fleischman,'[3] a German, who had cut 'an entirely new series of letters for the great foundry of the Enschedés at Haarlem during the years 1730 to 1768 ... some twenty alphabets all of which were of an elongated character, with thin hairlines and thin serifs.'[4]

Pierre Simon Fournier (1712-1768) or Fournier le jeune, the celebrated Parisian founder, whose father had been manager of the famous Le Bé foundry, started work on his own account in 1737. Of his tremendous industry (he cut over eighty types in twenty-eight years), and technical brilliance as a punch-cutter and founder, a wealth of evidence remains in his published works. But although he was technically brilliant he is not to be considered as an innovator of new type designs but

[1][2][3]A. F. Johnson. *Type Designs: their History and Development.*
[4]Stanley Morison. *Type Designs of the Past and Present.*

Parangon Romain, N°. 4.

Lors qu'Aspafie étoit concubi-
ne d'Artaxerxès. On ne fauroit
lui donner moins de vingt ans à la
mort de Cyrus: elle avoit donc
foixante - quinze ans lors qu'un
nouveau Roi la demande comme
une grace particuliere.

1 2 3 4 5 6 7 8 9 0
A B C D E F G H I J K L M N O P
Q R S T U V W X Y Z

J. M. Fleischman sculpsit. 1739.

Parangon Italique, N°. 4.

Aspasia, qui eftoit fort âgée, &
toutesfois très-belle, qui avoit efté
putain de fon feu frere. Darius son
fils en devint fi fort amoureux, tant
elle eftoit belle nonobftânt l'âge, qu'il
A B C D E F G H I K L N O P Q T V X Y Z

J. M. Fleischman sculpsit. 1739.

35. *Fleischman's roman and italic* [224]

rather as a clever adapter of the work of others in that field. Naturally inclined by upbringing to take as models the work of earlier celebrated founders (Le Bé had been a pupil of Claude Garamond) he was nevertheless swayed by the new fashions established by the Royal Printing House. His first roman and italic were based on those of Louis Luce—who complained that his ideas had been stolen. Fournier thought it necessary to make the capitals align with the tops of the ascending letters. And he wrote 'I squared the angles of these same capitals a little more, as well as some of the lower-case letters, where I removed a certain "rounding-off" in the angle between the perpendicular and horizontal strokes. This serves to give them more freedom, to distinguish one from another, and to make the strokes more clear.'[1] Of the twenty point size (see the example, page 68) Paul Beaujon wrote:'No more happy compromise has been found between "old" and "modern" styles; it is the first of the "transitional" faces, and so cleverly does it mingle tradition with precision of cutting that it seems at times to partake of almost contradictory virtues. It is smart but not forward, old-fashioned but not archaic.'[2]

England was not immediately affected by these changes in French typography but, in William Caslon I, had found her first real type designer. Starting his foundry nearly twenty years after the appearance of Grandjean's new type Caslon issued his first broadside specimen sheet in 1734. It is said that when it appeared 'his reputation was made.'[3]

While in France the use of old-face types was gradually being discontinued, in this country William Caslon I's old-face design gained steadily in popularity. But although type design in England was not at once affected by the changes on the Continent an influence had been at work from towards the close of the seventeenth century which eventually affected it profoundly: a new style of writing—the round hand —was developed during that period. The old-face design of Aldus was, as we have seen, based on the hands of the humanists—written with broad-nibbed pens held at an angle of approximately 30° to the direc-

[1] In his *Modèles des Caractères.*
[2] *The Monotype Recorder* March-April, May-June 1926.
[3] D. B. Updike. *Printing Types, Their History, Forms, and Use.* Vol II.

tion of the line of writing—thus producing in the round letter forms the characteristic NE/SW shading that we recognize in old-face types. (For a note on the examples of this writing shown below, see p. 263.)

turkey's quill

bamboo

But in executing the new hand the writing masters held their pens vertically or almost vertically, that is, at right-angles or almost at right-angles to the direction of the line of writing. In the new letters the vertical strokes were thickest and the horizontal ones thinnest. The works of the writing masters of the day, published in books printed from engraved copper plates (of which George Shelley's *Alphabets in all Hands*, *circa* 1715, a page from which is shown in our examples, is one of many), helped to give the new hand a wide advertisement & accustom people to it.

But no typefounder thought of adopting the new style of letter until the Birmingham lacquer manufacturer, John Baskerville (1706-1775), who in his earlier years had been a writing master, became interested in the art of letter founding. 'Baskerville was only the first to admit into the typefoundry a letter which had been clamouring outside its door for at least half a century. This, then, was what we owe to Baskerville: that at a time when abstract rules still were applied to works of beauty . . . he was sensible enough to base his design on the living pen-form which will always remain as a check and inspiration to typefounders'.[1]

Baskerville not only enriched the art of typography with his types—which to the readers of his day were over-brilliant, glittering and thus tiring to the eyes—but built new improved presses and produced improved inks and paper—all of which enabled him to print his type with

[1] *The Monotype Recorder*. Vol XXVI. No 221. September-October 1927.

the care that it demanded. And although Baskerville's founts 'never had much vogue in England, they did have an enormous influence on the later development of English type-forms, and on the type-forms of Europe.'[1]

Baskerville's types, and those of other founders which were based on them, for example, Alexander Wilson's romans as shown in his specimen sheet of 1772, the types of William Martin, whose brother Robert had worked with Baskerville, Vincent Figgins's roman of 1793, and the roman of William Caslon III, shown in his specimen of 1798, may be looked on as examples of the transitional group of faces, that is, faces which heralded those types which have been called 'modern'.

Characteristics of intermediate or transitional romans

STRESS OR SHADING
More nearly vertical. (In some cases vertical.) See Monotype Baskerville.

MODELLING, OR GRADATION FROM THICK TO THIN STROKES
More pronounced than in the old faces but slight when compared with Bodoni. In other words it is not abrupt.

SERIFS (FEET)
When bracketed the bracketing is usually finer than in the old faces. Some transitionals have flat, but not very thin, unbracketed serifs. See Monotype Fournier.

OTHER DISTINGUISHING FEATURES
Some transitional faces show a definite tendency to lateral compression or condensation.

[1]D. B. Updike. *Printing Types, Their History, Forms, and Use.* Vol II.

PETIT PARANGON ROMAIN.

NOUS ne devrions regarder comme bien réel &
indépendant, que ce qui peut contribuer à notre bon-
heur ; & pour lors il n'y auroit de véritable bien que
la vertu, puisqu'elle seule peut nous rendre heureux,
tous les autres étant rélatifs & ne devenant bien ou
mal que par l'usage qu'on en fait : mais nous enten-
dons par ce terme, tout ce qui est convenable, & ce
qui sert à augmenter nos plaisirs & à diminuer nos
peines.

PETIT PARANGON ITALIQUE.

*LA galanterie est l'art de séduire par la louange &
la coquetterie. On entend aussi par galanterie une amou-
rette, un commerce entre les deux sexes, dont l'esprit &
le sens font tous les frais, sans que le cœur y ait la moin-
dre part. On peut, dit M. de la Rochefoucault, trouver
des femmes qui n'ont jamais eu de galanterie ; mais il est
rare d'en trouver qui n'en aient jamais eu qu'une.*

*La galanterie n'est guere connue qu'en France, où la
mode, qui influe sur les mœurs, fait consister la gloire
d'un sexe dans ce qui fait la honte de l'autre, dans la fureur des bonnes fortunes.*

36. Luce roman and italic, Paris 1771 [225]

l'en empêche, en lui prouvant que la rade de Lisbonne avait été formée exprès pour que cet Anabatiste s'y noyât. Tandis qu'il le prouvait *a priori,*
le vaisseau s'entr'ouvre, tout périt à la réserve de
Pangloss, de Candide & de ce brutal matelot
qui avait noyé le vertueux Anabatiste; le coquin
nagea heureusement jusqu'au rivage, où Pangloss
& Candide furent portés sur une planche.

A peine ont-ils mis le pied dans la ville, en
pleurant la mort de leur bienfaiteur, qu'ils sentent
la terre trembler sous leurs pas; la mer s'élève en
bouillonnant dans le port, & brise les vaisseaux
qui sont à l'ancre. Des tourbillons de flammes &
de cendres couvrent les rues & les places publiques; les maisons s'écroulent, les toits sont ren-
versés sur les fondemens, & les fondemens se
dispersent; trente mille habitans de tout âge & de
tout sexe sont écrasés sous des ruines. Le matelot
disait en sifflant & en jurant : «Il y aura quelque
chose à gagner ici. — Quelle peut être la raison
suffisante de ce phénomène? disait Pangloss. —

37. *The roman of Louis Luce printed by modern methods* [225]

67

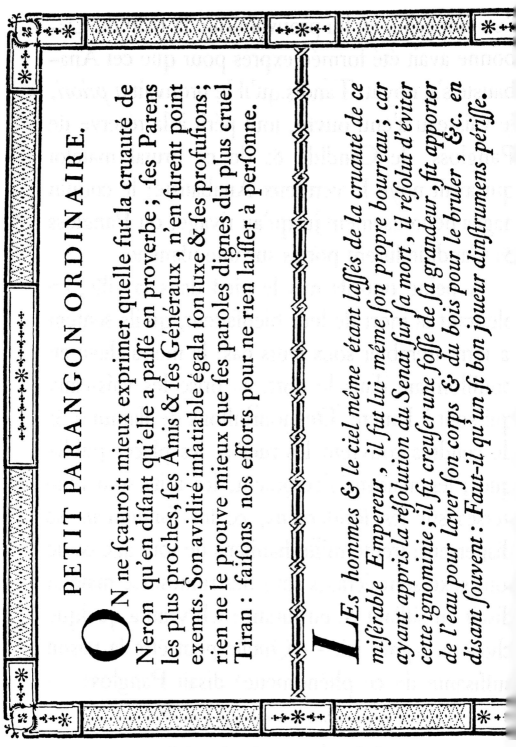

38. *Fournier le jeune's 20 point roman, 1742* [225]

CICÉRO ORDINAIRE.

L'AIR que nous respirons, nos alimens, les saisons, le climat, le tempérament, l'âge, l'extraction même, & ces dispositions intérieures au bien & au mal que le sang des pères communique à leurs enfans, sont autant d'ennemis qui attaquent notre raison & nos sens, & qui corrompent notre jugement.

L'habitude non seulement adoucit les disgraces de notre condition présente, mais encore elle semble changer la qualité des choses auxquelles nous nous accoûtumons.

On doit autant à l'habitude qu'à la raison.

39. *Fournier's Cicero ordinaire* [226]

DES INSTRUMENS
PRINCIPAUX
qui servent à la Fonte des Caractères.

DU PROTOTYPE,
*Servant de Justification générale pour la force de
corps & la hauteur des Caractères.*

L E *Prototype* est un instrument nouveau, de
fer ou de cuivre, dont la principale pièce faite
en forme d'équerre de quatre lignes d'épaisseur, est retenue à vis sur une platine dont le
bout arrondi qui excède l'équerre sert de man-
che : on en trouvera la figure parmi les Planches
gravées. Sa longueur contient 240 Points typographiques, qui font la mesure qu'il doit
avoir, & sur laquelle il faudra se régler. Mais
comme il seroit possible qu'en prenant cette

40. *Fournier's Cicero poetique* [226]

70

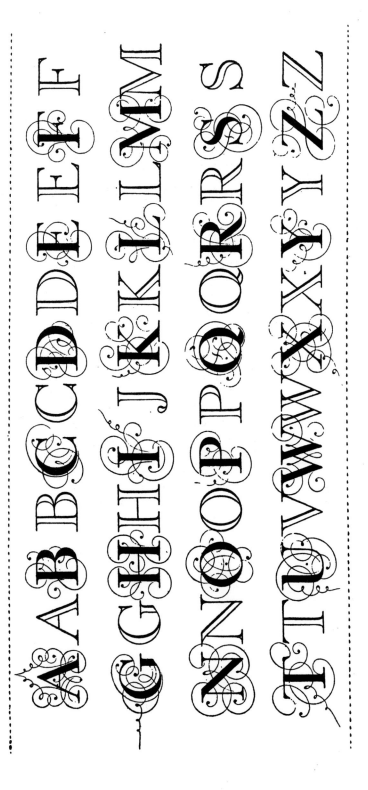

abcdefghijklmnopqrstuwxyz

A A B B C C D D E E F F
G G H H J K K L L M M
N O O P P Q Q R R S S
T U V V W W X X Y Y Z Z

Da Pacem, quae fumus, Domine, in diebus nostris. Shelly.

41. *A specimen of Round-hand 1710? [226]*

P. VIRGILII MARONIS

GEORGICON

LIBER PRIMUS.

AD C. CILNIUM MAECENATEM.

QUID faciat lætas fegetes, quo fidere terram
   Vertere, Mæcenas, ulmifque adjungere vites
Conveniat: quæ cura boum, qui cultus habendo
 Sit pecori, atque apibus quanta experientia parcis;
5 Hinc canere incipiam. Vos, o clariffima mundi
Lumina, labentem cœlo quæ ducitis annum,
Liber, et alma Ceres; veftro fi munere tellus
Chaoniam pingui glandem mutavit arifta,
Poculaque inventis Acheloia mifcuit uvis:
10 Et vos agreftum præfentia numina Fauni,
Ferte fimul Faunique pedem, Dryadefque puellæ:
Munera veftra cano. Tuque o, cui prima frementem
Fudit equum magno tellus percuffa tridenti,
Neptune: et cultor nemorum, cui pinguia Ceæ
15 Ter centum nivei tondent dumeta juvenci:
Ipfe nemus linquens patrium, faltufque Lycæi,
Pan ovium cuftos, tua fi tibi Mænala curæ,
Adfis o Tegeæe favens: oleæque Minerva
Inventrix, uncique puer monftrator aratri,
20 Et teneram ab radice ferens, Silvane, cupreffum:
Dique Deæque omnes, ftudium quibus arva tueri,
Quique novas alitis non ullo femine fruges:
Quique fatis largum cœlo demittitis imbrem.

Tuq

Some contemporary intermediate or transitional romans

Baskerville (Deberny & Peignot, Linotype, Monotype and other founders), Bell (Monotype), Fry's Baskerville (Stephenson Blake), Fournier (Monotype), Georgian (Linotype).

Ao. 1746.

No. 9

Oprechte

Dingsdagfe

HAERLEMSE COURANT.

NEDERLANDEN.

OMSTANDIG RELAAS *van het geen voor, in en na het Beleg van* BRUSSEL *van den 27 January tot op den 24 February gepasseert is, volgens de Berichten van binnen en van buyten.*

Den 27 January 's morgens ten 5 uuren trok het meeste gedeelte der Franse Guarnisoenen van Valencienne, Maubeuge, Condé, Doornik, Ryssel en Aath uyt, marcheerende omtrent 30000 Man sterk in 3 Colonnen, d'eene na Soignie, de tweede na Braine le Comté, en de derde na Tubio, by zig hebbende 40 Stukken Canon, 12 Mortiers en een groote quantiteyt Krygs-Munitien: Een van die Corpsen arriveerde den 28 dito met het krieken van den dag voor Nivelle, waar in 7000 Man Zwitzers van 't Regiment Constant, eenige Vry-Compagnien en de Hussaren van Waldek lagen, dewelke zig al te maal, volgens de Franse berichten, tot Krygsgevangen hebben moeten overgeven en na Aath gebragt zyn.

Den 28 January kreeg men door de uytgezonde Patrouillen kondschap, dat de Marschal Graaf van Saxen, die daags te voorent' Aloft overnacht had, met 30000 Man in Asche op Marsch was en verderna Lippelo, Willebroek en Grimbergen: Waar op terstond een Krygs-Raad by den Graaf van Caunitz gehouden en vervolgens en Hussaar na Leuven en Tirlemont afgezonden wierd, met ordre aan de daar leggende Hanoverse Troupen van zig ten eersten na Mechelen en Vilvoorden te begeven, en men zond die nacht 1200 Man met eene goede quantiteyt Krygs-Munitien van hier derwaarts.

Den 29 arriveerde de Marschal Graaf van Saxen te Marli en deed 2 Bruggen over het Canaal by de Konings-Moolen slaan, en de Grenadiers die zonder tegenstand gepasseert hebbende, volgde de overige Armée in 't gezicht van een sterk Detachement, het welk men 's morgens vroeg [...]

ven, alwaar ze ook eene Battery hadden. 's Avonds ten 8 uuren viel, eene Schermutzeling voor, dewelke tot 2 uuren 's morgens duurde, waar by wy echter maar 4 dooden en 14 gequetsten kreegen, en eenige Burgeren wierden door de Bomben verpletterт.

Den 11 vuurde men geduurig en met succes uyt onze Artillery op hunne Loopgraven: By het opkomen van de nacht wierpen de Franse verscheyde Bomben op onze Werken en op de Stad, en tusschen 6 en 7 uuren deeden ze met veel Verwoedheyd een Storm op het Hoornwerk buyten de Poort van Escarbeek, het welk zy ook met den Degen in de Vuyst zouden verovert hebben, ten waare de Zwitzers zig zo dapperlyk hadden gequeeten, dat ze dezelve weer eyzen door het werpen van veele Grenaden en met de Bajonetten op de Snaphanen wederom daar uyt dreven: Wy verlooren daar by 60 à 80 Grenadiers, en de Generaal van der Duyn, die op het sterk vuuren quam toeschieten, kreeg door een Kogel van een Snaphaan, die hem de Knoop van zyn Hoed wegnam, een ligte Quetzuur aan het Hoofd.

Den 12 's morgens begonnen de Fransen uyt 4 Stukken Canon van 24 ₶ Bresche op de Stad te schieten, en continueerden daar mede de geheele dag. Jegens de nacht deeden ze wederom een Storm op het gemelde Hoornwerk, en alhoewel zegeduurende dezelve tusschen 10 en 11 uuren over de 300 Bomben op de Werken wierpen, en wy daardoor vry meer Volk dan by de voorgaande Storm verlooren, wierden zenochtans wederom met groot Verlies afgeslagen.

Den 13 maakten ze zig door middel van hun Canon Meester van de uytterste Pallisaden, en attaqueerden jegens den avond het Hoornwerk voor de derde reys, waar van ze de twee Bolwerken geheel en al ruineerden: Wy verlooren in die Storm omtrent 100 Soldaten en 5 à 6 Officieren, maar de Fransen wel tienmaal zo veel. Op ordre van den Generaal vander Duyn wierden eenige Huyzen voor de Vlaanderse Poort in brand gestoken. Een Courier van Weenen gekomen, en dien de Fransen

THE
Modern-face
ROMANS

'The whole question of the evolution of roman from old face to modern face is largely a question of technique, rather than the rejection of one design for another on a definite principle. In typography we shall find that mechanical improvements in the printing press and changes in the texture of paper allowed the engraver of types to produce effects which would have been impossible in the early days. It was useless for a Garamond to cut a delicately modelled serif which the processes of reproduction available would have obscured.'[1]

Though founders were forbidden to copy the *romain du roi* many of them did so, but because of the fear of prosecution the plagiarists did not go as far as Grandjean himself in transforming the old-face design. Mr Johnson says that 'thin, flat serifs and vertical shading in capitals are frequently found in the first half of the eighteenth century, when the lower-case was still in the state of transition.'[2] See the example on the opposite page.

It has been said that Grandjean's *romain du roi* foreshadowed the modern face, but, in fact, it was a greater step towards the full development of that face than appears from the works in which it was first used. For this reason: Grandjean's type was well in advance of the printing techniques of his day. It needed the improved printing presses & wove

[1] [2] A. F. Johnson. *Type Designs: their History and Development.*

papers invented later in the century to do it justice. Examples of his types printed by twentieth century methods will be found on pages 77, 78. They show clearly how far Grandjean's design had advanced towards the modern face.

Other typefounders copied the types of Baskerville and Fournier. 'Baskerville was well-known on the Continent, and is generally said to have had much influence on Didot and Bodoni.'[1] But it was not until 1784 that the first modern face appeared. Cut in the typefoundry of F. A. Didot, of the famous family of Parisian founders and printers, it was used in a prospectus announcing a work of Tasso's. This book was to be printed on an improved press introduced by F. A. Didot, and on wove paper, then being manufactured in France for the first time. Both the improved press and the wove paper gave the sharper impression necessary for the modern faces which the Didots introduced, & which they proceeded to cut with ever increasing degrees of modelling—the thin strokes finally becoming hairlines. 'The full flower of the Didot modern face can be seen in the Virgil of 1798.'[2]

Though these over-modelled types were criticized strongly by some of Didot's own countrymen they set a style which became popular all over Europe: modern face is still largely used in France today. By 1787 the famous printer Bodoni of Parma had copied Didot's early modern faces, (see the example, p.82) & the German founder, J. E. Walbaum, & other European founders followed suit. England was introduced to the new style by Robert Thorne in 1800.

Characteristics of modern-face roman

STRESS OR SHADING
Vertical, i.e. thickest parts of curved forms East/West.
MODELLING, OR GRADATION FROM THICK TO THIN STROKES
Abrupt and exaggerated, that is, great contrast between thick and thin strokes.

[1] [2] A. F. Johnson. *Type Designs: their History and Development.*

SERIFS (FEET)
Flat and unbracketed.

OTHER DISTINGUISHING FEATURES
The uniform width of the capitals in some designs combined with
the features noted above make the modern faces rigid and mechanical
looking.

Some contemporary modern-face romans

Bodoni (many founders), Firmin Didot (Deberny & Peignot),
Walbaum (Berthold and Monotype).

---

loteries, l'imprimerie qui était établie près l'administration de
ces dernières fut transformée en *Imprimerie des administrations
nationales* & chargée des publications du Ministère de l'inté-
rieur, de la Trésorerie nationale & des diverses administrations
publiques.

Sur ces entrefaites, Anisson, directeur de l'Imprimerie nationale exécutive, c'est-à-dire de l'atelier du Louvre, fut arrêté
comme conspirateur & jeté en prison. Il proposa au Gouver-
nement de lui céder le matériel typographique qui était sa
propriété particulière tant à l'Imprimerie du Louvre que dans
ses succursales. Le Comité de salut public accepta, & l'on
procéda immédiatement à l'inventaire des ateliers en question.
Anisson ayant été condamné à mort & exécuté, l'Imprimerie
du Louvre fut exploitée pour le compte de l'État. Ensuite le
matériel qui la constituait fut, pour la majeure partie, trans-
porté à l'Imprimerie des lois installée en haut du faubourg
Saint-Honoré, dans la maison de l'ancien fermier général
Beaujon.

44. *Grandjean's type printed by 20th century methods* [228]

qu'à Dieu de le faire, & qu'au diable de le vouloir. Ne tentez donc pas de retomber à quatre pattes : personne au monde n'y réussirait moins que vous. Vous nous redressez trop bien sur nos deux pieds pour cesser de vous tenir sur les vôtres.

. . . .

Recherchons la première source des désordres de la société, nous trouverons que tous les maux des hommes leur viennent de l'erreur bien plus que de l'ignorance, & que ce que nous ne savons point nous nuit beaucoup moins que ce que nous croyons savoir. Or quel plus sûr moyen de courir d'erreurs en erreurs que la fureur de savoir tout?

45. *Grandjean's Corps 20 printed by modern methods* [228]

AVIS

AUX SOUSCRIPTEURS

DE

LA GERUSALEMME

LIBERATA

IMPRIMÉE PAR DIDOT L'AÎNÉ

SOUS LA PROTECTION ET PAR LES ORDRES

DE MONSIEUR.

L<small>ES ARTISTES</small> choisis par M<small>ONSIEUR</small> pour exécuter son édition de <small>LA GERUSALEMME LIBERATA</small> demandent avec confiance aux souscripteurs de cet ouvrage un délai de quelques mois pour en mettre au jour la premiere livraison. Il est rarement arrivé qu'un ouvrage où sont entrés les ornements de la gravure ait pu être donné au temps préfix pour lequel il avoit été promis : cet art entraîne beaucoup de difficultés qui causent des retards forcés ; et certainement on peut regarder comme un empêchement insurmontable les jours courts et obscurs d'un hiver long et rigoureux. D'ailleurs la quantité d'ouvrages de gravure proposés actuellement par

46. The first modern face, Didot 1784 [229]

PUBLII

VIRGILII MARONIS

GEORGICA.

━━━━━━━━━━

LIBER PRIMUS.

Quid faciat lætas segetes, quo sidere terram

Sit pecori; apibus quanta experientia parcis;

Hinc canere incipiam. Vos, o clarissima mundi

Lumina, labentem coelo quæ ducitis annum,

Liber, et alma Ceres, vestro si munere tellus

Chaoniam pingui glandem mutavit arista,

Poculaque inventis Acheloïa miscuit uvis;

Et vos, agrestum praesentia numina, Fauni,

Ferte simul, Faunique, pedem, Dryadesque puellæ:

Munera vestra cano. Tuque o, cui prima frementem

Fudit equum magno tellus percussa tridenti,

Neptune; et cultor nemorum, cui pinguia Ceæ

7.

47. The full flower of the Didot modern face, 1798 [229]

Quousque tandem abutêre, Catilina, patientiâ nostrâ? quamdiu etiam
furor iste tuus nos eludet? quem
ad finem sese effrenata jactabit audacia? nihilne te nocturnum præsidium Palatii, nihil urbis vigiliæ, nihil timor populi, nihil concursus bonorum omnium, nihil hic munitissi-
*mus habendi senatus locus, nihil
horum ora vultusque moverunt? Pa-
têre tua consilia non sentis?* con-

M. TULLIUS CICERO ARPINAS

ORATOR ATQUE PHILOSOPHUS.

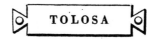

48. *Bodoni's modern face* [230]

Two Lines Great Primer, No. 1. New.

Quousque tandem abutere, Catilina, patientia nostra? quamdiu nos
etiam furor iste tuus eludet? quem
ad finem sese effrenata jactabit a-
udacia? nihilne te nocturnum præ
ABCDEFGHIJKLMNOPQRST
UVWXYZÆŒABCDEFGHIJKLM
NOPQRSTUVWXYZÆŒ£1234567890

49. *Robert Thorne's modern face, 1800* [230]

PEINTURES

ANTIQUES ET INEDITES

DE

VASES GRECS,

TIREES DE DIVERSES COLLECTIONS,

AVEC DES EXPLICATIONS,

ROME

IMPRIME PAR DE ROMANIS

M. DCCC. XIII.

nici, jam antiquissimis temporibus, ob libertatis avitæ immensum studium ac fortissimam defensionem, Romanis juxtà Græcisque monimentis cele-bratissimi, claritudinem vos nunc uni, cum vicinis atque fœderatis vestris, iisdem rebus, quibus olim majores vestri, per universum terræ orbem, apud omneis gentes, populos, atque reges, seduló summâ cum laude ac gloriâ tuemini. tum etiam constat, nullam gentem, nullos gentium reges vel prin-cipeis, bonarum literarum curam tam arcè cum armorum studio conjun-xisse, ac vos battenus fecistis; etiam in extremo bellorum ac pugnarum ar-dore armorumque crepitu scholas juventuti erudiendæ crebrias aperiundo, literarumque secretiorum cultores per ingentia præmia è longinquioribus terris exciendo. Vnde mihi etiam spes haud dubia, sed fiducia certa, bos quoque meos labores vobis fore non ingratos nec inacceptos: utique quum ipsum hoc opus potissimâ sui parte in vestro solo, id est, in inclyto ac grati-ssimo Musarum domicilio, Lugduno ad Rhenum, productum sit. Cui ego

* 2

luca

51. *Seventeenth century italic, Elzeviers 1631* [233]

The Modernized Italics

Of the italic faces, we have already noted the Aldine, the Vicentino and the group which is the contemporary of old-face roman. Here it is convenient to describe the fourth group—the modernized italics.

We have seen that the setting of whole books in italic was a common practice in the sixteenth century. This use of italic as an independent letter, that is, as a type form distinct from roman, continued throughout the seventeenth century also, no attempt being made to mate italic to roman until Grandjean cut the *romains du roi*. But in the first half of the seventeenth century appeared an italic which is remarkable for its condensation, an effect in part obtained by the designer romanizing certain letters—see the m and n, and also the a in our illustration.

In Grandjean's cutting of an italic for the *romain du roi* 'we find a deliberate attempt to make the secondary type conform to the roman.'[1] He romanized the a, m and n, & thus made the slope of the italic lower-case more regular. He was the first to introduce the straight-shanked lower-case *h* in italic (previously *h*). The slope of his italic capitals was to some extent regularized also.

Alexandre, Grandjean's successor at the Imprimerie Royale, maintained this trend towards modernization. By 1712 he had altered the cursive beginning strokes of the lower-case letters. He 'reduced these

A. F. Johnson. *Type Designs: their History and Development.*

Ne crions point contre les plaisirs que nous n'avons plus, ne condamnons point des choses agréables qui n'ont que le crime de nous manquer.

C'est par l'aversion secrète pour la justice qu'on aime mieux donner que de rendre, & obliger que de reconnaître : aussi voyons-nous que les personnes libérales & généreuses ne sont pas ordinairement les plus justes.

On peut vivre avec des indifférents, ou par bienséance, ou par la nécessité du commerce : mais comment passer sa vie avec ceux qu'on a aimés, & qu'on n'aime plus !

Saint-Évremond.

52. *Grandjean's italic for the 'romains du roi'* [233]

strokes until they were something half-way between serifs and the pen-strokes of the old face.'[1] Below, we show a five line example of Alexandre's italic, cut between 1712 and 1716, in which the alterations in these beginning strokes may be seen in the letters i, j, m, n, p, r and u.

La magnificence & la galanterie n'ont jamais paru en France avec tant d'éclat, que dans les dernières années du règne de Henry Second. Ce prince était galant, bien fait & amoureux; quoique sa passion pour Diane de Poitiers, Duchesse de Valentinois, eût commencé il y avait plus de vingt ans, elle n'en était pas moins violente, & il n'en donnait

Pierre Simon Fournier in his *Modéles des Caractères*, published in 1742, remarks how greatly his italic differs from all previous designs. Based to some extent on the formal hands of the engravers, & on the changes introduced by Grandjean and his successors, his italic shows not only a considerable differentiation between thick and thin strokes but an important innovation in the serif treatment of certain lower-case letters, e.g. *m, n, p* and *r*: he *romanized* the serifs of these letters. In his specimens of 1742 (our example is taken from his *Modéles*) it will be noticed also that they are inclined and bracketed. From the same examples it will be seen that Fournier regularized the slope of his italic letters and dispensed with ligatured, or tied, letters. He 'carried the idea of conformity with roman further than any earlier designer.'[2] Bodoni, in Italy, and Rosart in the Netherlands were among the designers who based their italics on those of Fournier.

Notwithstanding the popularity of Fournier's italics they were soon superseded by the italics cut by the Didots to mate with their fully developed modern-face romans. In the first of these Didot cursives the top serifs of the lower-case letters are roman (though unbracketed) but by 1812 they had discarded these serifs and were producing 'cursives of mechanical rigidity, with no life of their own, and not intended to be used on their own.'[3] See example on page 95. Mr Johnson says that cursives of this kind killed italic as an independent letter.

As Baskerville's roman foreshadowed the modern face roman in England, so likewise did his italic (which was a lighter, more regular,

[1][2][3] A. F. Johnson. *Type Designs: their History and Development.*

l'en empêche, en lui prouvant que la rade de Lis-
bonne avait été formée exprès pour que cet Ana-
batiste s'y noyât. Tandis qu'il le prouvait a priori
le vaisseau s'entr'ouvre, tout périt à la reserve d.
Pangloss, de Candide et de ce brutal matelot qu.
avait noyé le vertueux Anabatiste; le coquin nagea
heureusement jusqu'au rivage, où Pangloss et Can-
dide furent portés sur une planche.

Quand ils furent revenus un peu à eux, ils mar-
chèrent vers Lisbonne; il leur restait quelque argent
avec lequel ils espéraient se sauver de la faim aprè.
avoir échappé à la tempête.

A peine ont-ils mis le pied dans la ville, er
pleurant la mort de leur bienfaiteur, qu'ils senten
la terre trembler sous leurs pas; la mer s'élève er
bouillonnant dans le port, et brise les vaisseaux qu.
sont à l'ancre. Des tourbillons de flammes et d.
cendres couvrent les rues et les places publiques; le

53. *Italic of Louis Luce* [233]

and evenly sloped letter than the old face) foreshadow the modernized italics. The influence of Baskerville's design may be seen in the work of other founders—Isaac Moore of Bristol (1768), Alexander Wilson of Glasgow, William Martin, and that of Richard Austin (1786).

Robert Thorne produced, *circa* 1800, the first English modern face italic & other London founders were quick to follow him in producing a variety of lifeless modern italic faces.

Characteristics of modernized italics

Characteristics of the modernized group of italics are the great contrast between thick and thin strokes & the mechanical regularity of slope (as compared with the italics of the old-face group). The letters *m* and *n* are romanized, i.e. the tops or shoulders are squared. The use of the straight-shanked *h*, in place of the round-shanked *h*, is a feature of this group.

The serifs of the capitals, and of the ascenders of the lower-case are flat and unbracketed, and in some types in this group the letters m, n, p, r, have roman, unbracketed serifs at the tops of the stems, flat both above and below. This type of serif never appeared in English italics. The same serifs in other members of the group are flat on top but bracketed below, i.e. carefully shaped in a curve on the underside, and, in some, cursive beginning strokes are still used though these have lost any calligraphic quality.

Some contemporary modernized italics

Bodoni (many founders), Firmin Didot (Deberny & Peignot), Walbaum (Berthold and Monotype).

91

pu, en observant néanmoins de faire quelques changemens qui m'ont paru nécessaires, comme de mettre les Capitales au niveau des longues du bas de Casse, cela fait une plus belle uniformité, les anciens étoient dans l'usage de les faire un peu plus petites ; j'ai donné aux angles de ces mêmes Capitales un peu plus de quadrature ainsi qu'à quelqu'autres Lettres minuscules, où j'ai ôté un certain arrondissement qui se trouve dans l'angle des traits perpendiculaires & horizontaux, cela sert à leur donner beaucoup plus de dégagement, à les détacher les uns des autres, & à rendre les traits plus distincts. Mais la différence que l'on trouvera entre mes Italiques & celles des anciens, dont la plûpart servent encore aujourd'hui, sera beaucoup plus grande : on reconnoît toûjours dans plusieurs la main des grands Maîtres qui les ont faits, par la justesse & l'égalité des traits, mais on peut aussi y reconnoître un certain air d'antiquité que j'ai jugé à propos de réformer ; c'est pourquoi j'ai suivi mon goût sur cette sorte de Caracteres en le rapprochant un peu plus de notre maniere d'écrire, & distinguant bien surtout les pleins & les déliés ; comme on peut en faire la différence sur le champ, en prenant le premier Livre que l'on trouvera sous la main, & le comparant avec ceci ; je ne dirai rien de plus sur cet article.

Dans le dessein que j'avois formé de graver tous les Caracteres nécessaires pour faire une Fonderie complette, je me suis trouvé embarrassé pour sçavoir quelle force de corps je suivrois pour chacun, ces corps se diversifiant presqu'autant qu'il y a d'Imprimeries différentes. Un Cicero ou un petit-Romain, par exemple, est plus fort ou plus foible dans un endroit que dans un autre. J'entends ici par force de corps, l'épaisseur juste & déterminée que devroit avoir la matiere sur laquelle la lettre est figurée, ou la distance toûjours égale des lignes d'un même Caractere, & dont le défaut d'exécution cause beaucoup d'inconvéniens par le mélange qui arrive souvent des Fontes, Cadrats ou Espaces de différentes forces de corps, par le des-

54. *Fournier's italic, 1742* [234]

ANATOMICAL figures are made in two very different ways; one is the simple portrait, in which the object is represented exactly as it was seen; the other is a representation of the object under such circumstances as were not actually seen, but conceived in the imagination. Bidloo has given us specimens of the first kind; Euslachius of the latter.

That figure which is a close representation of nature, and which is finished from a view of one subject, will often be, unavoidably, somewhat indistinct or defective in some parts: the other, being a figure of fancy, made up perhaps from a variety of studies after NATURE, may exhibit in one view, what could only be seen in several objects; and it admits of a better arrangement, of abridgement, and of greater precision. The one may have the elegance and harmony of the natural object; the other has commonly the hardness of a geometrical diagram: the one shews the object, or gives perception; the other only describes, or gives an idea of it. A very essential advantage of the first is, that as it represents what was actually seen, it carries the mark of truth, and becomes almost as infallible as the object itself.

55. *Baskerville's italic* [234]

93

Quousque tandem abutere Catilina, patientia nostra? quamdiu nos etiam furor iste tuus eludet? quem ad finem sese effrenata jactabit audacia? nihilne. te nocturnum præsidium palatii, nihil consensus bonorum omnium, nihil hic munitissimus habendi senatus locus, nihil horum ora vultusque moverunt? patere tua consilia non sentis? constrictam jam omnium horum conscientia teneri conjurationem tuam non vides? quid proxima, quid superiore nocte

ABCDEFGHIJKLMNOPQRST UVWXYZÆŒ œ £1234567890

ABCDEFGHIJKLMNOPQRSTUVWXYZÆ

Quousque tandem abutere Catilina, patientia nostra? quamdiu nos etiam furor iste tuus eludet? quem ad finem sese effrenata jactabit audacia? nihilne te nocturnum præsidium palatii, nihil urbis vigiliæ, nihil timor populi, nihil consensus bonorum omnium, nihil hic munitissimus habendi senatus locus, nihil horum ora vultusque moverunt? patere tua consilia non sentis? constrictam jam omnium horum conscientia teneri conjurationem tuam non vides?

ABCDEFGHIJKLMNOPQRST UVWXYZÆŒ

56. *Robert Thorne's modernized italic,1800* [235]

AVIS.

J'ai dû suivre et adopter l'ordre numérique pour la dénomination de mes caractères, au lieu des noms insignifiants et souvent bizarres conservés encore aujourd'hui dans presque toutes les imprimeries, tels que Perle, Parisienne, Nompareille, Mignonne, Petit texte, Gaillarde, Petit romain, Philosophie, Cicéro, Saint Augustin, etc., lesquels n'offrent aucune idée de leurs proportions particulières ni de leur corrélation, qui en effet existe rarement entre eux d'une manière exacte.

Cet ordre numérique, le seul vraiment convenable, a été ainsi établi par mon père; et le nom de chacun de ses caractères particuliers en présentoit à-la-fois le signalement. Il a donc donné à celui qu'il a voulu prendre pour point de départ, et qui répond à peu près au petit caractère connu dans les imprimeries sous la dénomination de Nompareille, une proportion fixe et invariable, la ligne de pied-de-roi. Il l'a nommé le six, parceque le corps de ce caractère contient six points, ou six sixièmes de ligne. Le sixième de ligne, ou le point, est la plus petite partie qu'il soit possible de fondre, soit comme espace entre les mots, soit comme interligne. Ainsi donc le six comprend dans son corps, c'est-à-dire avec les lettres longues d'en haut et d'en bas, telles que b, p, etc. (ou simplement la lettre j, dont le point et la queue complètent la dimension totale); le corps six, dis-je, comprend une ligne juste de pied-de-roi: le sept comprend une ligne, plus un sixième de ligne, ou sept points, etc.

A ces dimensions établies j'ai ajouté des corps intermédiaires, ou demi-points, afin d'obtenir et de présenter plus de richesse et de variété dans les proportions des différents corps; et par là, du six au douze, j'ai augmenté de six le nombre de mes caractères. Leur progression graduelle est ainsi d'un demi-point seulement, ou d'un douzième de ligne; et ce douzième de ligne dans toute l'étendue du corps n'augmente que d'un trente-deuxième de ligne environ la grosseur la plus apparente dans chaque caractère, je veux dire celle des lettres médiales, telles que i, m, n, u, r, etc. Il est impossible d'établir des nuances moins sensibles entre les corps différents. Au-delà il n'y auroit plus que confusion, et mélange inévitable dans les caractères d'une imprimerie.

Tous ceux-ci ont été gravés sous mes yeux, d'après les modèles que j'ai fixés généralement pour les différents types, et les changements particuliers que j'ai fait subir à quelques uns d'entre eux, notamment au g, et à l'y. Depuis environ dix années consécutives, pendant lesquelles j'ai employé assez régulièrement à peu près trois heures par jour à ce travail avec M. Vibert, actuellement sans doute l'un de nos plus habiles graveurs en lettres, ou poinçons, mes retouches les plus multipliées, mes indications les plus minutieuses, peut-être même mes caprices de perfectionnement, qui souvent m'ont porté à recommencer deux ou trois fois les mêmes types, n'ont pu refroidir son zèle, ni me laisser entrevoir le terme de sa patience.

S'il est vrai que dans les arts industriels il existe un point où il faut s'arrêter, je ne pense pas y être parvenu. Aussi me proposè-je de rectifier successivement plusieurs types qui me paroissent susceptibles d'amendement: et les corrections enfin que je n'aurai pas su faire n'échapperont pas au goût sûr et déja exercé de mon fils, aujourd'hui mon associé, dans peu d'années mon successeur.

57. *Pierre Didot's italic, 1819* [235]

OLD STYLE SERIES.

———•———

Great Primer.

TYPE of the OLD STYLE of face is now frequently uſed—more eſpecially for the finer claſs of book work; as however the faces which were cut in the early part of the laſt century are now unpleaſing both to the eye of the critic and to the general reader, on account of their inequality of *ſize* and conſequent irregularity of *ranging*, the Subſcribers have been induced to produce this ſeries, in which they have endeavoured to avoid the objectionable peculiarities, whilſt retaining the diſtinctive characteriſtics of the mediæval letters.

Miller & Richard.

58. *Old Style, Miller and Richard, 1860* [236]

Old Style

During the first forty years of the nineteenth century English book typography, with the exception of some notable examples, had little to commend it. Some good work was produced in transitional types of near modern flavour.

William Blades regarded the year 1820 'as a boundary line between the old and new style of punch-cutting. About that time great changes were initiated in the faces of types of all kinds. The thick strokes were made much thicker and the fine strokes much finer, the old ligatures were abolished and a mechanical primness given to the page, which ... could scarcely be called improvement. At the same time, printers began to crowd their racks with fancy founts of all degrees of grotesqueness, many painfully bad to the eye and unprofitable alike to founder and printer.'[1] And Mr D. B. Updike writing of the fall in standards of type design in the early years of the nineteenth century blamed Robert Thorne, who introduced the full modern face into this country as 'responsible for the vilest form of type invented—up to that time' (1803) & further remarks that 'A tide of bad taste (in modern face) had swept everything before it by 1844—the precise year of the revival of Caslon's earliest types!'[2] This revival was the work of the Whittinghams of the famous Chiswick Press whose use of the original Caslon types in *The Diary of Lady Willoughby* (1844) marked the beginning of their return to favour. This revived use of the earliest Caslon types—in the com-

[1] William Blades. *Early Type Specimen Books of England, Holland, France, Italy & Germany.* London 1875.
[2] In *Printing Types, Their History, Forms, and Use.* Vol II.

petent hands of Pickering and of Whittingham—was regarded by Mr Updike as 'the chief typographic event of the mid-nineteenth century.'[1] Since that day Caslon Old Face has suffered no further eclipse but has gained steadily, if at times slowly, in popularity.

In 1860 Alexander Phemister cut for Miller & Richard a face which was first shown by those founders in a specimen issued in that year. It was called Old Style and the following note accompanied the specimen: 'Type of the old style of face (they meant, of course old-face designs such as Caslon Old Face) is now frequently used—more especially for the finer class of book-work; as however the faces which were cut in the early part of the last century are now unpleasing both to the eye of the critic and to the general reader, on account of the inequality of *size* and consequent irregularity of ranging, the subscribers have been induced to produce this series in which they have endeavoured to avoid the objectionable peculiarities whilst retaining the distinctive characteristics of the medieval[2] (*sic*) letter.' Below are shown 24 point roman and italic alphabets of the 1860 design.

ABCDEFGHIJKLMNO
PQRSTUVWXYZ
abcdefghijklmnopqrstuvwxyz

ABCDEFGHIJKLMNO
PQRSTUVWXYZ
abcdefghijklmnopqrstuvwxyz

In effect the typefounders had tried to remove what they thought were objectionable features in the original Caslon Old Face without

[1] In *Printing Types, Their History, Forms, and Use.* Vol II.
[2] For *medieval letter* read *old face*.

producing a modern face. Miller and Richard's Old Styles and the many copies thereof have enjoyed wide use both in book and in job-bing printing up to the present day, but now, in the work of the best publishing houses have been ousted by the many excellent revivals of old-face and transitional designs and by what have been called twen-tieth century type face designs, the group of faces next to be described.

When Phemister settled in America he produced a version of the Old Style design—Franklin Old Style. One German foundry bought matrices from Miller & Richard and named the face English Mediæval!

Characteristics of Old Style

STRESS OR SHADING
Vertical.
MODELLING, OR GRADATION FROM THICK TO THIN STROKES
Gradual, though this is not so in all versions of Old Style.
SERIFS (FEET)
Bracketed and inclined, lighter and more sharply cut than in the old faces.
OTHER DISTINGUISHING FEATURES
There is a regularity and certain sharpness of cut which are 'modern'. The uniformity of width in the capitals is a relic of the modern face.

Some contemporary Old Style types

The foundry responsible for the original Old Style design, Miller & Richard, no longer exists. Much of its material (matrices, etc) is now the property of Stephenson Blake but the purchases included only the punches and matrices of the 14 point size of Miller and Richard's Old Style. This size was bought to complete the range of Stephenson Blake's Old Style No 2. Monotype, Linotype and Intertype offer versions of the Old Style face.

ABCDEFGHIJKLMNO
PQRSTUVWXYZ
abcdefghijklmnopqrstuvwxyz
1234567890

Then said the other sister, And in faith I am married to a husband that hath the gout, twyfold, crooked, not couragious in paying my debt, I am faine to rub and mollifie his stony fingers with divers sorts of oyles, and to wrap them in playsters and salves, so that I soyle my white and dainty hands with the corruption of filthy clouts, not using my selfe like a wife, but more like a servant. And you my sister seem likewise to be in bondage and servitude, wherefore I cannot abide to see our younger sister in such great felicity; saw you not I pray you how proudly and arrogantly shee

ABCDEFGHIJKLMNOPQRSTUVWXYZ
abcdefghijklmnopqrstuvwxyz

Verily I live not, nor am a woman, but I will deprive her of all her blisse. And if you my sister bee so far bent as I, let us consult together, and not to utter our minde to any person, no not to our parents, nor tell that ever we saw her. For it sufficeth that we have seene her, whom it repenteth to have seene. Neither let us declare her good fortune to our father, nor to any other, since as they seeme not happy whose riches are unknowne: so shall she know that shee hath sisters no Abjects, but worthier than she. But now

A B C D E G H J K M N P
Q R T U Y
e k m n r t v w z

59. *Lutetia, Monotype 1930* [237]

Twentieth-Century

TYPES

'The appearance of Lutetia (roman) created something of a sensation
... because the face was in no recognizable way purloined from ancient
times, but instead rose freshly from the reasoned canons of type design.'
This extract from a review of Lutetia by Mr Stanley Morison[1] forms
an apt introduction to these notes on designs which Mr A. F. Johnson,
writing in 1932, described as *Twentieth-Century Types*. He said then that
'Our common book face has a tradition of some four centuries behind
it, and to depart from that tradition, outside certain narrow limits, is to
run the risk of being less legible. The exotic type can never be accepted
as a normal book-type ... It may be that a twentieth-century style
is now being evolved. Of all the types in this group we can say, that,
although they cut across the historical divisions (already described), they
have much more in common with the earlier type forms than with
those of the nineteenth century. Abrupt shading and mathematical verticality of stress are avoided by all. In serif treatment a new style is being
worked out. The old-face designs were cut originally when printing
methods were less perfect mechanically than they are today. Serifs were
blunt because they had to endure and to withstand heavy treatment. It
was useless to cut sharp and delicate serifs when crude presses and meth-

[1] *The Fleuron.* No 5.

101

ABCDEFGHIJKLMNO
PQRSTUVWXYZ
abcdefghijklmnopqrstuvwxyz
1234567890

CUTTING A PUNCH BY HAND means cutting on steel, with the appropriate gravers, chisels, or other tools, an exact model of the letter or other symbol in the mind of the punch-cutter or the designer for whom he is working. In addition to the 'face' of the letter, i.e. the actual printing surface of the punch, the punch-cutter is responsible for the right shaping of the punch seen in section. The 'bevel' must be right both from the point of view of the printing impression and the strength & quality of the type-metal in which the type will be cast. With these limitations and considerations in mind, the punch-cutter is at liberty to cut letters of any shape that pleases him or the designer; and if the punch-cutter & the designer are the same person, so much the better...

Until recent years all letter punches were hand cut, and the printing types derived from them, especially the faces cut before the industrial era... show a liveliness and variety otherwise unattainable. Moreover, pantographic enlargement or reduction is with hand cutting impossible, and each size of type has to be cut as though it were a new design.

Punch-cutting by machine involves substantially the following procedure: the designer, according to his experience and skill, draws the letters to be cut to an enlarged size (say one or two inches high). The drawing is then again enlarged, by reflecting it through a lens on to a sheet of paper

ABCDEFGHIJKLMNO
PQRSTUVWXYZ
abcdefghijklmnopqrstuvwxyz

60. *Perpetua, Monotype 1929–1930* [237]

ods of inking and the hand-made papers used would have obscured the result. Finely cut serifs, not the hair lines of Bodoni, but cut to a point, are characteristic of some of the latest types. Smaller serifs too, especially in the upper case, are favoured. Future generations will perhaps hold that printing types of the past were overweighted with serifs. The inscriptional capitals of the Trajan column, a famous model of roman lettering dating from the second century A.D., have small serifs, and have served as a basis for the design of more than one modern series.'[1]

Germany, France, Italy, Switzerland, Spain and the U.S.A. have all produced versions of twentieth-century faces. In terms of numbers Germany leads in this field but there is no doubt that the design of the most successful of these twentieth-century faces cut specifically with book composition in mind—that is to say types which the best of our English printers would want, and would feel happy to use—has so far been concentrated in this country and in Holland.

Characteristics of twentieth-century romans

STRESS OR SHADING
Sometimes oblique, sometimes vertical, or nearly vertical, but not with mathematical verticality of stress.

MODELLING, OR GRADATION FROM THICK TO THIN STROKES
Gradual. Never abrupt.

SERIFS (FEET)
Small and sharply cut, not as hairlines, but cut to a point. Often noticeably smaller in the upper-case than heretofore.

OTHER DISTINGUISHING FEATURES
The capitals in some designs reflect in their varying widths the general proportions of those on the Trajan column. Capitals often unobtrusive. Many of these twentieth-century romans are space savers, that is economical of space in setting.

---

[1] In A GUIDE TO PRESENT-DAY TYPES. *Paper and Print.* December 1932.

It was now the beginning of August, and the plague grew very violent and terrible in the place where I lived, and Dr. Heath coming to visit me, and finding that I ventured so often out in the streets, earnestly persuaded me to lock myself up and my family, and not to suffer any of us to go out of doors; to keep all our windows fast, shutters and curtains close, & never to open them; but first, to make a very strong smoke in the room, where the window or door was to be opened, with resin and pitch, brimstone or gunpowder, & the like; and we did this for some time. But as I had not laid in a store of provisions for such a retreat, it was impossible that we could keep within doors entirely; however I attempted, though it was so very late, to do something towards it; and first, as I had convenience both for brewing & baking, I went and bought two sacks of meal, and for several weeks, having an oven, we baked all our own bread; also I bought malt and brewed as much beer as all the casks I had would hold, & which seemed enough to serve my house for five or six weeks; also I laid in a quantity of salt butter and Cheshire cheese; but I had no flesh-meat, and the plague raged so violently among the butchers and slaughter-houses, on the other side of our street, where they are known to dwell in great numbers, that it was not advisable so much as to go over the street among them. ❡ And here I must observe again that this necessity of going out

ABCDEFGHIJKL
MNOPQRSTUVWXYZ
abcdefghijklmnopqrstuvwxyz

ABCDEFGHIJKLMNOPQRS
12345 *TUVWXYZ* 67890
abcdefghijklmnopqrstuvwxyz

61. *Times New Roman, Monotype 1932* [238]

Some twentieth-century romans

Besides the Lutetia, Perpetua and Times Roman which are shown
the following may be added as other representatives of this group of
romans:
Aldus (Stempel), De Roos (Amsterdam), Emergo (Enschedé),
Pilgrim (Linotype), Romulus (Enschedé and Monotype),
Solus (Monotype), Spectrum (Enschedé and Monotype).

THE DISPLAY TYPES

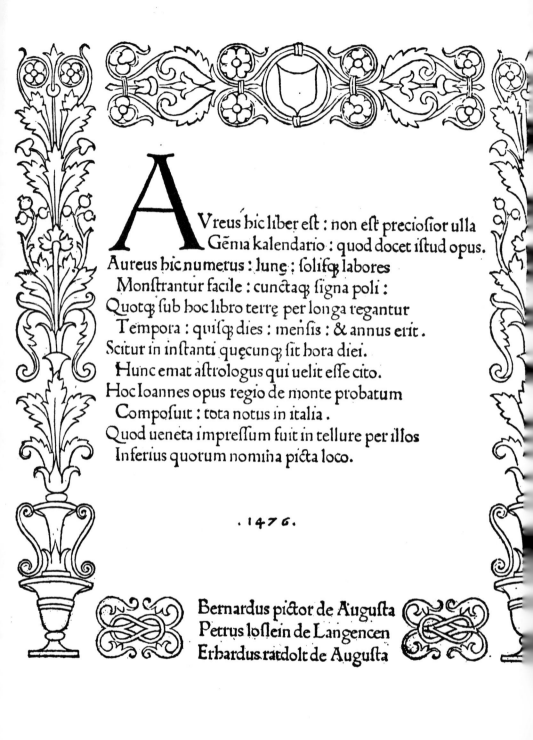

AVreus hic liber est : non est preciosior ulla
Gēma kalendario : quod docet istud opus.
Aureus hic numerus : lune : solifꝗ labores
Monstrantur facile : cunctaꝗ signa poli :
Quotꝗ sub hoc libro terrę per longa regantur
Tempora : quilꝗ dies : mensis : & annus erit .
Scitur in instanti quęcunꝗ sit hora diei.
Hunc emat astrologus qui uelit esse cito.
Hoc Ioannes opus regio de monte probatum
Composuit : tota notus in italia .
Quod ueneta impressum fuit in tellure per illos
Inferius quorum nomina picta loco.

.1476.

Bernardus pictor de Augusta
Petrus loslein de Langencen
Erhardus ratdolt de Augusta

62. *A nearly complete title-page, Venice 1476* [239]

PART TWO
THE DISPLAY TYPES
II

From the time of the invention of printing in Europe up to the beginning of the nineteenth century display types as we know them, that is, types designed specifically for use in jobbing or ephemeral printing did not exist: there was no call for them. Up to that time to be a printer meant to be a printer of books and even in books it was not until some time after 1500[1] that the page which of all others in a book affords the best opportunity for the use of display types began to be used and accepted as part of a normal format. In the sense in which we are familiar with them, title-pages in manuscript books were unknown, & in printing, the information later given on the title-page was, up to the early sixteenth century, usually to be found in the colophon.

When title-pages were first used they were frequently set in the size of type used for the text of the book. Occasionally a larger type was used or the words were cut on a wood block. But such simple arrangements were soon to be superseded by title-pages set in larger types, often in capitals. Black-letter was mixed with roman on these pages and lines in italic were frequently used. By about 1530 large sizes of lower-case began to be employed but in the following century printers reverted to the use of large, heavy capitals. They also crowded these pages, including for instance notes on the contents, the qualifications

---

[1] Of books with a 'fully developed title-page, giving title, author, and full imprint, Dr Haebler, the German authority on incunabula, knows of only one instance in the fifteenth century.' A. F. Johnson in *One Hundred Title-Pages, 1500-1800*. John Lane, London. 1928. The most interesting part of this rather dull and heavy page—it has four lines of large woodcut lettering in addition to a considerable amount of minor display matter—all in black-letter—is the pleasant, decorative initial I.

of the authors, etc. arranging this and other information in as great a variety of types as possible. This custom of crowding the title-pages appears to have sprung from the fact that copies were at that time exhibited as advertisements for the books themselves. Such practices did not make for excellence in the typographic arrangement of title-pages. Of the seventeenth century Mr Johnson has said that it was 'undoubtedly the worst in the history of typography.'[1]

In the eighteenth century title-page arrangement improved, becoming simpler & lighter. Baskerville, for example, thought that type could well stand alone, that is, without the support of blocks or any manner of decorative material. The classical school of printers (Didot, Bodoni) eschewed not only decoration, but the mixing of lower-case and italics with lines in capitals on their title-pages. They relied, in the main, on compositions in various sizes of roman capitals only, as can be seen from the example on pages 84, 85.

On the Continent, where 'from the middle of the sixteenth century the writing masters & the copper-plate engravers, especially the French, had been experimenting with all manner of decorated letters'[2] Pierre Simon Fournier, whose work has already been referred to in the notes on the intermediate or transitional types, was 'mainly responsible for one innovation, the introduction of shaded & other decorative capitals which were so successfully used at Paris.'[3] This innovation was soon taken up by other founders in France and in the Netherlands & towards the end of the century by founders in England.

Though these shaded & decorated types were designed for purposes of display it was with the book in mind that they had been cut. The advent of display faces designed for jobbing or ephemeral printing, that is, of types designed specifically for the purposes of advertisement and not of bookwork dates from the opening years of the nineteenth century. In this field England took the lead.

*   *   *

[1] In *One Hundred Title-Pages, 1500–1800.*
[2] A. F. Johnson. A GUIDE TO PRESENT-DAY TYPES (Display Types). *Paper and Print.* Spring 1933.
[3] A. F. Johnson. *One Hundred Title-Pages.*

The first three of our groups of display types were designed *for use in books*. Script types were originally used as types for continuous reading and whole books were set in them. Decorated and shaded types were of course used on title-pages, as initials, in chapter headings, & in other parts of the book.

*   *   *

In our notes on display types we cannot follow precisely the arrangement used in describing the various groups of book types. We shall adhere to the same plan in giving short historical notes & listing representative contemporary examples. But in the notes on characteristics a change will obviously have to be made. In writing of the infinite variety of display types it will not be possible to be as specific in these notes as it was in the case of the book faces, e.g. the stress or shading of decorated types may be oblique or it may be vertical, and the modelling may follow types of either the old-face or modern groups. In most cases however the characteristics given as peculiar to each group, combined with an examination of contemporary examples, will serve as sufficient guides for the purpose of identification.

*   *   *

The first group of display types, the scripts, is so large & so varied that only the briefest of descriptions of its two main divisions will be possible if the historical notes are to be kept within bounds.

III

Aabcd d e f g h i k l m m n n
n o p q r ſ ſ ſt ſſ t u x y z ʒ ʒ.

Nouiſſimis iam his temporibus uer-
ſantur mala plurima inter plures
chriſtianoʒ principes: Vnde multi
ſeniorum dominia non reſtant ſiti-
re aliena; ſuiſue ſubiugare ditionib⁹
que ſua non ſunt loca. ꝛcett.

A B C D E F
G H J K L M N
O P Q R S T
V X Y Z ꝛ

63. *Vicentino's 'Lettera da Bolle'* [240]

Gothic Scripts

Mr Johnson describes a script type succinctly as '... one cut in imitation of current hand-writing, not of the cursive book hands (e.g. Arrighi's Chancery hands), but of the ordinary script in everyday use ... As the scripts are based on current handwriting, they fall, like the hands, into the two divisions of gothic or mediæval, and Latin or renaissance.'[1]

The earliest script types date from about the middle of the sixteenth century and, initially at least, all script types were used as book types, that is, as types for continuous reading.

Italian calligraphers of the first part of that century—for example Vicentino, Celebrino, Palatino—showed examples of gothic scripts in their specimen books, for despite the efforts of the humanists, the businessmen of the time apparently preferred such scripts to the more legible humanistic hands. The illustration on p. 116 shows one of the earliest gothic scripts cut in type form. It was based on the hand used for writing out papal bulls. After some further trials the Italians ceased experimenting with either gothic or Latin script types and from the 1560's appear to have ignored them up to the time of Giambattista Bodoni.

But in other countries of Europe, including our own, versions of the gothic script were cut.

In Germany during the sixteenth century the professional penmen or scribes not only wrote an ordinary gothic script (currentschrift) but showed specimens of a more disciplined hand used in the German Chanceries (Kanzleischriften). The first two gothic scripts to be cut in

[1]In *Type Designs: their History and Development.*

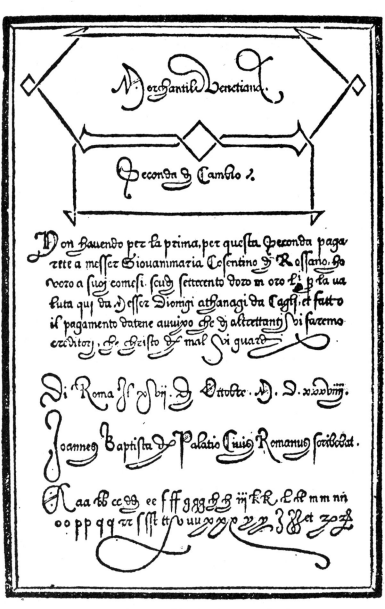

64. *A 'commercial' hand, Palatino 1540* [240]

Germany were based on these more formal gothic script hands. See the illustration on page 118. In Germany very few books appear to have been set in script types. Mr Johnson thinks that that was possibly because the German printers used them in the modern way, that is in the production of ephemera. During the seventeenth and eighteenth centuries the tendency of German script types to become lighter continued and towards the close of the latter century close-fitting of the letters was attempted in order to make the lines appear handwritten. See the example on p.120. In Germany, scripts of this kind 'remained the standard script throughout the nineteenth century.'[1]

Robert Granjon, the famous type designer, thought that his country should also have types based on current handwriting for books set in French. The popular name for his script types—civilité—derived from the titles of two books on good manners printed in 1559 and 1560 respectively. But though he printed many books in his civilité it was not a popular type in France. His 'intention of introducing a new "lettre française" entirely failed.... Books had ceased to be hand written and Granjon, in his attempt to introduce a rival to italic, was too late.... what he designed proved only an historical curiosity in typography, which is after all what most of the script types are. They have no bearing on the development of our principal book faces.'[2]

In the Netherlands however civilité enjoyed a wider use. Granjon supplied Plantin, among others, with his civilité types and Granjon's scripts were copied.

The earliest English writing book appeared in 1571. In it was shown a gothic script based on the ordinary Elizabethan hand and named *secretary*. It was not available in type form until 1576 and does not appear to have been used for the printing of books but in the modern manner, i.e. for wine licences, marriage licences, on circular letters demanding loans etc—and also in the printing of music, the latter a use to which script types were commonly put. At least two other varieties of secretary were cut, but in addition to these there was another gothic script of considerable antiquity, a legal, and upright script called Court hand. See the example on p. 124. The type cut from it was not much

[1][2] A. F. Johnson. *Type Designs: their History and Development.*

Fabricæ Basilicæ Principis Apostolorum de urbe Reveren

Salutem et sinceram in dño charitatem Sedis Aptica prouidentia circumspecta nonnunq̃ rigore q̃ i
quods̃. Et Canonum prohibent instituta de gratia benignitatis indulget prout personarum et negoc̃
libenter exidere agnoscit Sane ex parte
nobis meditum naperrone oct dicte Fabricæ Commissario oblata petitio continebat q̃ ipsi ex certis rōi
cu[?] urbes taliter copulari vero quia Tertio et Quarto   grauibus inuicem sint coniun
adimplere i ñ possunt dispensatione Aptica super hoc non obstanta Quare mediante eorum Commissa
ipsorum exponentes eis super his per nos super a Sede Aptica interq̃ pararetur de opportune dispensar
uteri Nos igitur quibus cura dicte Fabricæ ab eadem Sede commissa fuit eorum in hac parte
Aptica nobis concessa et nouissime confirmata Circumspectioni bre per presentes manu Commissary uri
ptas committimus que sicsit ita cum ipsis exponentibus qui eorum fabricæ de ceto subsidio ad illius uti
cum conuersatio iuxta ordinem sibi per eundem Commissarium statuam subuenerint q̃ impedimen
ab eorum stupite perueniant et nouale libere ualeant intersse maxime
huiōi non obstantibus taneq̃ Dummodo dicta mulier propter hoc ab
contrata fuerit licitæ remanere misericorditer dispensa   Iubilentes per easdem presentes omnibus et singulis ad quos
suscipiendam q̃ per legitimam declarari   Iubilentes per easdem presentes omnibus et singulis ad quos
suscipiendam q̃ per legitimam declarari   applicando preme cōrum exponentes sic dispensatos possint et pre
uentorum uincatorum anteri dicte Fabricæ applicando preme cōrum exponentes sic dispensatos possint et pre
molesto colore molestare inquietare uel perturbare audeant siue presumant   Datum

used, and its use 'for legal documents was abolished in 1753, and its place taken by the script known as Engrossing.'[1] This was a gothic script and the last example of an English gothic script was an engrossing cut *circa* 1765 by Thomas Cottrell for a law printer. See the example, p. 125.

Note on availability of gothic scripts

With the exception of Deberny and Peignot's La Civilité no gothic scripts appear to be available for use today. The American Type Founders Civilité, based on a French sixteenth century face, has many Latinized letters both in the upper- and the lower-case. Some letters in Bauer's Legend may be said to be based on gothic scripts like the sixteenth century civilité's.

A number of fine gothic scripts are held by the Enschedé foundry but are not available for general use: Berry, Johnson and Jaspert show a fine example in the 1958 edition of their *Encyclopædia of Type Faces*, under Private Press types.

[1]A. F. Johnson in *Type Designs*.

left, 'Lettera da Bolle' cut as a type [240]

die Befeſtigung zum tail verhindert/nichts deſtminder hat Herr
Bartolome von Liuian/ der vnſer öberſter Haubtman war/
ain Viſier gemacht / durch welche Sy ſich von aller beſchedi-
gung ſicher zuſein erzaigt.   Liguano/ welchs ah der Etſch
zwiſchen Padua vnd Mantua ligt/ weils für ain notwendig
ort geacht iſt/ trachten Sy wie Ich/ von denen ſo vnſer Comun
regiern/ gehört hab/ ſölches teglich zubefeſtigen.

    Das vierd/ zubetrachten was man ih die Stat vnd darauſ
fürt/ erforſcht auch mit vil wort. Dann offenbar iſt/ das vnſer
Stat Inns Waſſer gebawet/vnd Jr vonnöten iſt/das alle ding
ſo zu aufenthalt menſchlichs lebens notwendig zugefürt werden
die vom Land/ vnd mit vom Waſſer Jr herkommen haben.
Das ſo man daraus fürt / iſt nichts anders dann Kauffman
ſchatz / Als Tuech/ Seidin Gewandt/ vnd vil Kremerey/ di
man Jnn vnſer Stat macht.   Es bringen auch vnſere Kauff
leut vil kauffmanſchatz aus Barbaria/ Alexandria/ Baruti
dieſelbigen werden nachmals durch die andern Prouincien auf
getailt.

    Das letzt/ iſt die einfürung der Geſatz / Welches aber ai
Materi aines anndern Geſprechs iſt / das man thun möchte
wann Jr ſehen wolt ob vnſer Comun ainfeltig / oder zeſame
geſetzt. Iſts ainfeltig / was geſtalt es ſey / Iſts zeſamen geſetzt
ob es ſich naig zu ainem mer dann zu aim andern.   Diſe din
mügt Jr vaſt wol bey euch ſelbs betrachten /   So Jr verſtande
habt wie der Subiect beſchaffen ſey.   Wann Jr öber ſöllich
ainiches annder Vrtail wellt/mag euch vnſer Herr Nicolai
Leoncinus volkomenlich vergnügen/Welcher/vmb das Er ai
groſmechtiger Philoſophus iſt/ vnd vnſers Comuns zum alle
erfarnſten/kan Er von ſölchen dingen/ vil bas dann kain ande
rer diſputieren.

    Ich hab euch nun die Ordnungen diſer vnſers Comuns/m
der kürtz vnd fugſame ſouil mir müglich/ erzelt / Vnd ob Je
euch Je mit vergnüegt hett/Erbeut Ich mich noch/ſolches ſo of
zuerzelen/das Jrs volkomenlich verſtendig bleibt/vnd allen eir
ren guten freunden das mittailen möcht.

Buch gezeigt, welches mir sehr wohl gefallen, wegen der starken
Collection von gantz besonders sauberen Schriften, die meistens Herr
Fleischmann seel. graviert. Dieser war 1727. ohngefehr auf unserer
Schriftgiesserei und folgte Joh. Michael Schmid nach dem Haag zu
Herren Alberts und Uytwerff mit denen gedachter Schmid Arrows
errichtet. In Holland hat sich also der seel. Fleischmann völlig perfec-
tioniert, und so ihnen reichen Vorrath von mancherlei Schriften hinterlaßen.
Ich bin begierig Dero Probier-Buch selbsten zu haben, und ersuche dahero
mir drei Exemplaria davon mit nechstigem Post-Wagen einzu-

(a)

... von Kunstgebrauch; der Industriel aber
und Vorzug des Erfinders, wird wohl bleiben, und
wenn ich noch 3 Jubilaea erlebten, so kombt mir
nicht anders vor, als wie mit den Buchhändlern,
die vorgeben, als hätten sie den Vorzug vor den
Buchdruckern und wären eher gewesen, als die
Buchdrucker, weil sie damals mit Manuscript ge-
handelt hätten, ein schlechtes Erweisen; wann ich
mich einlaßen wollte, und ihnen auch ihre Schrift

(b)

Werck manchen Kunstverwandten zu kostbar fällt,
und lieber ist Gold vor den Einzaehen tragen,
so entschloß ich mich den Lehrjungen zu verfertigen,
welcher 20 gf kostet, merke dahero gantz wohl, daß
er gütig aufgenommen wird, Da ich doch immer
dachte, ob werde heißen: was will und dieser weisen
was gut ist, sehe aber doch daß mancher noch was
darinnen findet, was er noch nicht gewußt, dießes
danke ich Gott, und der Kunst.

(c)

67. German Schreibschrifts of 1660, 1772 and 1793 [241]

Und ob Sie gleich Ordre erthei-
let an Herren Krage daß er mir
dafür zahlen sollten, so sehen Sie
mich nicht vor einen solchen
Mann an, der Ihnen nicht
träumen sollte, und wären viel
mehr mir nachtheilig; befehlen Sie
mir, kan ich dienen, es sey worzu
immer es wolle, ich bin bereit,
denn davor bin ich in der Welt
meinem Nächsten zu dienen; die

68. *A Schreibschrift of unknown origin* [242]

pectora, et inuito pauat ixe per equora vento.
At Bessus facinus jam premeditatus acerbum,
Narbazanesqz suus, numeroso milite fultj
Jam definierant Darium comprendere viuum,
Et si Magnus eos sequeretur, munere tanto
Commodius possent victoris inire fauorem,
Quod si percelebres euadere principis alae
Fore parat, auderent Dario regnare perempto,
Et vires reparare, nouumqz lacessere martem.
Narbazanes igitur sceleri jam tempora nactus
Oportuna suo: Scio Rex que dixero dixit
Displicitura tibi, nec erit sententia cordj
Hec mea grata tuo: sed pregraue vulnus acerbo
Curatur ferro, grauis est medicina dolentj,
Asperior sanat grauiores potio morbos,
Naufragiumqz timens factura sepe redemit
Nauita quod potuit, et damnis damna leuauj.
Scio quod amara geris aduerso numine bella,
Seu vrgeue tuos non desinit aspera persas,
Omnibus est tentanda modis fortuna, nouisqz
Est opus ominibus, depone insignia Regni
Ad tempus bone Rex; alij concede regendam
Imperij summam, qui nomen Regis et omen
Possideat, donec martis cessante procella
Hostibus expulsis Asia justo tibi Regi
Restituat regnum: breuis expectatio factj
Huius erit, tot Bracta dabunt totqz Jndia gentes
Ut maior belli moles, maiora supersim
Robora, quàm bello que sum exhausta priori.
Cur in perniciem pallantum more bidentum
Iruimus? fortis animj est contemnere mortem,
Non odisse tamen vitam: sed amare virorum est
Degeneres, et quos constat tedere laboris
Compelluntur ad hoc vt vitam ducere vile
Quid reputem: quid mirum? Ignauo vincere mors est.
                              m iij   Econtra

proditionis consilium initum à besso et Nabarzano.

Nabarzanis oratio.

69. Granjon's civilité 1557 [242]

121

Abuses comitted by the Heaving, Sawing, and Measuring
of Timber, bordes, lathes, quarters, Joystes, punchions,
rafters, stabbe plankes, and such like stuffe:

Item Timber, bordes, & such like stuffe abide aboue spoken, is bought & solde noithe
in this realme of England, not by any Standard, Size, or measure, to any lawfull Size
or true measure, by reason will minded persons by subtill practise, knowing there is no
lawe to the contrary to binde them to keape any assise of true measure: and therefore it is solde
to her Maiestie & her bewowing subiectes, what measure or assise they please, Wherby her
Maiestie & her bewowing subiectes are greatly deceaued & abused, not onely in paying for the stuffe
But also for land and water cariage, Wherof her Maiestie the profit: & great deale more than
they receaue any measure for: for by comune timber bouldes bee well serued and keape true
measure, that is to say, 5 foote of assise or more to a loade, and as it is measured and solde there
wanteth by true measure 8, 10 or 12 foote of assise more or lesse in the most Loades.

Item all bordes and plankes, that are sawed, are measured so insufficiently, that in euery score
lande of bordes or plankes by true measure, there wanteth one hundreth or more.

Item all lathes are so insufficient in breath & thicknes, that lathes and latticed are in great
danger to stand vppon them on the rooses of houses: Besides my number there wanteth in a
bundell, which boundes containes 5 score lathes, of 5 foote long to the hundreth: and 6 score and 5
lathes of 4 foote long to the hundreth, 12, 16 or 20 lathes more or lesse in the most Bundles.

Item, there are a smalle number of... which are for wanteth which pieces the aforesaid stuffe, bothe

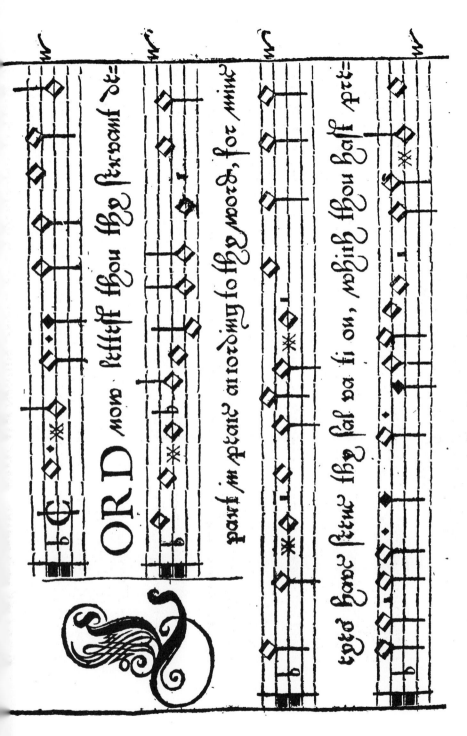

71. A third fount of Secretary, London 1641 [243]

COURT HAND.

Double Pica.

Ꝙuouſꝗuo tendom ebutoꝛo Ɛotiɛino potionbio

 noſtꝛo quemdiu nos obiom fuꝛoꝛ iſto tuuꝟ oɛudot

𝔍𝔰𝔱𝔰 ... (Byddel sample alphabet)

COURT-HAND.

Byddel 10.   Matrices 59.

Englifh.

Ꝙuonſꝗuo tendom ebutoꝛo Ɛotiɛino potibio on noſtꝛo

buemdiu nos obioni fuꝛoꝛ iſto tuuſ oɛudot quom od fuꝺoꝺ

(Byddel sample alphabet)

Byddel 10.   Matrices 67.

U N I O N.

. Double Pica.

𝒯hat about this time (1450) the

UNION.

Art of Printing and Cafting Sin-

ABCDEFGHIJKLM

Byddel 10.   Matrices 63.

72. *Court hand* [243]

Engroſſing

And be it further hereby enact
ed, That the Mayors, Baili=
ffs, or other head Offiters of eu
ery Town and plate torporate,
and City within this Realm
being Juſtite or Juſtites of P
eate, shall have the same au=
thority by virtue of this Art,
within the limits and pretintts
of their Jurisdictions, as well
out of Seſſions, as at their Seſſ=
ions, if they hold any, as is he=
rein limited, preftribed and ap=
pointed to Juſtites of the Pea

A B C D E F G H I J K =
L M N O P Q R S T U V

73. *Thomas Cottrell's Engrossing, circa 1765* [244]

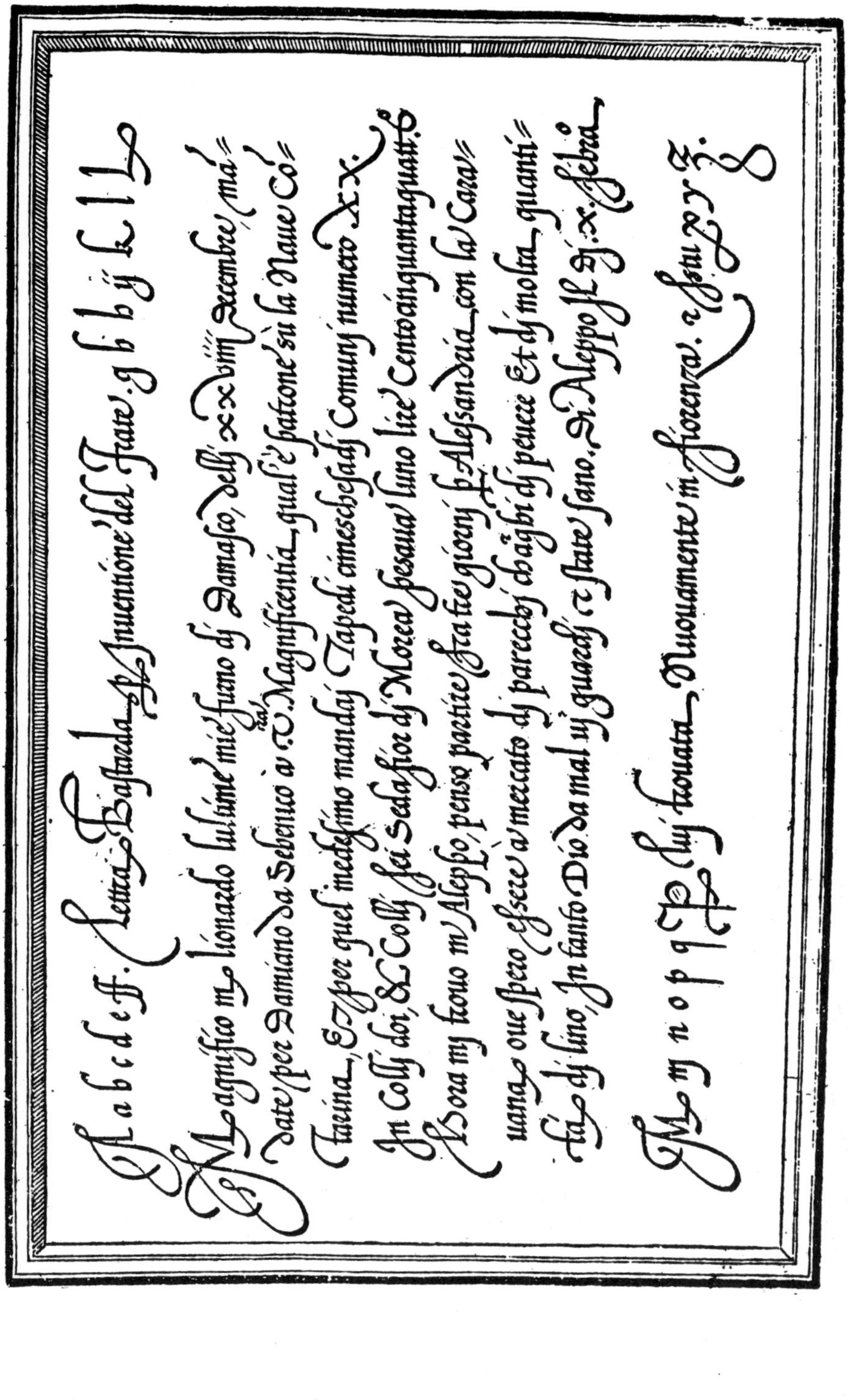

74. *Cancelleresca Bastarda, Amphiareo, 1554* [245]

Latin or Renaissance Scripts

This, the second division of the group of scripts, stems from the Italian hand. The invention of the hand from which Mr Morison derives these Latin scripts, a less formal and rounder style of writing than that of Arrighi—named Cancelleresca Bastarda[1]—was claimed by Vespasiano Amphiareo, the Venetian writing master.

Of the Latin scripts in France Mr Johnson says 'there are three groups … the ronde, a descendant of civilité which is largely gothic (frequently found as a decorative type in French books of the first half of the nineteenth century), the bâtarde coulée, also called financière, because used in the Ministry of Finance, and the bâtarde ordinaire or italienne, the purest form of Latin script. Fournier uses the word bâtarde alone instead of bâtarde italienne. The financière, originally a more cursive variety of the bâtarde, in the course of time became indistinguishable from it …. The Latin scripts, that is, those based on the Italian hand, are curiously late in typographical history, & in fact are comparatively rare before the

[1] 'The term *bastarda, bastarde, bâtarde, bastard,* was used in the fifteenth century somewhat arbitrarily to designate a current or cursive variety of a formal or text letter.' Stanley Morison. ON SCRIPT TYPES. *The Fleuron* No 4.

eighteenth century.'[1] Mr Johnson records only those of Pierre Moreau, a professional calligrapher who lived in Paris, and one English script type, in the previous century. Moreau first produced books printed from engraved plates and then experimented with script types, which like the earlier gothic scripts, he designed for book work, i.e. as types for continuous reading. Altogether, in six years (1643-1648) Moreau printed about a dozen books in his bâtarde italienne. See the example, p.135. His types, after passing through several hands, were finally bought by the Imprimerie Royale in 1787 and one of their last uses was in the printing of paper money.

Latin scripts in England in the seventeenth century were a rarity. Mr Morison shows specimens of the first Latin script that he had been able to discover in use in England as illustrations to his article on script types.[2] He remarks of it that it 'is a very fine one, so fine that one immediately suspects it of foreign manufacture.'[3] See illustration, p.138.

The next English scripts to be considered are the Cursorials issued by the Grover foundry about 1700. These Cursorials were described by Mores in his *Dissertation:* 'The Cursorial is a flimsey type imitating a pseudo Italian handwriting, and fitted for ladies and *beaux*.'[4] Five of the six sizes originally belonging to the Grover's Foundry (the largest English foundry in the seventeenth century) are still in the possession of Stephenson Blake of Sheffield, coming into their hands through those of three other founders. See the illustration, page 139. It is thought that the first cursorials were cut to imitate the MS news sheets circulated in the coffee houses of the day. All these cursorials were of poor design.

On the Continent from this time onwards Latin scripts appeared in great numbers. Even Germany, the home of gothic, succumbed, and German typecutters produced specimens of Latin scripts. In Italy G.B. Bodoni cut dozens of scripts, and, knowing little of the history of handwriting, gave them bewilderingly confusing titles.

In *Type Designs: their History and Development.*
In *The Fleuron* No 4.
Ibid.
Edward Rowe Mores. *A Dissertation upon English Typographical Founders and Founderies.*
London 1788.

Caractères

par Firmin Didot

Paris, rue du Regard, Faubourg S.-Germain.

Du Département de la Seine.

In England, Mr Johnson writes that 'after the cutting of the Grover cursorials, there is a long gap in the history of scripts. Neither William Caslon I, nor his son, nor Baskerville designed anything in this class.'[1] But Thomas Cottrell, a pupil of William Caslon, started his own foundry in 1757 and cut a script in which he tried to produce the effect of writing by fitting his letters closely together. Cottrell's type was copied by the other founders in this country. Of all these types Mr Johnson says that they 'still had considerable traces of the true Italian hand.'[2] On the Continent Cottrell's imitators (the Didots and other founders) called it Anglaise.

Scripts of this class were eventually influenced by the 'modern' cult in type design, i.e. there was a greater differentiation in modelling, or the gradation from thick to thin, and, Mr Johnson remarks 'increased ingenuity in imitating a current round hand. Then we get the typical Anglaise, admired & copied by the Didots, the script of the nineteenth century.'[3] He states that scripts of the Cottrell class 'were the last good scripts until we reach the work of the present generation; they perished at the same time as italic, with the introduction of the modern face.'[4]

Writing in the Spring of 1934 on script types Mr Johnson said that 'For good modern scripts, we have to go to German founders. Among the large number of "Roundhands", "Freehands", and fancy scripts shown by our founders, all are bad.'[5] Though the position here has improved a little in the intervening twenty-five years it is still a fact that if one wants a spirited script the chances are that one's final choice will be a letter from one of the Continental foundries. In this group the number of types is so great that the choice of representative specimens is not an easy one.

[1][2][3][4] In *Type Designs: their History and Development.*
[5] In A GUIDE TO PRESENT-DAY TYPES. *Paper and Print.* Spring 1934.

CARACTERE DE FINANCE,

Dit Batarde Coulée.

Nouvellement gravé par Fournier le jeune Graveur et Fondeur de Caracteres d'Imprimerie. Demeurant actuellement rüe S.t Etienne des grèa, proche l'Abbaye de S.t.e Genevieve. à Paris. 1749.

Le present Caractere est gravé à lusage des Imprimeura curieux, pour l'impression de certaina ouvragea legers qu'on voudroit faire passer pour être écrita. Il est utile pour lea Epîtrea dedicatoirea, Lettrea circulairea, Billets de Commerce, d'invitation d'Assemblée, de Ceremonie, &c. Necessaire Surtout pour lea ouvragea d'Intendance, comme Mandementa, Permissiona, Ordonnancea, Avertissementa, Ordrea, deffensea &c. Pour lea ouvrages du Secretariat des Evéchez, pour lea Bureaux lea Fermea, les Gabellea, les finances et autrea que le goût & la Curiosité dicteront. Le Prix est de Quarante sola la livre.

77. The Bâtarde Coulée script [245]

LETTRES ORNÉES,

Pour tenire lieu de petites Capitales
au le Caractere de FINANCE,
Batarde Coulée. Gravé par
urnieu le jeune.

Epistre.

tendre d' vostre Grandeur, en vous faisant

present si peu conuenable à cette haute Vertu,

nt vous honorez aujourdhuy la premiere Char-

e du Royaume? Certes, Monseigneur, c'est vne

ciuilité bien audacieuse, que de vous jnuiter à

scendre en ma faueur du Throsne d' la Ju-

ce au Theatre de la Comedie. Mais si les

ipions n'ont pas dedaigné de s'y treuuer quel-

es fois. à la priere des Terences, & d'embrasser

smes la protection de leurs Ouurages; J'espere,

onseigneur, que vous ne refuserez pas la vo-

e à celuy que ie vous presente; & que peut-estre

s luy donnerez quelques-vnes de vos heures,

ry qu'elles soient toutes precieuses. Vous n'y

rez pas, comme dans les leurs, tout ce qu'v-

Langue a d' plus pur & d' plus fleury, ny

t ce qu'vn beau Genie peut auoir de beaux

timens; mais vous y verrez quelques images,

tost d' ces charitables soins que vous prenez.

78. *Pierre Moreau's Bâtarde Italienne* [245]

LA

BELLE ESCLAVE,

Tragicomedie.

DE

Monsieur N.r L'Estoille.

A PARIS,

Se vendent l'Imprimerie des nouueaux Caractere.s
De Pierre Moreau, M.e Escriuain Iuré, à Paris,
& Imprimeur ord.re du Roy, proche le Portail
du grand Conuent des RR.PP. Augustins,

Et en la boutique au Palais en la Salle Dauphine,
Par F. Rouuelin, à l'Enseigne de la Verité. 1645.

Auec Priuil. du Roy.

79. Pierre Moreau's Bâtarde Italienne [245]

CHARLES by the Grace of God, King of England, Scotland, France and Ireland, Defender of the Faith, &c. To all Mayors, Bailiffs, Constables, and other Our Officers and Ministers, Civil and Military, whom it may concern, Greeting. In pursuance of Our Declaration of the fifteenth of March, 1672½: We do hereby permit and license James Briscoe of Toxteth Parke in Our County of Lancaster of the Persuasion commonly called Congregationall to be a Teacher, and to teach in any place licensed and allowed by Us according to Our Said Declaration. Given at Our Court at Whitehall the sixteenth day of may in the 24th year of Our Reign, 1672.

By His Majesties Command.

80. First Latin script to be used in England, 1672 [246]

Dawks's News-Letter.

Sʳ London

January 3. 1698.

Last night we had three French Mails, but they bringing nothing material, we shall entertain you with the Domestick News following.

Falmouth, Dec. 29. The Mary of London for Barcelona, and the Mary of and from the same place for Marseilles, both Laden with Fish. The new Africa of London for Leghorn, and some other outward bound Merchant Ships, having been cleared at the Custom House, are sailed hence to their respective Ports.

Plymouth, Dec. 30. We have had most terrible Storms of late; and his Majesties Ship the Chatham hath rode it out in great danger for these three days last past.

Harwich, Ian. 1. Yesterday the North Country Ships, and some Laden Colliers sailed hence for the River.

Portsmouth, Ian. 1. Seven Men of War are now at Spithead, where there has been very great Storms, but without any considerable damage.

A Servant of Esq; Bunches arriving here last Week from Venice, brings an Account that his Master being upon his Travels arrived there, in his Travels contracted an Indisposition of which he Died, before he attained to full Age, leaving 7000 l. per Annum behind him; he is much Bewailed by the Inhabitants of the Pall Mall, where he formerly resided.

Our Merchants have Advice from the Indies, that last Summer there happened cold unseasonable Weather there, by which a great part of the Silk Worms were Starved to Death, and the Fruits much damaged; so that it seems the Bad Season has been universal.

Its Discoursed that the Ships belonging to the Scotch East India Company are arrived in the mouth of the River Darien in America, but no Letters mentioning any such thing, we shall suspend our Belief for the present, till we hear the same confirm'd by very good hands.

The two Yorkshire Stingo Houses, near Paddington, were three times Robb'd within this Fortnight, and two of the Gang are seized for the same.

Yesterday an unfortunate Accident happened in Soho, viz. A Child not a Year Old, being left in a Room, in which was no living Creature besides but a Cat, upon the Mothers return, the Child was found Dead, and upon searching its Body, no marks of violence were found, nor that the Door had been opened; so that it's presumed the Cat Smothered the Child by sucking its Breath. Last Night the Coroners Inquest sat on the Childs Corps, but we don't yet hear what the Verdict is.

81. *One size of the Grover Cursorials, circa 1700* [246]

Double Pica Script.

Then Agrippa said unto Paul, Thou art permitted to speak for thyself. Then Paul stretched forth the hand, and answered for himself: I think myself happy King Agrippa, because I shall answer for myself this day before Thee, touching all the things whereof I am ac= cused of the Jews: especially, because I know thee to be expert in all customs and questions which are among the Jews: wherefore I beseech thee to hear me patiently. My manner of life from my youth, which was at the first among mine own nation at Jerusalem, know all the Jews; which knew me from the beginning (if they would testify) that after the most straitest set of our religion, I lived a Pharisee. And now I stand and am judged for the hope of the promise made of God unto our fathers: unto which promise our twelve tribes, instantly serving God day and night, hope to come: for which hope's sake, King Agrippa, I am accused of the Jews. Why should it be thought a thing incredible with you that God should raise the dead? I verily thought with myself that I ought to do many things contrary to the name of Jesus of Nazereth: which things I also did in Jerusalem: and many of the saints did I shut up in prison having received authority from the chief priests; and when they were put to death I gave my voice against them. And I punished them oft in every synagogue and compelled them to blaspheme; and being exceedingly mad against them, I persecuted them

A B C D E F G H I K L M N O P Q R
S T U V W X Y Z A B C D E F G H I

J'ai l'honneur de vous adresser une Epreuve de quelques=uns de mes nouveaux Caracteres d'Ecriture, et de vous pré=venir que ma Fonderie est actuellement en état d'exécuter les Fontes qu'on pourrait en desirer. Elles seront faites avec le plus grand soin, en très=bonne matiere, et au prix le plus modéré. On trouve aussi chez moi les Casses qui leur conviennent.

L'accueil extremement flatteur que ces nouveaux caracteres, pour lesquels j'ai obtenu un Brevet d'Invention, ont reçu de Son Excellence le Ministre de l'Interieur, ainsi que du Jury, à la derniere exposition des objets d'art, me donne lieu de croire que cet avis vous sera agréable. J'au-rais desiré mettre sous vos yeux plusieurs lignes de mes Caracteres d'écriture Ronde, Coulée, Bâtarde, et Anglaise; mais la disposition et la largeur de la page qui tient à cette Circulaire ne m'ont pas permis d'y placer un texte ou ils pussent tous être employés.

83. Firmin Didot's Anglaise, 1809 [247]

Some contemporary Latin or Renaissance scripts

Scores of these Latin scripts are available today for most
founders seem to have produced at least one design in this
group. Unfortunately it is impossible to be fair to all designers
and founders of Latin scripts if at the same time we are to keep
this list of representative examples within reasonable bounds.
Ariston (Berthold), Artista (Schelter & Giesecke, now Typoart),
Bernhard Cursive (Bauer, and Stephenson Blake, who call the type
Madonna Ronde), Cantate (Bauer), Cigogna (Nebiolo), Constance
(Klingspor), Copperplate Bold, Francesca Ronde (Stephenson Blake),
Graphic Script (Bauer), Invitation Script, Marina (Stephenson Blake),
Mistral (Olive and Amsterdam), Palette (Berthold), Parisian Ronde
(Stephenson Blake), Pepita (Monotype), Rondo (Amsterdam),
Scribe (Deberny & Peignot), Signal (Berthold), Sketch (Ludwig
& Mayer), Trafton (Bauer), Virtuosa (Stempel).

84. *Decorated initial, Paris 1487* [248]

DECORATED

The history of decorated letters—from the lapidary inscriptions of the fourth century up to the present day—has been traced in some detail by Mr Stanley Morison in his article on decorated types.[1] Here it will be sufficient to note that decorated capitals were first used in printing during the 1450's. In those early days they were used singly, i.e. as initial letters only. Had title-pages then been part of the book it is possible that decorated letters might have been used on them for the composition of complete words or lines.

From about the middle of the sixteenth century French writing masters were showing specimens of a variety of ornamented or decorated letters in their writing manuals (some of these books were printed from wood-engravings, others from copper plates) and French scribes continued to produce all kinds of ornamented letters during the seventeenth and eighteenth centuries. Mr Morison refers readers to 'A remarkably various collection of *lettres fleuragées* of a most delicate kind'[2] intended for the use of goldsmiths and jewellers which was published in M. Pouget fils: *Dictionnaire de Chifres et de lettres ornées a l'usage de tous les artistes.* (Paris 1767). What may have been the first French decorated capitals in type form date from 1680, but the real pioneer of decorated letters in typography was Pierre Simon Fournier whose first ornamented types appeared *circa* 1749. By the time Fournier had published his *Manuel Typographique* (1764-1766) he had cut nine different decorated and shaded letters in sizes ranging from 6 point to approximately 108 pt and shows specimens of them therein.

[1] *The Fleuron* No 6. Cambridge University Press 1928.
[2] *ibid.*

ner des

ftoíres

the Tryal of the Alderman for his Life ; of the Jury that found him and other worthy Citizens, guilty of a Ryot; and of the Sums they were fin'd in ; of the Perfons who kept fix Aldermen, and many of the Citizens out of Guild-hall, by Military Force ; of the Grand and Petty Juries againſt my Lord Ruſſel ; and of Colonel Sidney's Jury ; with Part of ſome Informations, taken upon Oath, by a Committee of the Houſe of Lords, who enquir'd into the Adviſers and Proſecutors in the Tryals of the Lord Ruſ-ſel, Colonel Sidney, Sir Thomas Armſtrong, Mr. Corniſh, &c. Sold by B. Bragge in Pater-Noſter-Row. Price 6 d.

Scriptographia ; *or,* Written Print-Hand ; *(which can't be imitated by any other Printer) fit for Bills of Lading, Bills of Sale, Bonds of all ſorts, Receipts for the Land=Tax,&c. Sea=mens Bills and Tickets of Leave, Letter of Attorney, Warrants of all ſorts, Releaſes, In-dentures, or any other blank Law=Forms. Such as have Occaſion for any of theſe, may have them printed on this, or larger Characters of the like,* by H. Meere, *Printer, at the Black-Fryer in Black-Fryars, London.*

¶ Compleat Sets of the Obſervator, or ſingle Ones, ever ſince it was begun by Mr. Tutchin, to this Time, are to be had of B. Bragge at the Raven in Pater-Noſter-Row, and H. Meere at the Black-Fryar in Black-Fryars

¶ Any Gentleman, who us'd to ſend Notice of Things formerly to Mr. Tutchin, are defir'd now to direct them to H. Meere, at the Black-Fryar in Black-Fryars, for the Obſervator, Poſt pay'd. Where Advertiſements are taken in.

Widow of the late Author, JOHN TUTCHIN.

U N I O N.

Double Pica.

That about this time (1450) the U N I O N.
Art of Printing and Caſting Sin-
ABCDEFGGHIJKLM

Byddel 10.　Matrices 63.

85. *Union Pearl, circa 1690* [248]

It should be noted here that one of the earliest of all decorated types was of English provenance. Union Pearl dates from about 1690 & may be regarded as the first English decorated letter. Little is known of its history. It is available from Stephenson Blake who inherited the original matrices.

Fournier's types were copied by other French founders, and abroad by J. F. Rosart for the Enschedé foundry at Haarlem. In the 1780's the first shaded and decorated types were cut in this country. They may be seen in the specimen books issued in 1786 by William Caslon III, in 1794 by the Frys, and in 1796 by S. & C. Stephenson.

In Paris the Didot and Gillé fils typefoundries produced decorated and shaded versions of the modern face. Some of Didot's (Pierre Didot l'ainé) decorated capitals are now in the possession of the Enschedé foundry.

Such is the variety and nature of decorated letters that they defy precise analysis. The Oxford English Dictionary gives the meaning of the word *decorated* as: *Adorned; furnished with anything ornamental; invested with a decoration*. Succinct in itself, this description serves to emphasize the extraordinary variety to be found in decorated types.

Some contemporary decorated types

Demeter (Schriftguss, now Typoart), Gill Floriated (Monotype), Fournier le jeune (Deberny & Peignot), Fry's Ornamented, June (Stephenson Blake), Modernistic (American Type Founders), Molé Foliate (Enschedé, Stephenson Blake), Ornata (Klingspor), Sapphire (Stempel), Union Pearl (Stephenson Blake), Vesta (Berthold).

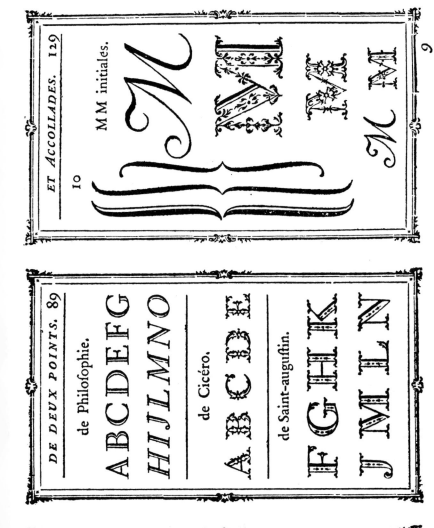

86. *Decorated types of Fournier le jeune* [249]

Non dubito fore ple-
rosque, Attice, qui hoc
genus fcripturae leve et
non fatis dignum fum-

Deux Points de Cicero Romain Orné, N°. 1.

ABCDEFGHIJ
KLMNOPQRS
TUVWXYZ
ÉÈÊËÇÆŒ,,'

Deux Points de Cicero Romain Orné, N°. 2.

ABCDEFGH
IJKLMNOP
QRSTUVWX
·;'YZÉÈÊŒ

87. *The Rosart's decorated types* [250]

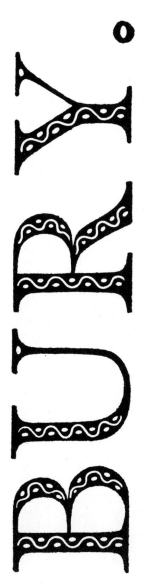

BURY.

FRY'S ORNAMENTED

ABCDEFGHIJKLMNOPQRS
TUVWXYZ&ÆŒ

CANON ORNAMENTED.

TYPOGRAPHY.

88. *Decorated letters in England from the 1780's* [250]

ABCDE
LMNO
UVW

ABCDEFG
OPQRSTU

FGHIJK
PQRST
XYZ

HIJKLMN
VWXYZÆ

n capitals [251]

153

90. *Fournier le jeune's shaded types* [252]

SHADED

We have already noted that Fournier, pioneer in cutting decorated letters in typography, produced the first shaded types also and showed several sizes in his *Manuel* of 1764-1766.

Later, when advertising faces were cut these were equipped with shaded versions but 'the earlier shaded letters fell out of use as decorative material for bookwork'[1] and seem rarely to have been used for the next hundred years.

The simplest form of shaded type is one in which a single white line runs down either the left or the right (but more usually the left) of the thick strokes. Types of this kind are still called hand-tooled, the term originating perhaps in the compositor's efforts to tool white lines on display types, i.e. on actual metal sorts. The best of these shaded types may be used with distinction in bookwork and, of course, in many kinds of ephemeral printing. But there are others, designed for use in jobbing printing in which the shading is (a) on the left *and* on the right of the same stem (b) formed by three or more white lines running parallel with the sides of the thick strokes and (c) formed by *horizontal* white lines.

There is yet another form of shaded type probably owing its birth to the shaded letters of the early nineteenth century which in the past has been grouped under the name *Inline*. Present day examples vary in their basic design, some being normally seriffed romans and italics and others sans serifs. All have one thing in common—a white line (often a fine

[1] A. F. Johnson. A GUIDE TO PRESENT-DAY TYPES. *Paper and Print.* Summer 1933.

Ornamented Two=line Letters.

Five Lines Pica.

MABC

Four Lines Pica.

ABCDH
FGIJKL

Double Pica.

ABCDEFG
HIJKLMN

Great Primer.

ABCDEFG
HIJKLMN

91. *Edmund Fry's shaded capitals, 1788* [252]

white line) running down the centre of the thick stems. This line sometimes cuts right through the serifs at head and foot.

Roman and italic types, sloped romans, and sans serif types are among
those to be found with shading.

Some contemporary shaded types

WITH SINGLE WHITE LINE ON THE LEFT:
Cameo (Ludlow), Castellar (Monotype), Dominus (Stephenson
Blake), Gresham (Stevens Shanks), Imprint Shadow (Monotype),
Narciss (Klingspor), Othello Shadow (Monotype).

WITH SINGLE WHITE LINE ON THE RIGHT:
Cooper Hilite (American Type Founders), Maximilian Antiqua
(Klingspor), Rex (Genzsch & Heyse).

WITH SINGLE WHITE LINE CENTRALLY:
Adastra (Stempel), Colonna (Monotype), Delphian Titling (Ludlow),
Elegant Inline (Stempel), Erbar Inline or Phosphor (Ludwig & Mayer),
Lutetia Open (Enschedé).

WITH WHITE LINE ON LEFT AND ON RIGHT:
Gallia (American Type Founders), Trio B (Schriftguss, now Typoart).

WITH THREE OR MORE WHITE LINES:
Alfrodita (Nacional), Atlas, formerly Fatima (Française), Prisma
(Klingspor).

WITH SHADING HORIZONTALLY:
Eclair (Deberny & Peignot), Excellent (Bauer), Kombinette (Ludwig
& Mayer), Minster Symbol (Schriftguss, now Typoart).

A

SPECIMEN

OF

PRINTING TYPES,

BY

FRY and STEELE,

𝕷𝖊𝖙𝖙𝖊𝖗=𝕱𝖔𝖚𝖓𝖉𝖊𝖗𝖘

TO THE

PRINCE OF WALES,

TYPE-STREET.

PRINTED BY T. RICKABY.

MDCCXCV.

92. Title page of the 1790's [253]

CANON ITALIC OPEN.

CUMBERLAND.

TWO LINES ENGLISH OPEN.

SALISBURY SQUARE.

93. Shaded types—early nineteenth century [253]

Twelve Lines Pica.

A S
B G
C E

94. *Twelve lines pica letters of Thomas Cottrell* [254]

FAT FACE

The shaded types cut for use in jobbing printing were not the first to be designed specifically for the purposes of advertisement. The earliest advertising types were what we now call Fat Faces. Nicolette Gray says that the first step in their evolution 'was the introduction, for advertising purposes, of normal letters enlarged beyond the scale of normal book work. According to Edward Rowe Mores this innovation was due to the English typefounder, Thomas Cottrell. His book of *c.*1765 shows a twelve-line pica letter. The idea was taken up by other founders and later letters tend to grow bigger and fatter.'[1] But Mr Johnson says that the lottery handbills of the early nineteenth century 'illustrate the development of the design from the Bold Faces, (i.e. thickened versions of the normal book types) and suggest that these Bold Faces rather than the placard types of Cottrell were the begetters of the Fat Faces.'[2]

Fat Faces were originally referred to simply as fat types and this term probably included types from other groups, for example, the antiques, (that is egyptians). All these fat types were extraordinarily bold and (unlike the bold faces of the day) not intended for use in bookwork.

Two early nineteenth century writers ascribe the development of Fat Faces to Robert Thorne the typefounder, pupil of Thomas Cottrell.

[1]In *Nineteenth Century Ornamented Types and Title Pages.* Faber and Faber. London **1938.**
[2]In *Alphabet & Image* No 5. September 1947. FAT FACES: THEIR HISTORY, FORMS AND USE.

Lottery Draws 8th *June*, 1810.

A SINGLE TICKET may gain

£100,000,

A SIXTEENTH may gain

£6,000,

IF BOUGHT OF

BISH,

STOCK-BROKER,

4, Cornhill, or 9, Charing Cross,

LONDON.

CAPITAL PRIZES

Shared and Sold by

BISH,

IN THE

LAST LOTTERY,

VALENTINE'S DAY,
14th FEBRUARY, 1810.

	Class.	
3,734	....A....	£20,000
4,654	....A......	5,000
591	....B......	1,000
591	....C......	1,000
999	....A......	1,000
999	....B....	1,000
999	....C......	1,000
2,952	....A......	1,000
2,952	....D......	1,000
388	....C......	500
4,540	....A......	500
4,694	....A......	500

CAPITAL PRIZES

Shared and Sold by

BISH,

IN THE

LATE LOTTERY,

DRAWN 20th OCTOBER, 1809.

	Class.	
3,618	....A....	£20,000
2,618	....D......	20,000
4,090	....D......	5,000
383	....B......	1,000
830	....A......	1,000
830	....B......	1,000
548	....D......	500
4,855	....C......	500

95. *A lottery hand bill of 1810* [254]

In his *Practical Hints on Decorative Printing* (1822) William Savage said that Thorne 'has been principally instrumental in the revolution that has taken place in Posting Bills, by the introduction of fat types.' And T. C. Hansard writing in 1825 in his *Typographia* remarks that 'the extremely bold and fat letter, now prevalent in job printing, owes its introduction principally to Mr Thorne.' Thorne's last specimen book was dated 1803. William Thorowgood who bought Thorne's foundry shows the first specimens of the latter's jobbing types in 1820.

The other English foundries soon copied the original fat face design and these types were widely used in much of the ephemera of the day, e.g. broadsides, ballads, pamphlets, newspapers, etc. This early popularity waned however as the nineteenth century advanced, and though never entirely out of fashion (they were used on royal proclamations for example) it was not until the 1920's that their use was revived—not in England initially, says Mr Johnson but in the United States and in Germany.

In the same article he wrote 'The American Typefounders showed their *Ultra Bodoni* in 1928, well named, for that is exactly what a Fat Face is, an exaggerated design after the true classical modern face or *Bodoni*.' And he defines the characteristics of these faces as types with 'thin, flat serifs, vertical stress & abrupt contrast of thick & thin strokes. To these characteristics we must add exaggeration of the contrast between thick & thin. The thickness of the main strokes as compared with their height is in the proportion of 1 to $2\frac{1}{2}$. At what particular point a type ceases to be a Bold Face and becomes a Fat Face is hard to decide.'[1]

It may be noted in passing that Nicolette Gray in the work already quoted from writes of Fat Face serifs that they 'may be unbracketed or slightly bracketed, but those terminating a thin vertical stroke are always bracketed.'[2]

[1] In *Alphabet & Image* No 5.
[2] Students should note the triangular or wedge-shaped serifs used in some Fat Face designs, e.g. A.T.F. Ultra Bodoni's A, E, F, K, L, M, N, U, V, X, Y etc.

How far, O Catiline, wilt thou abuse our patience?
How long shall thy frantic rage baffle the efforts of
Justice? To what height meanest thou to carry thy
daring insolence? Art thou nothing daunted at the
nocturnal host to secure the Palatium? Nothing by
the City Guards? ABCDEFGHIJKLMNOPQRSTUVWXYZ
ABCDEFGHIJKLMNOPQRSTUVWXYZÆŒ

How far, O Catiline, wilt thou abuse our patience?
How long shall thy frantic rage baffle the efforts of
Justice? To what height meanest thou to carry thy
daring insolence? Art thou nothing daunted at the
ABCDEFGHIJKLMNOPQRSTUVWXY £1234567890
ABCDEFGHIJKLMNOPQRSTU MAN MAN

96. Robert Thorne's fat face [255]

SIX LINES PICA No. 1.

THORN

Berkshire

Gloster

97. William Thorowgood's fat face [255]

TWELVE LINE PICA ROMAN No. 2.

MINT
main.

98. *William Thorowgood's fat face* [255]

Some contemporary fat faces

Normande (Haas), Normandia (Nebiolo), Nubian (American
Type Founders), Roman Extra Bold (Bauer), Sphinx (Deberny &
Peignot), Thorowgood (Stephenson Blake), Ultra Bodoni (American
Type Founders, Monotype).

Two Lines Pica, Antique.

ABCDEFGHIJKLMNOPQR
STUVWXYZ&;:;.-
£1234567890

Two Lines Pearl Antique, No. 2.

ABCDEFGHIJKLMNOPQRSTUVWXYZÆŒ& ;:;.-' £1234567890
FREEHOLD & COPYHOLD ESTATES.

Brevier Antique.

ABCDEFGHIJKLMNOPQRSTUVWXYZÆŒ& ;:;.- £1234567890
PRINTING - TYPES, FOR EXPORTATION.

V. FIGGINS.

99. *Vincent Figgins's Antique, 1815* [257]

ANTIQUE OR EGYPTIAN

The types which we know by the name of *Egyptian* were first shown by Vincent Figgins in his specimen book of 1815, under the name Antique,[1] but at least one historian of the day (Hansard) gave Robert Thorne the credit for designing them. Contemporary writers cannot agree on the name of the innovator of Egyptian types, but Thorne, who before his death in 1820 had actually cut several sizes and had set up specimens of them, named them Egyptian in the title lines to those specimens. William Thorowgood (neither founder nor printer), who as we have already noted purchased Thorne's foundry in 1820, used these settings of Thorne's and in them we probably have the first use of the name Egyptian for types of this kind.

Exactly why the term Egyptian was used has been the subject of much conjecture.[2] The most reasonable explanation for the coining of the name seems to lie in the heightened interest in the early nineteenth century for all things Egyptian, occasioned by Napoleon's expedition to that country. While this seems to be a perfectly valid reason for first using the name, the whys and wherefores of the invention of the slab-

---

[1] Today the term remains an alternative name for Egyptian faces.

[2] "These characters were often called in type-specimens and elsewhere "Egyptian" (no doubt in allusion to their "darkness"); and a London jest-book of 1806, under the heading "Fashionable Egyptian Sign-Boards," says: "An Irishman describing the Egyptian letters which at present deface the Metropolis, declared that the thin strokes were exactly the same size as the thick ones!" ' D. B. Updike. *Printing Types, Their History, Forms, and Use*. Vol II.

TWO LINE GREAT PRIMER EGYPTIAN

Quosque tandem abu-
tere Catilina patientia
FURNITURE 1820

TWO LINE ENGLISH EGYPTIAN.

Quosque tandem abutere Catilina
patientia nostra? quamdiu nos
W. THOROWGOOD.

seriffed letter itself remain a mystery. It is not known whether the originators were signwriters or typefounders.

The distinctive features of Egyptian (or Antique) types are (1) the slab serifs (unbracketed or bracketed) often of the same thickness as the stems of the letters though in some of the early Egyptians the designers made their lower-case letters follow modern-face patterns (2) the lack of any differentiation between the thick and the thin strokes in some designs. In others differences in stem thickness are apparent, e.g. the thinning of curved forms where they meet vertical straights, e.g. as in the lower-case a, d, g. This thinning is very noticeable in some of the earliest Egyptian designs (3) the descenders, & the ascenders are often very short (4) the stress is vertical (5) a uniformity in the width of the capitals.

All the earliest Egyptians (or Antiques) were very bold types but typefounders in our time have cut them in weights ranging from light to Extra Bold.

When the Egyptians appeared Hansard in his *Typographia* referred to the new letter as 'a typographical monstrosity.' But extravagances based on them called *Italian* or *French Antique* followed in which the heaviest strokes are *horizontal*. Contemporary versions of these types, now called reversed Egyptians, are Figaro (Monotype), Hidalgo (Amsterdam), Italienne (Fonderie Typographique Française).

Some contemporary antiques or egyptians

Beton (Bauer), Egyptian Expanded (Stephenson Blake, originally Miller & Richard), Expanded Antique (Stevens Shanks, formerly V. Figgins), Karnak (Ludlow), Memphis (Stempel), Rockwell (Monotype).
Reversed Egyptians, that is egyptians with the serifs thicker than the main strokes: Figaro (Monotype), Hidalgo (Amsterdam), Italienne (Française), Playbill (Stephenson Blake).

R.T.THORNE
ashbourn &.
£12£67890

101. *William Thorowgood's Egyptian* [258]

Next FRIDAY, July 15,

ALL IN ONE DAY,

4 of £21.000

AND MANY OTHER CAPITALS; TOGETHER WITH

64 Pipes of Old Port Gratis!

Presented by HAZARD & Co. as an addition to the Four Prizes of One Thousand Guineas—being
SIXTEEN PIPES for EACH TICKET, Shares in Proportion, so that EACH SIXTEENTH
will receive ONE PIPE.

NO BLANKS! As every Number is sure of £5.

HAZARD & Cº

STOCK-BROKERS,

AT THEIR OLD-ESTABLISHED AND FORTUNATE OFFICES,

Royal Exchange Gate; 26, Cornhill; and 324, Oxford Street, end of Regent Street:

Who Shared and Sold on the 31st of last May,

No. 1,804······£30,000 | No. 3,627············£5,000

Also in the Last Year's Lotteries alone FIVE Prizes of £30,000 and £20,000; and the following
Prizes drawn on the 19th of April last,

8,185, £20,100—9,579, £2,000, and Eight other Capitals.

102. *Another early nineteenth century lottery bill* [258]

FIVE LINES PICA, IN SHADE.

ABCDEFGHI
IJKLMNOP
RSTUVWX.

V.FIGGINS.

103. *Vincent Figgins's Five lines pica, in Shade, 1815* [259]

SHADOWED OR THREE-DIMENSIONAL[1]

'Unable to press any more novelty out of the modern letter as inherited from Grandjean through Fournier, Bodoni and the Didots, the nineteenth-century typefounders resorted to the exploitation of colour. It is true that Firmin Didot and Gillé enfeebled their types until they were positively unreadable by artificial light but, taking a hint from Bodoni's bolder letter cut *ca*.1780, Thorne, after imitating Wilson and Caslon, all but sent printing to perdition at one stroke by his invention of the extreme fat-faced type. For a generation or more English and continental book printing suffered from these bad types. A worse novelty was reached when, in order to provide a trick three-dimensional fount, heavy black types decorated with white outline flowers were provided with a perspective-shadow. Finally, there came a queer piebald fatuity, the upper half of which is black and the lower white, or vice-versa. This monster also is found in a three-dimensional form; but, we are gratified to add, its creation seems to have exhausted both the resources of the trade and the patience of the public.'

[1]'Between 1810 and 1815 were developed not only the two principles for the variation of lettering, by modification of the form and by decoration of the face, but also that idea which enormously enriched the possibilities under either principle, that of the three dimensional letter. The first shadowed letters (1815) are characteristic and distinct from all the hundreds of letters to follow. They are all fat faces, white outline letters with a heavy black shadow . . . The introduction was immediately enormously popular. Every founder came out in a wide range of sizes, many with italic.' Nicolette Gray. *Nineteenth Century Ornamented Types and Title Pages.*

Two-Line Letters in Shade.

Great Primer.

ABCDEFGHL

Pica.

ABCDEFGHIKM

Long Primer.

ABCDEFGHIJKLMNOPR

Brevier.

ABCDEFGHIJKLMNOPQR

Nonpareil.

ABCDEFGHIJKLMNOPQRSTUVW

Pearl.

ABCDEFGHIJKLMNOPQRSTUVWXYZ&.

Pearl Italic.

ABCDEFGHIJKLMNOPQRSTUVW.

Two-Line English Ornamented.

ABCDEFGHIK

V. FIGGINS.

104. *Shadowed types, Vincent Figgins, 1833* [259]

These remarks by Mr Stanley Morison in his article on decorated types[1] brings his survey to the middle of the nineteenth century. By that time the Victorian typefounders, whose first shadowed or three-dimensional types appeared about 1815, had produced a whole range of fantastic letters, fat faced, egyptians or antiques and sans serifs (the group of faces next to be described) in shadowed or three-dimensional form.

The terms shadowed or three-dimensional used to describe types in this group, that is, types possessing in addition to the normal characteristics of a face, a third dimension—that of depth—includes types which our nineteenth century founders issued under a wealth of titles (some thoroughly confusing—as *open* or *shaded*) including Tuscan, Ornamented and Perspective.

Some contemporary shadowed or three-dimensional types

Figgins Shaded (Stevens Shanks), Orplid (Klingspor), Profil (Haas), Sans Serifs Shaded (Stephenson Blake), Stridon (Warnery), Thorne Shaded (Stephenson Blake), Umbra (Ludlow), Verdi (Bauer).

[1] In *The Fleuron* No 6.

CUMBERLAND.

CANON ORNAMENTED.

TYPOGRAPHY.

TWO LINES ENGLISH EGYPTIAN.

W CASLON JUNR LETTERFOUNDER

TWO LINES ENGLISH OPEN.

SALISBURY SQUARE.

105. *The first sans serif type,1816* [259]

SANS SERIF

This group of faces represents the next essay on the part of the early nineteenth century typefounders in types cut specifically for the jobbing printing field. The first sans serif type appeared as a single line specimen under the name *Egyptian* in William Caslon IV's specimen book of 1816. This type, roughly the equivalent of Gill Bold in weight, was repeated in a specimen issued about 1819. Then apparently no more was seen of the new letter form until black, clumsy versions appeared under their correct name, sans serif, in Vincent Figgins's specimen book of 1832. In the same year William Thorowgood showed a specimen under the apt name of grotesque, a name admirably suiting many contemporary revivals of nineteenth century sans faces also. Besides the descriptive *sans surryphs* used by Blake and Stephenson of Sheffield in 1833 curious names were coined for these early sans serif types including Doric and Gothic, the latter 'presumably due to the fact that the early types in this style were heavy, black letters, which by their colour recalled the early gothic or black-letter types.'[1]

Besides being heavy & black most of the early sans serifs were titlings, with letters of monotonously uniform width, this trait, of course, deriving from the 'modern' face. Lighter cuttings of sans serif faces came later. No lower-case appears to have been cut in England before the 1870's though in America and in Germany sans serifs equipped with lower-case were in use long before that time. The Schelter and Giesecke foundry appear to have issued such a letter in 1830.

The most important characteristic of types in this group is implicit in the name—the absence of serifs. The letters are monoline, or, in other

[1] A. F. Johnson. *Type Designs: their History and Development.*

TO BE SOLD BY AUCTION, WITHOUT RESERVE; HOUSEHOLD FURNITURE, PLATE, GLASS, AND OTHER EFFECTS. VINCENT FIGGINS.

106. *Sans serif, Vincent Figgins, 1832* [260]

words appear to have strokes of equal thickness. The widths of the strokes does of course vary, e.g. curved forms are often thinned where they meet vertical strokes or other curved forms as in the lower-case b and g respectively. These are the more obvious examples: an examination of sans serifs will reveal other, subtler variations in stroke widths. 'The sans serif is in fact an Egyptian with the serifs knocked off, and it is probable that that was the manner of its creation.'[1]

The manner in which contemporary sans serifs 'have been modified is in accordance with the change in our general typography; the letters have been made to conform to earlier and better designs, and the bad features derived from the modern-face roman have been eliminated.'[2]

Some contemporary sans serif types

Erbar (Ludwig & Mayer), Futura (Bauer), Gill Sans (Monotype). Nineteenth century sans serif: Grotesque No 9 (Stephenson Blake).

[1] [2] A. F. Johnson. *Type Designs: their History and Development.*

SIX LINE REVERSED EGYPTIAN ITALIC,

HOMERTON

MOLDER

THOROWGOOD, LONDON.

EIGHT LINES PICA TUSCAN REVERSED

MODERN

REVERSED OR
CAMEO

These types are of early nineteenth century origin. The first examples were Egyptians, Fat Faces, and Tuscans[1] reversed white on a black ground. Thorowgood shows a Reversed Egyptian italic in his specimen of 1828 and the Sheffield founders, Bower & Bacon a Four-line White—fat face capitals reversed white on a black ground—in a specimen of 1830. Unlike the contemporary versions of reversed types the earliest examples appeared on continuous black grounds—there were no white lines separating adjoining letters as there are in present day examples.

Enjoying a relatively brief period of popularity these reversed types went almost entirely out of fashion about forty years after they had first appeared and the design was not resuscitated until the 1920's.

Today types of this kind are sometimes called *Cameo*[2] and are usually sans serif capitals reversed white on a black or shaded ground.

[1]'The Tuscan, was, as Mr Morison points out, invented in the fourth century by Pope Damasus I. Its characteristic is that the points of the serifs are extended and curled, probably bifurcating the stem. In the nineteenth century it tends also to acquire a bulge in the middle of the stem . . . The first nineteenth century English Tuscan was brought out by Figgins in 1815. Between 1815 and 1875 the letter form was subjected to various devices to vary its colour, shape or shadow.' Nicolette Gray in *Nineteenth Century Ornamented Types and Title Pages.*

[2]A precious stone, as the onyx, agate, sardonyx, etc, having two layers of different colours, in the upper of which a figure is carved in relief, while the lower serves as ground. This is the definition of *Cameo* given in the Oxford Dictionary.

TEN LINES WHITE EGYPTIAN.

HORN

TWO LINES GREAT PRIMER.

NOTTINGHAMSHIRE

FOUR LINES WHITE.

ABCDEFGHIJKL

108. *G.W.Bower's White types, 1837* [260]

Some contemporary reversed or cameo types

Gill Cameo, Gill Cameo Ruled (Monotype), Granby Cameo
(Stephenson Blake), Lucina (Ludwig & Mayer), Razionale, Fregio
Razionale (Nebiolo).

IONIC.

TWO-LINE LONG PRIMER.

ABCDEFGHIJKLMNOPQRSTUV

TWO-LINE BREVIER.

ABCDEFGHIJKLMNOPQRSTUVWXYZ

TWO-LINE NONPAREIL.

ABCDEFGHIJKLMNOPQRSTUVWXYZÆŒ & ,;:-'?.
THEATRE ROYAL DRURY LANE, A GRAND BALL.

TWO-LINE DIAMOND.

ABCDEFGHIJKLMNOPQRSTUVWXYZÆŒ & ,;:-'?. CITY OF LONDON.
THE LORD MAYOR, ALDERMEN, AND COURT OF COMMON COUNCIL.

NONPAREIL.

ABCDEFGHIJKLMNOPQRSTUVWXYZÆŒ & ,;:-'?. HER MOST GRACIOUS MAJESTY VICTORIA.
THE HOUSE OF LORDS. THE HOUSE OF COMMONS. PARLIAMENT OF THE UNITED KINGDOM.

109. *Henry Caslon's Ionic titlings, circa 1844* [261]

Ionic

The name *Ionic* seems to have been used by early Victorian founders
as an additional name for Egyptian types. *Ideal* was an early Victorian,
and *Cushing Antique* an early American synonym for Ionic. The latter
is thought to have been first used by Blake and Stephenson in 1833:
their specimen is of a modified form of the earliest Antique/Egyptian.
A comparison of this type with those of Figgins and of Thorne shows
that the serifs are bracketed and not as slab-like, that there is a greater
differentiation between the thick and thin strokes, and that the letters
are not as heavy and certainly not as sharply cut. Types of this kind are
now classed as modified egyptians. Present day revivals would include
Stephenson Blake's Consort in its various forms, and Stevens Shanks
Antique Nos 3 & 5, and a variety of clarendons, for example that of the
Haas'sche Schriftgiesserie.

Originally display types, the types in this group are now primarily
newspaper text faces. Some use of them is also made in Bible printing,
magazines and advertisements. The present day versions of the Ionics
having been designed specifically with newspaper production in mind
are usually monoline letters of large x-height, with very short ascenders and descenders, open counters and sturdy, flat, or slightly bracketed,
serifs.

'A primary defect of Ionic—from the point of view of text composition—is a certain monotony resulting from the complete uniformity
of line throughout every character . . . having no thick and thin, it
does not look 'customary' to eyes habituated to the old faces, old styles
and moderns employed in 99 per cent of the reading matter which is

Quousque tandem abu-
tere, Catilina, patientia
nostra? quamdiu nos e-
tiam furor iste tuus elu-
det? quem ad finem sese
effrenata jactabit auda-
cia? nihilne te noctur-
num præsidium palatii,
nihil urbis vigiliæ, nihil
ABCDEFGHIJKLMN
ABCDEFGHIJKLMNOPQR
£ 1234567890

**In the State Lotteries,
now wisely abolished by
the Legislature, the risk
was so greatly against
the adventurer, that, ac-
cording to the Schemes,
the buyer of the whole
Lottery would lose half
his money. Few, there-
fore, but the imprudent,
the inconsiderate, & the**

110. *Henry Caslon's Double pica Ionic, circa 1844* [261]

produced in this country . . .The more careful the press-work given
to it the more Ionic looks what it is, namely, a somewhat superior catalogue or jobbing type. There is no consensus that Ionic provides the
finally satisfactory newspaper face.'[1]

Some contemporary ionic faces

Excelsior (Linotype), a lighter and somewhat modified version of
Linotype Ionic, Ideal (Intertype), Ideal News (Amsterdam),
Ionic (Linotype), Ionic No 2 (Monotype).

[1]THE TIMES & MODERN TYPOGRAPHY. *The Monotype Recorder* Volume XXI No 246.
September–October 1932.

HOUSEHOLD FURNITURE,
PLATE, CHINA-WARE, JEWELS,
WATCHES,
AND OTHER EFFECTS.
ABCDEFGHIJKLMNOPQRSTUVWXY

BREVIER SANS-SERIF, OPEN.

FOR THE BENEFIT OF THE PRINTER'S
PENSION SOCIETY,
GRAND CONCERT OF ANCIENT AND MODERN
VOCAL AND INSTRUMENTAL MUSIC.
ABCDEFGHIJKLMNOPQRSTUVWXYZÆŒ
VINCENT FIGGINS.

TWO-LINE PEARL, OUTLINE.

STANDARD NOVELS
&
THE WORKS OF LORD BYRON,
WITH EMBELLISHMENTS.

Mʀ. Cº. Nº. &c. −,;:.'!
ABCDEFGHIJKLNMOPQRSTUVX
WYZÆŒ!

VINCENT FIGGINS,
LETTER FOUNDER,
17, WEST STREET, SMITHFIELD,
LONDON.

111. *Some of the first outline or open types, 1833* [261]

OUTLINE OR OPEN

The designers of the first outline or open types may possibly have been influenced by Fournier le jeune's cutting of decorated and shaded letters. If we accept the definition given below as being a reasonable description of a true outline or open type then Fournier himself does not appear to have cut one.

The earliest designs in this class appear to have begun as jobbing types. William Thorowgood shows examples of what he calls open types in his specimen books of 1821, 1828 and 1832, but *open* as a description of those types is a misnomer: they are without exception shaded versions of jobbing faces. But on the title-page of the specimen book issued by Thorowgood in 1834 appear three examples of jobbing types in outline or open form. Vincent Figgins showed outline faces in his specimen book issued in the previous year.

Nicolette Gray in her *Nineteenth Century Ornamented Types and Title Pages* says: 'One hardly notices the introduction of the first outline types in 1833; for not only are they very light, but also very small...The outlines are delicately cut and very fine so that the faces are aethereal'.

The names of the types in this group should be sufficiently descriptive of them: the thick stems of the letters are *outlined* (i.e. the stems are *open*) and not solid as in normal type. But the typefounders and manufacturers of type composing machinery have so thoroughly bedevilled our typographical nomenclature that the terms open, outline, shaded,

FOR THE
INSTRUCTION OF YOUTH
IN THE VARIOUS
BRANCHES OF MATHEMATICAL,
COMMERCIAL & CLASSICAL
EDUCATION.

ABCDEFGHIJKLMNOPQRSTUV
WXYZ, &c. Co. No.

BREVIER TUSCAN.

BLAKE & STEPHENSON,
LETTER FOUNDERS,
SHEFFIELD.

ABCDEFGHIJKLMNOPQRSTUVWX
YZ&&

TWO LINES NONPARIEL SANS-SURRYPH.

SOCIETY OF ARTS.
NOTICE TO STUDENTS.
THE LECTURES AT THE ANTIQUE
ACADEMY,
WILL COMMENCE ON
MONDAY NEXT.

ABCDEFGHIJKLMNOPQRSTUVWX

112. *Two outline types of Blake & Stephenson, circa 1833* [262]

'hilite', and hand-tooled have been freely interchanged in their specimen books! In the true outline type the outlining is of the same weight round the whole of the stem, but some letters may be admitted to this group which have outlines fractionally thicker on one side of the stem (usually the right) than on the other. True outline letters are therefore lighter than shaded letters—white & not black preponderating in their designs.

The chapter heading shows a fine contemporary outline letter.

Some contemporary outline or open types

Columna (Bauer), Moreau le jeune (Deberny & Peignot), Old Face Open—but an outline face in its smaller sizes only—the 60 point size, for example, is a *shaded* letter (Stephenson Blake), Open Capitals (Enschedé), Normandia Outline (Nebiolo).

TWO LINES ENGLISH CLARENDON

Quosque tandem abutere Catilina, patientia nostra? quamdiu nos etiam furor iste tuus eludet? quem ad finem sese effrenata jactabit audacia tua? nihilne te nocturnum præsidium palatii, nihil urbis vigiliæ, nihil timor

£1234567890

METROPOLITAN IMPROVEMENT.

113. *The first Clarendon* [262]

Clarendon

The first Clarendon, a modified Egyptian style of letter, was registered byW. Thorowgood and Co. of the Fann Street Letter Foundry in
1845.[1] No sooner had the copyright period of three years (with which
the letter was invested) expired, 'than the trade was inundated with all
sorts of Piracies and Imitations . . . . .' We have seen that the earliest
Ionics were bold display types, but if Besley's rather rough letter was
somewhat compressed, a comparison of *weights* shows scarcely, if any,
differentiation between it and the earliest Ionics. While our contemporary Ionics are no longer bold display faces but are designed in the main
as newspaper text faces, i.e. normally weighted types for continuous
reading, the Clarendons have remained dark-faced types & their main
field of employment has been for distinguishing words in works of
reference. Such has been their popularity for this kind of work that
Clarendon has long been a synonym for bold or dark-faced types—to
many old-established printers it is a generic name for bold composition-
sized faces. The feature noted, which marked Besley's Clarendon from
its predecessors, the Ionics, though not a characteristic of all nineteenth
century Clarendons is one which marks contemporary versions of the
type also. They are, in the main, somewhat condensed faces.

   Clarendon is now classed as 'an Egyptian with more differentiation
of colour and rather lighter serifs than the original model. Some letters
follow the roman model rather than what we now think of as Egyptian,

---

[1]'There had been types of similar design before Besley's, which went under the name of
Ionic.' *A History of the Old English Letter Foundries.* T. B. Reed.

Quousque tandem abutere Catilina, patientia nostra ? quamdiu nos etiam furor iste tuus eludet ? quem ad finem sese effrenata jactabit audacia ? nihilne te nocturnum præsidium palatii, nihilne urbis vigiliæ, nihil timor populi, nihil consensus bonorum omnium, nihil hic munitissimus habendi senatus locus, nihil horum

£1234567890

SALES BY PUBLIC AUCTION.

Quousque tandem abutere, Catilina, patientia nostra ? quamdiu nos etiam furor iste tuus eludet ? quem ad finem sese effrenata jactabit audacia ? nihilne nocturnum præsidium palatii, nihil urbis vigiliæ, nihilne timor populi, nihil consensus bonorum omnium, nihil hic munitissimus habendi senatus locus, nihil

£1234567890

MORNING PROMENADE CONCERT.

114. *Other sizes of the first Clarendon* [262]

such as the a, e, g, and t, and the capital R with its curls. This was also a characteristic of the first English Egyptians.'[1]

Some contemporary clarendons

Clarendon (Monotype, Series 12), Consort Bold Condensed (Stephenson Blake).

[1] *Encyclopædia of Type Faces.* W. Turner Berry/A. F. Johnson. Blandford Press London 1953.

The Foundational Hand Fig. 1

abcdefghijklmnopqr
stuvwxyz

Three essentials of form

① Angle of thin stroke of each letter shd. be constant at about 30 degrees to the horizontal writing line

② whole alphabet is based on a circle

③ good average height 4½ times the width of nib

"i" has foot

"l" and "t" have round limb

Exception
v and w pen held more steeply

\# note springing ½ of arches Notice inside shapes of letters

ABCDEFGHIJKLMNOPQRSTUVWXYZ

115. *Part of a Writing Sheet designed by Mrs Irene Wellington* [263]

Calligraphic

We include in this group only those designs which are patently derived from broad-nibbed pen forms—in other words types based on what Edward Johnston called slanted, or straight, pen writing—these terms referring of course to the angle of the pen nib in relation to the line of writing—slanted-pen writing giving round letters with an oblique stress and straight-pen writing giving round letters with vertical stress. There are a number of types that on cursory examination appear to have been based on one or other of these styles but which prove on closer scrutiny to have been produced with drawing instruments other than the broad-nibbed pen.

Below are examples of an italic hand and of built-up letters or versals, both written with broad-nibbed pens.

abcdeffghijklmnopqrs

ABCDE

Some contemporary calligraphic types

Bologna (Stephenson Blake), Carolus (Berling), Hyperion (Bauer), Klang (Monotype), Lydian (American Type Founders), Offenbach (Klingspor), Runnymede (Stephenson Blake), Steel and Wallau (Klingspor).

Fig a here the pen is held with the thin stroke horizontal giving a beautiful writing but remote from present day use.

Fig b here the pen is held with the thin stroke at 30 degrees giving good form, greater speed in writing and more legibility. It is nearer to the printed Roman that our eye is used to.

Fig c here the pen is held too steeply giving heavy shoulders & feet. This is to be avoided as ugly

Fig. 3 — pad / writing / paper / level / guard

Fig. 4 — writing board at angle of about 45°

Fig. 2 — oblique nib

Of wealth and fame and power
These masons did not know:
'Let's build,' they said, 'a tower,
Square to the winds that blow;
We are not men of culture,
Yet we are here to build
Room for a king's sepulture
And worthy of our guild!

So came each beam and rafter,
Each wingèd flight of stone.
Their deathless work lives after,
Their names were ne'er known:
For beauty did they plead not,
Yet beauty they did win,
And, like a child you heed not,
The grace of heaven crept in.

from 10th Cent. Card the Builders.

4.VIII.1945.

Footnote concerning the diagrams:—

Since the Foundational Hand is stated as being based on a circle, this form should be repeated in the arched letters as well as in the round ones. So the letter 'p' is similar to a reversed 'q' in form, or an inverted 'd': an 'n' is like an inverted 'u' in shape and the 'h' and 'm' have the same unity, and contain part of an 'o'; as does the top arch and bottom loop of an 'a'. The diagram does not strictly carry out this essential unity of form.   Irene Wellington 26 November 1947.

Borne out in;— benediction prebendary illuminate

116. *The completion of the Writing Sheet shown in the previous example* [263]

STENCIL

Stencil types are of this century. Despite the Industrial Revolution it does not appear to be a design with which Victorian founders experimented at all and though it is possible that such faces were cut—accidentally rather than as a result of conscious effort on the part of the punch-cutters—none have survived either for re-casting or for re-cutting. Most of the stencil types that contemporary typographers would recognize unhesitatingly as such date from the early 1930's—one of the earliest known to the writer is Schablone, Schmalfette. Otto Weisert, Stuttgart, 1931.

Luxemburg

In the stencil plates cut to produce stencilled letters used by manufacturers on cases of goods for export, for instance, a thin band of metal (or other material from which the stencil plate may be cut) supports the counter of the letter O, for example. In types designed to imitate stencilled lettering a representation of this device is used—and in some designs the thin band may *form* the whole of the counter of a particular letter.

Some contemporary stencil types

Braggadocio (Monotype), Futura Black (Bauer), Stencil (American Type Founders and Ludlow), Tea-chest (Stephenson Blake), Transito (Amsterdam).

Typewriter

Type forms based on the alphabets employed on standard typewriters would appear to date from sometime after 1878 when the first shift-key typewriter appeared on the American market. A very early italic Schreibmaschinenschrift is that of the Schriftgiess foundry: it appeared in 1897. Versions of the more normal roman have been cut in this country and in Germany, for example the Ribbon Face of Stevens Shanks the face of which is pitted with white to simulate the effect of actual typing on certain papers. Monotype Series 301 is an underlined face.

It is a well-known fact that all the characters on a given (normal) typewriter, i.e. both upper- and lower-case occupy the same space setwise. The types in this group are based on such characters, & besides having short descenders, a large x-height and open counters (if we except the m and w), have a further characteristic in common with contemporary Ionics: they are monoline faces.

Most typefounders have typewriter faces in their range, the normal sizes being 8, 10 and 12 point. The American Bulletin face is cut in sizes up to 36 point. The weights of typewriter faces vary from light, through normal weights, to darker versions.

Some contemporary typewriter faces

Bulletin (American Type Founders), Remington (Linotype), Ribbon Face (Stevens Shanks), Typewriter (Monotype) No 1, 2, 3 (each of these includes an underlined version), 4, 5, 6, 7, 8 and Monotype IBM 'Executive'.

ABCDEFG
HIJKLMNOPQRSTU
VWXYZÆŒƷ
1234567890ƷSCG

ABCDEFG
HIJKLMNOPQRSTUVWXYZ
1234567890 &£+✶

ABCDEFGHIJKLMNO
PQRSTUVWXYZ
1234567890
abcdefghijklmn
opqrstuvwxyz

117. *Bifur, Neuland and Koloss* [263]

MISCELLANEOUS
DISPLAY
TYPES

So far eight groups of book faces and sixteen groups of display faces have been described.These represent a very large proportion of the types extant today. If to these are added the bold or semi-bold versions of many of our book faces, for example Baskerville, Bembo, Ehrhardt, 'Garamond', Imprint, Perpetua and Romulus, and the bolds of jobbing faces like Plantin Series 110 and Times (which though born as jobbing faces are nevertheless used as book faces) &, further, if we remind readers of the enormous number of poorly designed faces mentioned in the introduction to this book it would seem that all type designs must surely have been accounted for. But that is far from being the case.

There are many interesting display types which cannot be placed simply in one or other of the groups described in this *Introduction*. Some are hybrids, a mixture say of a sans serif and a three dimensional face: others are types which have been modified in some way.

It will be agreed that Gill can be considered as a perfect example of a sans serif type. But what of Bifur and Neuland and Koloss? These can be called sans serifs only if we accept seriflessness as the sole criterion of sans serif types. But of course it is not. Bodoni divested of its serifs does not look like anything we have been taught to recognize as a sans serif type! Koloss is of course a hybrid. It has been described as an extra bold sans serif which suggests a fat face. Neuland has been described as a bold sans serif with modifications. Bifur is one of those types which

207

appears to have no recognizable group. It is a part-letter titling fount.

Students who read this *Introduction* will be wise if at first they learn to recognize the types in the groups we have described before attempting to place (let alone devise their own categories for) the many borderline types; and then, if after mastering some of the problems connected with type identification, they will face the fact that the nomenclature of type face design is unlikely ever to be settled satisfactorily, they will find themselves able to continue their studies of the subject with a measure of equanimity.

We list some examples of the kinds of types which we feel must be classed as miscellaneous display faces.

Some other contemporary miscellaneous display faces

Besides Bifur, Neuland and Koloss which we show by way of examples students may like to look at: Banco (Olive), Boul Mich (American Type Founders), Film (Deberny & Peignot), Grock and Kino (Monotype), Lilith (Bauer), Motor (Ludwig & Mayer), Robur Pale (Deberny & Peignot), Suggestion (Bauer), Wolfram (Ludwig & Mayer).

Notes on the Illustrations

Notes on the illustrations of gothic types

1. In the opening paragraph of the text a reference is made to block-books, the forerunners of books printed from movable type. The front endpapers of this book show a leaf from the first edition of the *Biblia Pauperum*, a block-book printed in the Netherlands, *c.*1460-1470 '. . . consisting of scenes illustrative of the New Testament, with Old Testament prefigurations and prophecies'. It was a popular work and was issued in many editions.

    An interesting description of this 'Bible of the Poor' appears in the catalogue of *Books printed in the Fifteenth Century now in the British Museum*: '40 leaves arranged in single sheets of two leaves each, printed with very thin ink, usually brown, on one side only, each sheet containing two woodcuts printed from a double wood block. The space between the two woodcuts is sometimes no more than one fifth of an inch, making it impossible to fold and bind them without concealing part of the text. The cuts may thus have originally been intended to be pasted on walls, rather than made up into books'. The narrowness of this division between the blocks may be seen in our example which is printed same size. [SEE FRONT END PAPERS]

2. From a manuscript containing the letters of the Apostles written on parchment at Mainz *circa* 1440 in the Textura script. The name of the scribe is not known. [4]

3. From the Gutenberg, Mazarin, or 42-line Bible printed at Mainz *circa* 1455 (not after 1456) in one of the texturas, or earliest versions of the formal gothic or black-letter types. The text pages of this magnificent folio bible are double-columned and the example on page 4 shows part of the first page of the Book of Matthew.

    Some of the characteristics of the texturas are noted on page 7. Types of this kind were used throughout the fifteenth century in Germany as the standard letter for Bibles and church service books, but with the appearance of the Italian Rotunda the texturas waned in popularity. See note 5 below. In France this style of letter is called 'lettre de forme'. [6]

4. A page from the Gospel of Nicodemus printed by Günther Zainer at Augsburg, 1460?. Mr Johnson writes 'For the printers of Latin texts, scholastic, theological or classical, the early printers cut a less formal letter (than the texturas), following, of course, the manuscripts . . . . the first of these

less formal designs is the Durandus type of Peter Schöffer of 1459. This is a rounder & more open letter with decenders like roman, but with neither the serifs of roman nor the feet of Textura; the descenders and the strokes which end on the line, including the long s, end bluntly; the a is open as in roman; the g has sometimes an open tail, but more often is shaped like the figure 8; the d is found in two varieties, one like roman & the other like the rounded gothic; ligatures of the round forms such as b & d with e and o are a characteristic. The effect of the increased height of the ascenders and length of the decenders is to add to the amount of white on the page & to impart a lighter appearance in comparison with Textura. There is a greater differentiation of letters and therefore increased legibility. On the other hand it still has not the full roundness of roman. Its upper case varies considerably, and in some cases is almost purely roman. The letter shares some characteristics of the Renaissance and others of the Middle Ages (hence the names) . . . The hand is gothic but with considerable roman tendencies. It was the formal book-hand of the earlier Italian humanists of the fourteenth century, and in particular of Petrarch . . . . . The history of the group is a short one, for after one generation it was superseded by the Rotundas. But between 1459 and 1485 some of the finest incunables were printed in types of this class'. The French name for this group is 'lettre de somme'. [9]

5. Page from a splendid missale speciale printed by Georg Reyser at Wurzburg in 1495. Text set in Rotunda (the Italian form of Textura) & printed in black and orange. In the page we show, the following words and initials are in colour—Quando cor/pus christi accipit in manus di/cat P—Et dicat ter D—Qn̄/sumit dicat C. 'In contrast with Textura', Mr Johnson writes, 'Rotunda is full of curves, e.g. the b, c, d, e, h, o, p, etc. The feet of Textura have in part disappeared . . . In contrast with Fere-humanistica it is without the tendency to roman, the a is closed, and the ascenders and descenders are shorter . . . Towards the end of the fifteenth century its larger sizes vied with Textura for use as heading types and in liturgical works, while the smaller sizes took the place of the Fere-humanisticas, and finally became the stock type in Europe for theological, legal and scholastic texts. Though round, Rotunda was not so broad as Fere-humanistica & was thus more economical. There are many fine books printed in Rotunda, but it suffered degradation by the end of the (fifteenth) century . . .' [10]

GENERAL NOTE ON THE VERNACULAR TYPES OR BASTARDAS

Unlike the three groups of gothic types described above the four which come under the heading of the Bastardas are based on bastard scripts. Mr Johnson describes a bastard script as 'current or cursive, written quickly and without the deliberation of the texturas, Fere-humanisticas or Rotundas. It is further characterized by its descenders running down to points ... while the ascenders are frequently looped. A typical letter is the a, which like our italic *a* is one-storeyed ... the g has the tail open. The earliest founts of this group are the small types of the Mainz Indulgences of 1454 and 1455'.

'...the gothic Bastardas, were confined to the countries north of the Alps, and the chief variety outside Germany was the national French hand, the 'lettre bâtarde which ... passed out of use about the middle of the sixteenth century; but in Germany the Bastarda has remained the national type, at first in the variety known as Schwabacher, and afterwards in the more familiar Fraktur'. Mr Morison has described the Bastardas as 'scripts answering to the need for a speedy letter appropriate for the copying of books or documents of minor value or importance'.

6. From a slim volume by Conradus Celtes, printed by Friedrich Kreusner at Nuremberg, *circa* 1487 in a type (first used 2 years earlier) which became 'the most popular German type for books in the vernacular & received the name of Schwabacher . . . . .' Mr Johnson continues 'Schwabacher has the usual Bastarda characteristics, the closed, one-storeyed a, the pointed descenders to (long) s and f; the tail of the g is open; the b, d and h are sometimes looped and sometimes not. The design of the upper-case as well as that of the lower-case is fixed, with few variations. In all the earlier gothic founts the variations among majuscules are so numerous as to defy classification. The upper-case was a separate fount, often revealing little attempt at harmony with the lower-case. But with these later Bastardas we can take account of the capitals also in defining groups ... (note in Schwabacher the M, A and S) ... Finally in colour, throughout its history, the letter was essentially black ... There were roughly only three sizes of Schwabacher'.

'Of the three German Bastardas which preceded Fraktur, Schwabacher was easily the most widespread. In Nuremberg, where it originated, it is all but universal. Schwabacher, together with its variant the Upper-Rhine type, remained the standard German text type down to about 1550 ... In the second half of the century it declined into its ultimate position as a secondary type, used in much the same way as italic was used with roman'. Mr Johnson writing in 1959 said 'German printers of today have revived Schwabacher, & it is now being used to a greater extent than at any time since the sixteenth century'. [11]

7. From a German passional by Jacobus de Voragine, Archbishop of Genoa, printed by Ludwig Renchen at Cologne, 1485. This is set in a type of the second definite group of Bastardas which has, says Mr Johnson 'in modern days been given the name of the Upper-Rhine type from the district in which it originated, and was principally used (in the Rhineland towns from Mainz southwards with a few examples at Cologne. It was common at Basle . . .). The earliest founts . . . are found with Ludwig Renchen at Cologne (1484) . . . In the lower-case the design differs from that of Schwabacher by the presence of more looped ascenders; in the upper-case the chief distinguishing letter is the M . . . In fact the M is the test letter, by the presence of which a type is included in the group . . . This grouping is not altogether satisfactory because . . . the Upper-Rhine type is not essentially different in design from Schwabacher . . . (it) is a convenient sub-group within the larger Schwabacher group'. [13]

8. Writing of the third group of Bastardas Mr Johnson observes that it 'is a genuine classification with some marked differences in design. It was of much more local use than the others, and mainly confined to Wittenberg and the neighbourhood, whence the name. The design appears first at Leipzig at the press of Melchior Lotter . . . in 1508. In the lower-case the distinguishing characteristic is the shortness of the ascenders, resulting in a comparatively large-faced type . . . Wittenberg letters vary little in size, they measure round about 95mm. to 20 lines, that is to say, they are much the same size as the medium sizes of Schwabacher & Upper-Rhine type. The fact that the Wittenberg letter looks bigger is a matter of height of ascenders. For the same reason a page in this letter has an unusually close-set appearance'. Of the capitals the M should be noted. Printers at Magdeburg, Erfurt, Dresden, Berlin, Breslau, & in Copenhagen (from 1559) had the type of which there were two copies. Our example is part of a letter, dated 1510, from the press of Melchior Lotter at Leipzig. [15]

9. From a work by Albrecht Duerer on the proportions of the human figure. Printed at Nuremberg in 1528. This 'fourth Bastarda group is the last to appear in type', writes Mr Johnson 'but historically the most important . . . a hand called Fraktur, meaning broken, was in use before 1450, and (there are)

214

instances of earlier uses .. In modern days it has been called "Deutsch". Certainly no type has a better claim to be called "The German Letter". Duerer was certainly closely connected with the originators . . . . . but there is no evidence that any of the designs are due to him. In design Fraktur is a narrow and pointed letter . . . There is a marked difference from Schwabacher in the width of the letters & also in the serif formation of the ascenders. In Schwabacher the b, for example, if not looped, ends bluntly, but in Fraktur the ascender runs up to a point. The upper-case is essentially a calligraphic letter, further removed from early gothic than is Schwabacher. The loose ends of the capitals have been aptly called by the Germans "Schnörkel", elephants' trunks . . . . these and . . . the pointed ascenders in the lower-case (make for) a spiky and restless design . . . decidedly inferior to Schwabacher. Two reasons may be given for the ultimate defeat of the better design by Fraktur. Just as the Rotundas had driven Fere-humanisticas out of the printing offices, because they were more economical of space, so again the narrower Fraktur appealed to the printer's pocket . . . (and) the printers after 1550 actually seemed to have preferred the fussiness of the new letter'.

'Between 1513 and 1524 eight varieties . . . were cut . . . In 1522 appeared the first Fraktur in the design which became traditional, that of Hieronymus Andreae of Nuremberg, designed by Neudörffer (the writing master: the text in our example is in this type). In spite of these eight designs it was quite a generation before Fraktur became a serious rival to Schwabacher as a text type (but) when Sigismund Feyerabend at Frankfurt in 1560 printed the German Bible in Fraktur, Schwabacher was doomed. By that date Frankfurt had become the centre of the German book trade . . . & Fraktur had become the fashionable type for books in the German language.

'Even before it became the normal text type, Fraktur had won popularity as a heading type. The type-designers (and woodcutters) exaggerated the Schnörkel of the upper-case for the purpose of decorating title pages . . . . . (allowing German 17th century printers to produce the very worst title-pages in the history of the book). The lower-case was subjected to various experiments in condensation and in enlarging . . . However, the design in general was not radically altered, and the best founders of the 18th century . . . . observed the original tradition . . . (and) it was not until we reach Unger that any serious attack was made on the letter'.

Johann Friedrich Unger (1753-1804) who began as a woodcutter, later becoming a printer and typefounder in Berlin, was a friend of Firmin Didot. He decided to reform Fraktur. He did, says Mr Johnson 'make a Fraktur as legible as any hitherto cut; in fact, by smoothing out the angles of the lower-case he approached more nearly to the despised design, Schwabacher. But in colour he went to the other extreme and by copying the lightness of roman produced the pallidness which is the chief ground of complaint against him'.

[16]

Notes on the illustrations of Venetian romans

10. From a manuscript, once at Quedlinburg, written in the Abbey of St Martin of Tours in the early part of the 9th century. Sir Edward MaundeThompson wrote of this MS that it 'shows the Carolingian reformed hand brought to perfection'. The script of our example is the 'consummate result' of Charlemagne's reform. When transcribing the works in which this hand had been used the humanists of the Italian Renaissance, whose perseverance 'had resulted in the re-discovery of numerous forgotten classical texts', modified it, and the beautiful humanistic or neo-caroline hands thus developed from it served the printers of fifteenth century Italy as splendid models for their types. On page 20 we show an example of a humanistic hand. [18]

11. Part of a page of Cicero: *Orationes in Verrem* written on vellum by the scribe Ioni. Venice, *circa* 1476. From the library of Sir Sydney Carlyle Cockerell.

   The following note on Francesco Petrarca, by an anonymous hand, is apposite here. 'Petrarch, who was born at Arezzo in 1304, was one of the first of the Renaissance scholars. By his studies of the classical authors he contributed much to the revival of interest in the Greek and Roman world. He himself wrote much in Latin & we owe to him the re-discovery of Cicero's Letters and other classical texts.

   'He was not only the first of the humanists but also one of the greatest poets Italy has produced. It has been said of him that he has often been imitated but never equalled. Petrarch . . . . lived at Avignon from 1313, where his father was exiled from Florence for political reasons. The second half of his life was spent in travel, study and political activity. He died at Arquà, near Padua in 1374'.

   Over two hundred editions of the various works of Cicero alone were produced in Italy before 1500 many of them by the printers of Venice who surpassed the total output of all the other (Italian) cities combined. [20]

12. Lactantius' *Opera* printed by Conrad Sweynheym and Arnold Pannartz at Subiaco, 1465, one of the first Latin books to be printed in Italy, and the first book printed in that country to bear a date. It is in the type used by the same printers for their edition of Cicero's *De Oratore* which came off the press earlier in the same year. In an article in *The Library* June/September 1943, EARLY HUMANISTIC SCRIPT AND THE FIRST ROMAN TYPE, Mr Morison writes: The Subiaco type presents the appearance of a truly handsome piece

of calligraphy. The design of the letters and the competence of the engraving and casting enable a composed page to reproduce a manuscript written in 'lettera anticha formata' (the most formal and handsome of the humanistic book hands of the early period). This was clearly the intention, and it must be allowed the intention was, for novices in the new art, brilliantly realized. That it was chosen for re-cutting by St John Hornby, Robert Proctor, and Sydney Cockerell, at the Ashendene Press, is proof enough of its outstanding aesthetic value. It can, indeed, hardly be questioned that the Subiaco fount is authentically humanistic'. Mr Morison concludes his article by saying that 'the Subiaco fount . . . is entitled to rank as the first humanistic or roman type'.

This book was also the first in which 'a real Greek type was used'. For many years after this printers left blank spaces where Greek quotations appeared in Latin books. The Greek characters were filled in by hand.   [23]

13. Part of a page from a handsome folio—Saint Augustine's *De Civitate Dei*—printed by Johannes and Vindelinus de Spira at Venice in 1470. 'Many roman types of varying degrees of purity and attractiveness were used by Italian printers of this period' wrote D.B. Updike, and, 'It was reserved for John and Wendelin de Spire to show a roman type which to-day appears roman to us. In the fount used in the Venice editions of Cicero's *Epistulæ ad Familiares* and Pliny's *Historia Naturalis* of John de Spire, printed in 1469, & the *De Civitate Dei* printed in the next year by John and Wendelin de Spire, this very modern quality can be clearly recognized'. The two lines immediately above the initial have been written in in a contemporary hand—that is, a humanistic or neo-caroline hand.   .   [25]

14. From the *De Præparatione Evangelica* of Eusebius printed by Nicolas Jenson at Venice in 1470. This fine, much-praised roman has been used as a model by many printers and type designers including the Doves Press, and the late Mr Bruce Rogers, who used it as a basis for his Montaigne & Centaur types. Jenson's roman is marred by its over-large capitals which make for spotty composition and some of his lower-case characters have been criticized also but there is no doubt that they compose exceedingly well.   [27]

15. From Appian's Roman History printed by Erhard Ratdolt at Venice in 1477 whence he had come from Augsburg. This printer's books are famous for their fine borders and initial letters and are said to be the first with decorative title-pages. For an example of a part title-page printed by Ratdolt see illustration, No 62, page 108. What is presumed to be the only known example

from the fifteenth century of printing in gold ink (powdered gold being substituted for the lamp black) appears in the dedication to the Doge in a volume of Euclid's works printed by Ratdolt, Venice 1482.   [28]

Notes on the illustrations of old-face romans

16. Page from the tract *De Ætna* written by Pietro Bembo and printed by Aldus Manutius at Venice, 1495. This example is referred to on page 31. It represents the Aldine roman in its 'first-state'. Mr Morison has said that in this type we have 'the origin of all old-faces'. In a comparatively short time it superseded Jenson's letter.   [30]

17. From the *Hypnerotomachia Poliphili* by Francesco Colonna printed by Aldus at Venice in 1499 and set in his roman in its final and perfected form. We refer to this illustration on page 31. Mr Johnson does not think that Aldus was especially interested in the design of roman letters—'his interest was in Greek literature & in the publication of the classics—& that the chief credit (as designer) should be given to his type-cutter, Francesco Griffo'. It may be noted here that Aldus had no gothic types.   [33]

18. From another beautiful Aldine volume, Saint Catharine de Siena's *Epistole* printed at Venice in 1500. The earliest Italian literature has come down to us from the thirteenth century. It was not until the time of Dante—who was born in 1265, two hundred years before the first book was printed in Italy, that Italian effectively began to compete with Latin as a literary language.
                                                                           [34]

19. From a philological work by Jacques Du Bois *In Linguam Gallicam Isagoge* published by Robert Estienne, Paris, January 1531 in his roman—in three sizes. '. . . *the* lower-case', wrote Paul Beaujon 'of French book printers for two centuries to come, as far as general design goes, though modified in the course of time by imitation'. Derived from the Aldine type of the *De Ætna*. Cutting attributed to Garamond in the Egenolff-Berner sheet of 1592. [35]

20. From *L'Histoire de la terre neuve de Péru* by Gonzalo Fernandez published in Paris in 1545. Paul Beaujon refers to the types in which this volume is set as 'possibly an earlier impression of the types' used in Dominique Jacquinot's *L'usaige de l'astrolabe*. See descriptive note for illustration 21, below. [36]

21. From *L'usaige de l'astrolabe* by Dominique Jacquinot printed by Jean Barbé, Paris 1545. Set in roman (2 sizes) and italic which are believed to have been cut by Claude Garamond. 'As there is only one other roman of normal book

size that we can definitely attribute to him, and no other italic' wrote Paul Beaujon in THE 'GARAMOND' TYPES, *The Fleuron* No 5, 'the founts deserve careful study'.   [37]

22. From Christopher Plantin's famous Polyglot Bible printed at Antwerp 1569–1573 (actual width of type matter 181 millimetres). The rather heavy lower-case is Plantin's Canon Romain & that below it is his Moyen Canon Romain, which Mr Harry Carter has said is Garamond's Gros Canon with capitals and shortened letters by Henri du Tour. Plantin bought material of Garamond's after the latter's death in 1561 and employed a number of punch-cutters, including Granjon and Le Bé to furnish his printing house with a wide range of types—gothics, romans, italics, scripts, exotics (including Greek, Hebrew and Syriaque) music types, etc.

   During recent years much about Plantin's life has been brought to light through the researches of Mr Harry Carter, Mr Colin Clair & others. Ample material therefore exists for those readers who would like to know more about this great French printer and his work.   [38, 39]

23. Part of the splendid broadside specimen issued by William Caslon (the first) in 1734. Mr Johnson writes 'The last of the distinguished type designers who were, consciously or unconsciously, pupils of Garamond was William Caslon ... He stopped the importation of Dutch types ... (and) took as his model the best Dutch types of the seventeenth century ... However (he) was not better than the designers he took as models. He owes his success in England, not to any originality, but to the fact that he was the first really competent engraver and caster of types in this country ... It was William Caslon who first began the practice of setting the text of his specimens in that notorious passage from Cicero's Catiline Orations which begins: *Quousque tandem* ...'
                                                                          [40]

Notes on the illustrations of italic types

24. From the Poems of Cardinal Bembo. A beautiful example of the cursive writing perfected in Italy during the first half of the 16th century. Possibly written after 1534. Formerly in the library of Sir Sydney Carlyle Cockerell and now in the Victoria and Albert Museum. [42]

25. From the Virgil printed on vellum by Aldus at Venice in 1501, the first book in which the new italic type was used for the purpose for which it had been designed, i.e. as a conserver of space—to make it possible to compress volumes of the classics into small compass. The type was cut by Francesco Griffo of Bologna, the engraver Aldus employed for cutting all his types. The wide distribution of this new type which the Aldine volumes secured for it was further promoted by the plagiarists: the design was widely copied throughout Europe. Despite its initial popularity it did not live because of the serious faults in its design—it is not to be compared with the beautiful italics of the Vincentino group. [44]

26. From the second part of Arrighi's beautiful writing manual *Il modo de temperare le Penne Con le varie Sorti de littere ordinato* per Ludovico Vicentino, printed at Venice in 1523. This continuation of his writing manual issued in the previous year (*La Operina*), is printed from wood blocks but also contains several pages printed from italic type, the earliest showing of this italic. [46]

27. From a book of poems, *Coryciana* by B. Palladius printed at Rome in 1524. Arrighi was one of the printers and the book is set in the first italic designed by him. Nineteen small books printed in this cursive in 1524 and 1525 are listed by Mr Johnson in his *Type Designs*. [48]

28. From H. Vida *De Arte Poetica* printed by Vicentino at Rome in May 1527 in a new formal chancery cursive. Only six books printed in this type by Arrighi have been recorded, writes Mr Johnson, the last being that from which our example is taken. It is thought that Arrighi may have perished in the disaster which overtook Rome in that year. Note the serifs which have taken the place of the rounded terminals of Arrighi's first type and the absence of swash letters. In body size it approximates the earlier type but it is of larger face. [49]

29. Camillo Agrippa. *Trattato de scientia d'arme* printed by Antonio Blado, Rome 1553 (Blado was a connection of Aldus). Arrighi's second type came into this printer's hands and his first use of it dates from about 1530. It 'proved to be' writes Mr Johnson, 'the forerunner of an even larger group of formal cursives' and was widely copied throughout Europe, 'the best example of the school (Vincentino) outside Italy and France turns up in an English law book printed in London in 1531'. [50]

30. *Epigrammata* of Claudius Rosselettus printed by Sebastien Gryphius at Lyons, 1537. A pleasant book, set, as were so many sixteenth century books, in italic throughout, except for the crossheads—the earliest recorded work set in this italic. Note the considerable slope of the lower-case and the greatly differing degrees of slope of the capitals (the O for instance is upright or may even be said to lean very slightly backwards!)—designed during the period when printers were experimenting and apparently finding great difficulty in producing a satisfactory upper-case—one which would accord with the slope of the lower-case. A further note on this italic will be found on page 53. [52]

31. From the *Emblemata* of Joannes Sambucus printed by Christopher Plantin at Antwerp, 1566 in an italic (Littera Currens Ciceroniana) by Robert Granjon, the famous French typecutter and designer of many old-face italics. Granjon appears to have supplied this printer, who had a very large and interesting range of italic types, with at least half-a-dozen italics in addition to romans, exotics and scripts. Plantin appears to have enjoyed producing illustrated works. Such was the demand for these Emblem books that he printed many editions in various languages. [54]

32. 'One of the few surviving types of the distinguished designer of the seventeenth century, Christoffel van Dijck, is an italic of this (old-face) school, a vigorous design cut without any idea of accompanying a roman, however it might be used'. In this note Mr Johnson refers to the type used in the prefatory matter to *Plinianæ Exercitationes*. C. Salmasius. Utrecht 1689, & shown in our example. [56, 57]

Notes on the illustrations
of intermediate or transitional romans

33. From the facsimile of the *Espreuve de Caractères* of Jean Jannon, originally issued at Sedan in 1621 (The facsimile is edited & has an introduction by Paul Beaujon, Paris 1927). Jannon's roman was based on Garamond, and his types, acquired by the Imprimerie Royale in 1642 who called them their 'caractères de l'université' were, after a period of use, left lying unused for more than 200 years and then in 1845 labelled by their owners as 'Garamond 1540'. These Jannon types have been widely copied in our own time & the resulting designs sold under the name of 'Garamond'. Paul Beaujon's brilliant, painstaking enquiries cleared up the muddle which for so long enwrapped the names and works of Claude Garamond and Jean Jannon.   [58]

34. *Médailles sur les principaux événements du règne de Louis le Grand.* A Paris de l'Imprimerie Royale 1702. The new type cut for Louis XIV by Philippe Grandjean for the exclusive use of the Royal Printing House foreshadows the style which we know as modern. Mr Johnson has listed the distinctive features of this face (cut finally in 21 sizes of roman and italic—the best of which were employed in the *Médailles*) as: Flat, unbracketed serifs. On ascenders of lower-case the serifs run across to the right as well as the left. Shading more vertical and modelling rather more than in old face. On left of l there is a small flick, at one time usual in gothic faces. He thinks that this and the cross-serifs may have been distinguishing marks. There are no hairlines. The modernness of the design is more evident when used with modern methods of printing—early eighteenth century methods almost make it appear an old face. The 'romains du roi' were widely copied despite the fact that type-founders were forbidden to do so. Grandjean died in 1714 and work on his types was continued by his friend and pupil, Alexandre.   [60]

35. Two of the types cut by Johann Michel Fleischman from the specimen issued by Joh. Enschedé et Fils, Haarlem 1870. Both 'Louis Luce & Fournier derived their taste for condensed romans from Fleischman', a German who worked in Holland. He was with the Enschedé foundry for eighteen years. Johan Enschedé praises Fleischman considerably in the preface to his specimen of 1768 and says that 'Seventy different founts engraved by Fleischman enrich this foundry, including Greeks, Latins, Arabian, Malay, Black-letter and Scripts'.

But D. B. Updike wrote 'His (Fleischman's) types are singularly devoid of style, & usually show a drift toward the thinner, weaker typography which was coming in Holland as everywhere else. But Fleischman's work was much the fashion in the eighteenth century . . .'

Of this founder's work Mr Johnson writes that 'he has been accused of taking all the life out of his types, an accusation which is certainly well founded in the case of his italics'. The handwritten notes on our example are by William Blades. [62]

36. *Essai d'une Nouvelle Typographie* . . . . . Louis Luce, Paris 1771. Luce, Jean Alexandre's son-in-law, worked at the Imprimerie Royale and completed the range of the 'romains du roi' by cutting the smallest size, perle. But he also worked on his own account. In his specimen of 1771 he shows a number of romans remarkable for their condensation & explains in what particulars (serif treatment & condensation) they differ from the 'romains du roi'. Luce complained that his ideas (he had, he said, published proofs of his types in 1732) had been stolen—Fournier (a better designer) not only copied his ornaments but his roman and italic also. [66]

37. So that the reader may be better able to judge the qualities of the roman designed by Luce this example is set in his Corps 20 and printed by modern methods. It is reproduced by courtesy of M. Arnoult of the Imprimerie Nationale. [67]

38. From Fournier's splendid volume *Modèles des Caractères*, Paris 1742. Paul Beaujon refers to this type as the first of the transitional faces. Fournier explains in his *Modèles* why he has modified certain features in designing his types (lining capitals with tops of lower-case ascenders, squaring the angles of capitals and of some lower-case letters). Fournier is to be regarded as a brilliant adapter (and sensitive improver) of the designs of others rather than as an innovator. Tremendously industrious, in a little over a generation, he not only published his observations regarding a point system of measuring type bodies, cut over eighty types, including music types, besides a wealth of flowers & ornaments, developed what we now refer to as the type family (he offered printers six variations of the normal roman—light, bold, condensed, etc all on the same body) and though not allowed to print his books, with the exception of his *Manuel*—set up the formes for some of his specimens with what exciting effects in regard to the arrangement of his ornaments and flowers students of his work will have observed, but, wrote Paul

225

R

Beaujon, 'He lived long enough to see his establishment the foremost and the richest of privately-owned foundries in Europe, & when he died, at fifty-six, he had made more changes in typography & set a more distinctive personal mark on the printed book than anyone else of his day'. [68]

39. From Fournier le jeune's *Manuel Typographique*, Vol 2. Paris 1766. This 12pt ordinary roman of Fournier's is a somewhat condensed letter. It has flat bottom serifs to the b, d, u (after Grandjean), but the top serifs are not flat and the shading is not vertical (see c, e). Despite the condensation & other changes and the fact that there is more 'modernity' about the upper-case Mr Johnson feels that 'on the whole the type impresses one rather as an old face. Both Fournier and Luce were more 'modern' in their treatment of italic.... (this type) may be looked at as an example of a transitional roman of the eighteenth century'. [69]

40. Fournier's *Manuel Typographique*, Paris 1764/1766, was published in two volumes—it was to have been a work of four volumes but 'the author did not live to finish it'. The first, which appeared in 1764, is a text book, devoted to instruction in the whole art of type-founding: to complete it Fournier inserted at the end of the book sixteen beautifully engraved plates showing the instruments used by the type-founder. The second volume published two years later, is filled with an extraordinary range of type specimens, each page enclosed within a border. Our example is from the first volume, the body of which is set in Fournier's very condensed Cicero (12 pt) Poétique. Mr Johnson writes that '.... the idea of his "poétique", a condensed letter intended for the printing of the long verses of the French Alexandrine without breaking into a second line, was derived (both in style and name) from Luce'. Fournier also cut a type which he called 'œil serré', a less condensed face with shorter descenders than the poétique type. [70]

41. From *Alphabets in All the Hands* by George Shelley, London ?1710. (Engraved by George Bickham) one of several writing books published in London early in the eighteenth century. Mrs Warde, in an article on the Baskerville types, wrote in 1927: 'Shelley of London had published a writing book ... in which the thickness of stroke in the roman alphabet came almost directly up-and-down. The serifs, too, were at a sharper angle than any printer could afford to press upon his soft paper, and the whole lower-case exhibited a magnificent breadth of proportion only made possible by this increased sharpness of outline'. [71]

42. From the Virgil, the first book printed by John Baskerville, Birmingham
1757. Baskerville, a former writing master became a type-founder (he started
work on his types in 1750) and printer. He was an admirer of the work of
his contemporary, William Caslon, but in designing his types followed the
style of calligraphy fashionable in his day & produced letters which diverged
from the old-face design in several particulars. Mr Johnson has summarized
them thus: His types are rather more modelled & their shading rather more
vertical than that of the Caslon letters, (see the e). As a result of the greater
modelling the counters of the round letters are larger & the type as a whole
is lighter. But the serifs are still inclined & bracketed, nor are the thin lines
excessively thin; therefore the roman has in general much more the appearance of old face than of modern face. He notes the Q with its new tail, the
curly-tailed (in some sizes) R, the lower-case g in which the tail is not quite
closed, and the w (capital and lower-case) without a central serif.

Despite the fact that no English founder offered to buy the contents of
Baskerville's foundry on his death in 1775 (it was sold practically in its en-
tirety to Beaumarchais at Paris in 1790: the original punches and matrices
were returned to this country in 1953, a gift from Charles Peignot to Cambridge University Press where Baskerville was for a time appointed Printer)
the leading type-founders in this country (the Fry foundry, Alexander
Wilson, William Martin, Vincent Figgins and William Caslon III copied his
types. Mr Johnson says that 'The last quarter of the eighteenth century might
well be described as the Baskerville period in English printing, both on account of the number of Baskerville designs which had been put on the market and because his formula for book-production (his spaced capitals, leaded
pages and almost complete absence of ornament—traits which appeared
later in the books of the so-called classical printers) had been widely adopt-
ed. Some of Baskerville's volumes are magnificent examples of printing and
arrangement—it was as a printer rather than as a designer of types that his
influence is said to have made itself felt on the Continent particularly on
Didot and Bodoni—but others are marred by his extraordinary spacing of
capitals, examples of which may be found in his folio Bible of 1763 particularly in the openings to the Books of Ruth and of Job.

For an excellent account of John Baskerville students should refer to the
new, revised and enlarged edition of Talbot Baines Reed's *A History of the
Old English Letter Foundries* by A. F. Johnson.   [72]

Notes on the illustrations of modern-face romans

43. From the *Haerlemse Courant*, 1st March 1746. Unfortunately only part of this very handsome page can be shown. It is reproduced from Charles Enschedé's *Fonderies de Caractères et leur matériel dans les Pays-Bas du XVe au XIXe siècle*, Haarlem 1908 & shows the first number of the journal to be printed in Fleischman's gaillarde roman engraved by him in 1745. The capitals are examples of the kind often found in the first half of the eighteenth century with thin, un-bracketed or only slightly bracketed, serifs and vertical shading 'when the lower case was still in the state of transition'. Mr Johnson mentions specimens of J. F. Rosart's capitals, and those issued by the Luther firm at Frankfurt in the years 1716 and 1718 as examples.   [74]

44. From a page of A. Christian's *Débuts de l'Imprimerie en France*, L'Imprimerie Nationale, Paris 1905, a quarto, each chapter of which is set in a different type, thus making it a specimen book of the Imprimerie Nationale. Many interesting types are shown including Jannon's Caractères de l'Université. One chapter is devoted to Jaugeon and the 'romain du roi': modern cuttings based on Jaugeon's report (Caractères Jaugeon, cut in 1904); and this chapter includes one of Jaugeon's squares divided into 2,304 small squares. There are also, among others, the *types poétiques* engraved in 1740 by Louis Luce and the caractères millimétriques engraved by Firmin Didot, 1812. A preliminary note to the chapter from which our specimen was taken reads 'Le présent chapitre a été composé avec les caractères . . . désignés sous le nom de *types de Louis XIV* gravés en 1693 par Phillipe Grandjean and Jean Alexandre'. A comparison of Grandjean's type as printed in 1702 (see illustration No 34, page 60) with the same type printed by twentieth-century methods shows clearly how much was lost by earlier methods of presswork (in which, of course are inextricably bound up not only the physical attributes of the press itself but the quality of ink, the method of inking, and the paper surfaces also). This illustration shows clearly that 'the modern face was implicit in (Grandjean's) design'.

    Grandjean's type was also used in an article on Arthur Christian, Director of the Imprimerie Nationale, which appeared in *Signature*, No 9, 1949.   [77]

45. This further example of Grandjean's romain du roi Corps 20, printed at the Imprimerie Nationale in 1955 on a smooth-surfaced paper shows even more clearly than illustration 44 how early eighteenth century methods of print-

ing to a large extent obscured the changes he had made in transforming the
old-face design.   [78]

46. Prospectus for Torquato Tasso's romantic epic on the Crusades, *La Gerusalemme Liberata* printed by F. A. Didot (l'aîné), 1784. 'The house of Didot',
says Mr Johnson,'is one of the illustrious families in the annals of typography.
About the year 1789 there were no less than seven members of the family
engaged in the various branches of the book trade at Paris', F. A. Didot,
l'aîné,was both printer and type-founder. He and his brother P. F. Didot,
were appointed printers respectively to the Comte d'Artois, & to the King's
eldest brother and it is thought that those appointments played a part in the
Didot's experiments in cutting new types.There is uncertainty as to the engraver of the early Didot types and to the dates of their appearance. In 1783
F. A. Didot printed three French classics in an excellent but very light transitional roman. Other light types followed—D. B. Updike speaks of one of
them as 'so thin and fragile . . . .This results in faded-looking pages that are
perfectly legible, but give an insecure feeling to the eye'. But while these
'maigre' romans were being used the type shown in our example appeared.
It had been cut in the foundry of F. A. Didot and Mr Johnson says of it that
'Following the definition of modern face—as a roman embodying the three
following characteristics (1) Flat & unbracketed serifs, (2) abrupt & exaggerated modelling, (3) vertical shading—we must accept this type as a modern
face and the first of its class.The thin, flat serifs, the verticality and abruptness
of the shading (contrast the e of this type with that of any earlier roman)
make this roman different only in degree of shading from the founts which
Firmin Didot (F. A. Didot's younger son, 1764-1836) was later to cut'. But
he remarks that this roman is, because the shading is not too exaggerated and
because of the great skill of the engraver, a far better type than the later cuttings which the Didots themselves came to prefer.
    All the types (even the approximately 10 point) in this prospectus print
beautifully.They are sharp and clear—a tribute not only to the types but to
the improved presses (with larger platens) which the Didots were using by
1784, and also to the *papier-vélin* (a highly finished wove paper modelled on
that used by Baskerville) which showed their precisely engraved types to ad-
vantage.The idea of using wove paper was probably taken from Baskerville.
                                                                    [79]

47. The type of the splendidly printed Virgil, edited and printed by P. Didot,
Paris 1798. From the time of the appearance of the first modern face used in

the prospectus issued in 1784 (see illustration No 46), Firmin Didot proceeded to cut types with ever greater degrees of modelling. He had cut types from the age of nineteen & Mr Johnson remarks that 'His delight at his own skill in cutting fine hair-lines led him on to an over-modelling of his types, which became a European fashion and the hall-mark of what are called classical types . . . The full flower of the Didot modern face can be seen in the Virgil of 1798 & the famous Louvre editions. These books won universal, or almost universal, praise, (& despite sharp criticism by some of his countrymen) . . . The Didot modern face remained the standard letter in France, and for the mass of books is still the normal design in use today . . . . . and most of the European typographers (of his day) were seduced by Didot'. Of these Bodoni was the most famous. [80, 81]

48. Page from the first of the two volumes of the *Manuale Tipografico*. Giovanni Battista Bodoni, Parma 1818, completed (with the help of his foreman) and published, after his death in 1813, by his widow. Bodoni was born at Saluzzo in 1740, and was the son of a printer. For a time he worked in his father's press and then struck out on his own. His work has been divided into two periods by D. B. Updike: (1) when he employed old face or transitional types and used decorations somewhat profusely, and (2) when he depended on his own type-designs & unadorned typography for his effects. During the first period, that is up to about 1780 he was greatly influenced by French printing and especially by the work of Fournier le jeune and some of his early books are 'so far from his later style' says Mr Updike 'that it is at first sight difficult to believe that he printed them'. But, writes Mr Johnson 'By 1787 he had cut types like the early Didot modern faces . . . & his name is especially associated with the fully developed modern face (students will note the *bracketed* serifs of some of his larger sizes of capitals). This was because he was the most famous printer in Europe in his day, although as a designer of roman types he was never anything but an imitator of the French. His *Manuale Tipografico* . . . . is the most sumptuous display of modern-face types in existence'. The two quarto volumes, printed on a very beautiful smooth wove paper run to over 500 pages & contain an enormous range of types, including exotics, and over a thousand decorative border units, besides rules, typographic signs, etc. [82]

49. From Robert Thorne's *Specimen of Printing Types*, London 1803 (the last this founder issued). Thorne took over the foundry of Thomas Cottrell, to whom he had been apprenticed, nine years after the latter's death in 1785. His speci-

men book of 1794 shows 'elegantly shaped large letters' (from five- to nine-teen-line) much of which material was, it has been surmised, based on Cottrell models; and ordinary sized types for which Thorne probably made use at first of Cottrell's specimen book as the latter had left it. 'It appears to have been no uncommon practice in the trade', says Mr Johnson 'to make use of a predecessor's book, corrected on the title-page in pen and ink. The St. Bride (Library) copy of Cottrell's specimen is thus altered to the name of a broker; and the specimens of the Type Street Foundry (Edmund Fry) are many of them similarly corrected to adapt them for the frequently changing style of that firm'.

But in Thorne's specimen of 1798 none of these types (except for the large letters) remain. His new types according to Reed 'more closely resembling the beautiful faces of Jackson and Figgins. His specimen of 1798—the year in which the full flower of the Didot modern face appeared—is indeed one of the most elegant of which that famous decade can boast. For lightness, grace, and uniformity, the series of romans & italics...excels that of almost all his competitors'.

But soon all these were to be swept away, for Thorne, together with other English founders, was very soon compelled to abandon the production of types of that kind because of the sudden public demand for types in the 'modern' style. Thorne, in his specimen of 1803, in which he showed the new letter, referred to them as Improved Printing Types and did not share the re-gret of his fellow founders at being forced to abandon what they regarded as better founts ('the ... entire abandonment of the time-honoured & grace-ful characters of the first Caslon'—among others) and indeed appears to have enjoyed his success with the new face. In Thorne's letter of 1800 (the date of its cutting) writes Mr Johnson 'we have an undoubted modern face—which ... appears to be the first to answer (in England) the definition of modern face which we have given (see descriptive note, illustration No 46, page 229). So far as the evidence of the type specimen books goes, Thorne appears to be the founder who was responsible for sponsoring the full modern face in England'. [83]

50. An example of a title-page in the so-called classical style from J.V. Millengen's *Peintures Antiques et Inedités de Vases Grecs* . . . . . Rome 1813—the year of G. B. Bodoni's death. It is one of the very few illustrations in this book which is not in facsimile as regards size. The page size of this large folio volume measures 21 inches deep by 14⅝ inches wide. The actual width of the second line of the setting is 260 millimetres.

Mr Updike has an interesting chapter on the origin of pseudo–classical types which he traces back, typographically, to beginning with the *romain du roi*, and, among other things to the growing taste throughout Europe 'for a lighter and more delicate style of typography; sometimes arrived at by actually cutting a lighter letter, sometimes by greater leading of the type'. Another influence on the development of these types and of the way in which they were arranged, was the worship during the early nineteenth century of the antique 'to the men of those days (something which was) brilliantly and thrillingly new'.

The printers who used these modern–face types set their title–pages wholly or almost wholly in different sizes of letter–spaced, widely leaded lines of roman capitals, with no roman or italic lower–case, and often without ornament. It is in the later work of the Didots that we reach the quintessence of the so–called classical in type face design. [84, 85]

Notes on the illustrations of the modernized italics

51. During the course of the eighteenth century the design of italic types was radically changed. The beginning of these changes dates from towards the end of the sixteenth century when italic types were being cast on the same body as the romans: of course, attempts had been made since before the middle of that century to regularize the slope of both the upper- and the lower-case.

'The reform' (of italic), writes Mr Johnson, 'if it may be so called, begins with Philippe Grandjean's "romain du roi", with the first step in the evolution of the modern-face roman. But already in the first half of the seventeenth century there is one peculiar italic which may be recorded, as being in some ways a forerunner of later developments . . . The most striking peculiarity of the type is its condensation, and in order to achieve the condensation the designer has romanised some of his letters; notably the m and n, in which the shoulders are squared up. The a also is a rounder letter, though condensed, than the typical old-face a.' The founder of this unusual italic is unknown. When the importation of Dutch types into this country was in full swing, that is, roughly in the seventy years (1650-1720) preceding William Caslon I, this italic was freely used in England. Our fine example of it is from the introduction to the second edition of Philip Cluverius's *Germania Antiqua*, printed by the Elzeviers at Leyden in 1631. [86]

52. While the romanizing of the unusually condensed italic described under (51) above may simply have happened as part of the process of condensation, with Grandjean's italic for his 'romain du roi' we find, writes Mr Johnson, 'a deliberate attempt to make the secondary type conform to the roman. He designed his a, m and n like those letters in the Elzevier fount; one effect of these forms was to remove some of the irregularity of slope from the lower case. In the upper-case he also gave a more consistent slope to his letters . . . That Grandjean, when designing his cursive, had in mind the roman, is shown by the fact that he introduced the straight shanked *h*, a form new in italic. His v too was new, at least in typography, and remained a form peculiar to the eighteenth century'. Our example of Grandjean's italic, the Corps 20 size, is from *Les Caractères de l'Imprimerie Nationale* by Florian le Roy. The volume was printed in 1955. [88]

53. This example shows the italic of Louis Luce, Corps 20 size, printed by modern methods on a smooth-surfaced paper. The Petit Parangon size of his italic

S

from his *Essai d'une Nouvelle Typographie* . . . . . Paris 1771, is shown in our illustration, No 36 on page 66. Luce said of his italic that he had purposely simplified its shape; reduced the number of angles; made it narrower; made the connecting lines lighter & reduced the number of letters with tails (kerns).

[90]

54. From Fournier's *Modèles des Caractères*, Paris 1742, the introduction to which is set almost completely (ten and a half pages of his twelve page *Avis*) in the Gros Romain or 18 point size of his italic, within, for this book, very simply bordered pages. Notes on Fournier's italic will be found on page 89 and some of his own interesting ideas on the design of italic type are to be read in the page from his *Avis* which we show as an illustration. Basing his italic on the formal hands of the engravers he took into account all the changes in the secondary type introduced by Grandjean, Alexandre & Luce (the latter complained that Fournier had copied his types, proofs of which had been published in 1732) and 'carried the idea of conformity with roman further than any earlier designer'. Though his italic was popular with European printers during the middle of the eighteenth century it was soon superseded by the italics of the Didots, cut to mate with their fully developed modern-face romans. [92]

55. Paragraphs from the preface to W. Hunter's *Anatomia Uteri Humani Gravidi*, a magnificent folio (paper size 25½ x 18⅜ inches) printed by John Baskerville, Birmingham 1774. It is in Latin and English and is illustrated with over thirty large, superbly printed plates by various engravers—both text and plates are on a very heavy laid paper (Baskerville appears to have printed few of his books on wove paper). The italic is Baskerville's Great Primer size.

The design of italic types in England during the eighteenth century followed a course, says Mr Johnson, which was similar to that of their development in France and they 'met the same end'. But, he continues 'There is one exception to be noted: roman serifs never appeared on an English italic . . . . . . As in the case of the modern-face roman, the beginning of the revolution (in the design of italic type faces) is to be traced to John Baskerville. His italic has received much less praise than his roman; it has been described as pinched and wiry'. He summarizes the changes Baskerville made in designing his italic as: It is more evenly sloped than the old face; it has the rounded a, the m and the n shaped as in Grandjean's type—and the straight shanked h—copied from the same source—but not Grandjean's v—a letter absent from English cursives; the g and s are other letters, he says, which bring the Baskerville lowercase into close harmony with the roman; & he notes the inconsistently retain-

234

ed calligraphic capitals K and N, and adds 'Baskerville's italic influenced the design of cursives in England for the next half-century, until the introduction of the modern face'.

How far Baskerville's influence extended as a designer of roman and italic types may be seen by reference to the descriptive note for illustration, No 42 on page 227. [93]

56. From his *Specimen of Printing Types*, London 1803. Thorne's activities and his gradual development as the founder responsible for sponsoring the full modern face in England are briefly described in the note to illustration 49, page 230. His specimens of the new modern-face romans introduced about the year 1800 were, writes Mr Johnson, 'accompanied by italics which are in several ways parallel to the later work of the Didots in France. The serifs of the upper-case and of the ascenders of the lower-case are flat and unbracketed; cursive beginning strokes are still retained, as in all English italics, but have quite lost the quality of flowing pen-strokes. The mechanical regularity of the slope adds to the lifelessness of Thorne's design . . . the tendency to over-modelling, characteristic of nineteenth-century types, is already in evidence. The other London founders rapidly followed Thorne's example. As the English founders missed the stage of cursives with roman serifs, they arrived at the modern italic even before their French colleagues'. [94]

57. Born in 1764, Firmin, the youngest son of François Ambroise Didot (1730-1804) designed a modern-face italic at the age of nineteen which his brother Pierre Didot l'ainé used to print his *Epître sur les progrès de l'imprimerie* issued in 1784. From the time of the appearance of the Didot's modern face in that year, Firmin Didot continued to cut types with ever greater degrees of modelling. Besides this increasing contrast between the thick strokes and the thin strokes, in the Didot italics the foot serifs of the p and q have disappeared; the serifs at the tops of the lower-case letters are roman serifs &, unlike Fournier's, are not bracketed, but flat both above and below and thus made to harmonize with those of the Didot modern-face romans. Further, the slope of Firmin Didot's italics was mechanically regular and in colour they were lighter than Fournier's letter. Bodoni, and the German founder Erich Walbaum, followed the Didots in designing their italics. By 1825 the modern style had become popular in Germany.

Then the Didots changed the design of their italic. They dispensed with the roman serifs and, says Mr Johnson 'designed the lifeless italics which were ultimately to prevail in the nineteenth century . . . . cursives of mechanical rigidity, with no life of their own, and not intended to be used on their own. The 'Avis' to Pierre Didot's specimen is set in one of these spineless letters, and the reader is immediately conscious that this is only an introduction and that he will not be expected to read a book in such a type. However, the Didots, if their intention was to kill italic as an independent letter, had attained that end. Although italics with flat roman serifs continued to be used for some years . . . . it was the latest of the Didot designs that was destined to survive'.

The example we show is the page headed *Avis* on which Mr Johnson comments above. It is from Pierre Didot's *Specimen des Nouveaux Caractères*, Paris 1819. [95]

Note on the illustration
of Miller and Richard's Old Style

58. From *Specimens of Old Style Types*. Miller & Richard, Edinburgh & London, 1860. These original Old Style types of Miller and Richard were based on old-face designs but with what the founders considered were the objectionable peculiarities of such faces removed—in effect they set out to produce a modernized version of a typical old-face design. In their revision they kept the bracketed and inclined serifs and the gradual stress of old face but made the latter vertical. The cutting of the letters is sharper and Miller and Richard borrowed another feature of modern face—they made the capitals of a more uniform width, narrowing the H, M and W and widening the P and R. The C appears without a lower serif. The bowl of the a and the eye of the e were made more open, and the lower-case t is taller than in Caslon.

The italic is quite steeply inclined but more regular in its inclination than Caslon. In the h, m, n and r the thin up-strokes commence from the *feet* of the thick down strokes.

Unfortunately the name OLD STYLE is not confined to Miller & Richard's designs and the adaptations of them (by other founders), but is used in a promiscuous and utterly confusing way as a designation for Venetian, old face and transitional types. [96]

59. Designed by Jan van Krimpen for Messrs Joh. Enschedé en Zonen in 1923–1924: the italic was designed in 1924–1925. Interesting notes on both will be found in Van Krimpen's *On Designing and Devising Type*, 1957, including the versions he was persuaded to produce for use by the Monotype Corporation on their machines, and of the alternative sorts he was persuaded to cut for the roman (a greatly improved E, F, L and e, besides others, which cannot be considered in the same light). Lutetia italic he based on his own reformed handwriting, which in turn had been based on 'certain Italian chancery hands'.

Writing of Lutetia in the December 1932 issue of *Paper & Print* Mr Johnson listed the distinctive features of the roman as: serifs bracketed but small; on the lower-case they are inclined, but only slightly. The incidence of colour is like old face, and the gradation from thick to thin is slight. E is a wide (and unfortunate) letter with the middle arm above the centre. G has a tall, vertical stroke below the final serif. H has the bar a little above the centre. M is square. Q has a long tail. T has parallel serifs, extending just above the top. U has the lower-case design. In W the middle strokes meet a little below the top. In the lower-case, a is a narrow letter with a tapering top arc; e has an oblique stroke to the eye (a feature Van Krimpen later regretted—he designed an alternative with horizontal bar); g has a moderately large bowl; the t is very short above the bracketed cross-stroke. The figures are old face.

Of the italic he wrote: The capitals resemble the roman, except W, in which the middle strokes cross. There is a swash series, with very prolonged strokes in A, K, M, N and R. The lower-case, very slightly inclined, has a considerable resemblance to the Blado italic, except for the y, the greater width of some letters, and the g, which has the tail drawn from right to left (a calligraphic form). The slight inclination and the angular beginning strokes are as in Blado; but the serifs at the top of ascenders are flat.   [100]

60. Eric Gill was commissioned to design this type by the (then) Lanston Monotype Corporation. Experimental founts (12 and 14 point—starting with the larger size) were cut by hand in Paris in 1926, the punches being engraved by the late Charles Malin. Malin's work together with Gill's drawings provided, wrote Mrs Warde, 'the starting-point from which Monotype Perpetua gradually emerged through successive trial cuttings and discussions at the Type Drawing Office in Salfords'. Gill acknowledged his debt to Monotype when Perpetua made its first appearance—in an inset to *The Fleuron* No 7.

He said: 'The Perpetua type . . . was cut (in a 13 point size) by The Lanston Monotype Corporation from drawings of alphabets made by me. These drawings were not made with special reference to typography—they were simply letters, drawn with brush and ink. For the typographical quality of the fount, as also for the remarkably fine and precise cutting of the punches, The Monotype Corporation is to be praised. In my opinion Perpetua is commendable in that, in spite of many distinctive characters, it retains that commonplaceness & normality which is essential to a good book-type'. By that time (1929) the italic, originally called Felicity had also 'undergone considerable modification from its first version'.

In the *Encyclopædia of Type Faces* by Berry, Johnson and Jaspert, 1958, the outstanding characteristics of Perpetua are named as: Serifs, small, sharply cut and horizontal. The stress and gradation of colour are akin to old face though the stress of O o appears vertical. A has a flat top; M is slightly splayed; there are two R's, one with a more extended tail, both ending in a serif on the line. There are two U's, one with the lower-case design. In the lower-case the only slightly abnormal letters are the a with the top arc tapering and the g with a long link. The figures are old face. Stephenson Blake have cut their version of the design.

The italic is slightly inclined and is much as the roman. The a is one-storeyed but has a roman foot serif; g has a calligraphic tail.

The quotation in this example is from Eric Gill's *An Essay on Typography* J. M. Dent & Sons Ltd. 1954. [102]

61. A design 'created by and for THE TIMES' newspaper under the supervision of Stanley Morison, and called the first 'twentieth century' newspaper type. Based initially on experiments with a specially cut 9 point size of Monotype Perpetua (at the time designated, No 3) 'it was only after exhaustive trials and comparisons that it was resolved to design a new face'. The new face was first used to print the issue of THE TIMES dated October 3, 1932. The paper reserved for itself the use of the new face for a period of one year & then released it for general use. Since October 1933 it has been used widely, for an ever increasing variety of book and ephemeral printing. The design had, of course, to be adapted for the Linotype machine before the first issue of THE TIMES could be printed in its new dress. In 1954 it was also made available by Intertype and a year later by Stephenson Blake.

Times New Roman has short ascenders and descenders. The serifs are small and sharply cut (to counteract the effect of stereotyping). The type is rather strong in colour. Capitals same height as short ascenders—stress appears ver-

238

tical. Stress or shading of lower-case is biased. Head serifs on b, d, h, i, j, k, l, m, n, p, r, are oblique and fine bracketed. The g has a wide tail. The g, j, p, q, y have been cut as long-descendered sorts also. Figures are ranging. The italic is 'regular, of a moderate inclination'. It has oblique and fine bracketed head serifs.

The quotation is from *A Journal of the Plague Year* by Daniel Defoe. [104]

*　　　*　　　*

2. *Calendarium.* Johann Regiomontanus. Printed by Pictor, Loslein and Ratdolt, Venice, 1476. We show the nearly complete title-page of this interesting book: printed in black & red it bears 'a verse panegyric on the book instead of a title'. The type used for the verse is used for the text also. There are some beautiful open floriated initials in this book. [108]

Notes on the illustrations of gothic scripts

63. Among examples of various hands in the second part of Arrighi's beautiful writing manual, *Il modo de temperare le Penne* (Venice 1523) is one entitled 'Lettera da Bolle'. This form of gothic script was used for the writing of papal Bulls (edicts or mandates) in the sixteenth century. Mr Johnson describes it 'as an upright, round, gothic hand, which in the lower-case has some resemblance to Schwabacher (see page 11), or to the later French hand called Ronde (see page 130). The form was established by tradition and most of the Italian calligraphers, who published their work, display a specimen.   [112]

64. Italian calligraphers of the first part of the sixteenth century showed a variety of gothic scripts in their writing manuals, for despite the efforts of the humanists (who were responsible for the Renaissance hands), conservative businessmen of the time preferred such scripts to the more legible humanistic hands displayed in the same writing books. Our example is one of a number of gothic scripts used by businessmen shown in the writing manual *Libro nuovo d'imparare a scrivere tutte sorti lettere . . . .* published by the celebrated writing master G. B. Palatino at Rome in 1540. In Italy one such variety of gothic script was translated into type but was not much used, and from the 1560's up to the time of Bodoni the Italians appear to have ceased experimenting with either gothic or Latin scripts.   [114]

65. In our example the text is a form, printed on a single sheet of vellum, granting a licence to marriage. Mr Johnson, who was the first to record the cutting of the hand as a type says of this form that it is set in a type which is 'a faithful transcript of the "lettera da bolle". . . The word Collegium at the head is set in a line of curious, rather ugly, initials, which again can be paralleled in contemporary writing books. The initial C (mutilated unfortunately) includes a woodcut of St. Peter, which certainly looks like work of the sixteenth century. The sheet . . . . was probably printed about 1550, and the printer would no doubt be the official church typographer, Antonio Blado. It seems likely that a search in Roman archives would bring to light other specimens of the use of this remarkable type'.

Readers will find three-quarters of the text of this form among the examples of gothic script types: that is all our page would accommodate. But by turning to the back of the book the whole form may be seen (*very* slightly reduced in size) reproduced as an endpaper.   [116]

6. Though the Italians appear to have ceased experimenting with script types from about the 1560's up to the time of Giovanni Battista Bodoni, interesting experiments were made in Germany, in France, in the Netherlands and in England, script types of both varieties being cut. In Germany during the sixteenth century the specimen books of the writing masters not only offered an ordinary gothic script (currentschrift) but showed specimens of a more formal hand used in the German Chanceries (Kanzleischriften). Some of the latter remarks Mr Johnson 'are very like Fraktur, while others are even more fanciful.. Two of these varieties (of Kanzleischriften—some Kanzleischriften sloped to the left, some to the right, & some have been described as tortured) were cut as types, the two earliest gothic scripts in Germany'.

Our example is from the German version of Donato Gianotti's history of Venice printed by Hans Kilian at Neuberg (on the Danube) in 1557. The whole text is set in the earlier of the two scripts. Notice that some of the down strokes in this type, which Mr Johnson has described as one of the best scripts ever designed, are bent backwards, though it may be described as an upright letter with capitals which are Fraktur. [118]

7. In sixteenth century Germany not only were the varieties of Kanzleischriften (the formal hands used in the German Chanceries) employed as types but a more usual form of script type (Schreibschrift) was used for book (with Schwabacher, which it was dark enough to accompany), & newspaper (Berlin, 1626) printing. After about 1567 no further examples of these Schreibschrifts have been found by Mr Johnson until about a hundred years later when they begin to appear in the specimen sheets of German typefounders. 'Perhaps', he writes 'the German printers used their scripts more in the modern fashion for ephemeral publications, since remarkably few books have been recorded set in script types'.

Of our three examples of Schreibschriften, reproduced by kind permission of Dr Frans Enschedé, the first is that shown by the Jean Henry Stubenvoll foundry, Frankfurt, in 1713, which however appeared originally on the specimen of Reinhard Voskens of about 1660. The second is an Enschedé letter dated 1772 and the third was shown by John Frederic Unger, Berlin, in 1793. The latter, though lighter and simpler than some Schreibschrifts of the mid-sixteenth century has not changed much in design. Examples 67b and c illustrate the development of German cursive handwriting during the eighteenth century. [119]

68. The latest script shown by the Enschedés, writes Mr Johnson, 'the "Klein Kanon", of unknown origin, has lost all colour; it corresponds among gothic scripts to Didot's "Anglaise" among the Latin. It is like the Anglaise not only in colour, but also in the attempt to conceal the fact that it is type by the close fitting of the connecting strokes. Again, like Anglaise among the Latin scripts, it remained the standard script throughout the nineteenth century'. Our specimen is reproduced by permission of Dr Frans Enschedé.   [120]

69. From *P. Galtheri Alexandreidos libri decem* printed by Robert Granjon at Lyons in 1558, in a gothic script he had designed which was popularly called civilité, a name derived from the titles of two books on good manners printed in the new type in the years 1559 and 1560 respectively. Granjon called his new type 'lettres françaises' and based it on the contemporary current script. He printed about twenty books in it between the years 1557 & 1562. Not greatly popular in France the type was nevertheless used in that country occasionally at all periods: examples are shown in specimen books of the eighteenth century & a book was printed in the middle of the nineteenth century in civilité. Besides books treating of manners the script was used for books on the art of writing. It was thought, remarks Mr Johnson 'to be an advantage that children should learn to read from a book printed in a type resembling the ordinary current script'.

   Granjon's type was copied despite the fact that he had been granted a monopoly for ten years in 1557 by Henri II. Granjon himself supplied other printers—notably Christopher Plantin at Antwerp, who had three civilité's cut by Granjon as well as others by Flemish typefounders (the French design is better than the rather restless Flemish). There are longish passages set in civilité in the preface to Plantin's famous Polyglot Bible (1569-1573). And there are instances on record of one of Granjon's civilité's actually being used in this country in the 1570's.   [121]

70. The earliest English writing book, that of John Baildon, published in 1571, shows a script based on the Elizabethan current hand which he calls the secretary hand (a gothic script employed as the normal handwriting of commercial circles of the time). 'It was', says Mr Johnson, 'a hand used throughout Europe, with national peculiarities, in Italy as well as in the countries north of the Alps. In Italy it was called "lettera francese" or "lettera mercantesca"... In France and the Netherlands it was known as civilité... A genuine English script was apparently not cut until towards the end of the century'.

This type (one of at least three) was first used in the colophon of a book printed in 1576 (but it was not used for the text of books as were the civilité types
on the Continent). After that it appears in various forms of ephemera: official
& semi-official notices, circulars, marriage & wine licences, the recognizances
entered into by victuallers, and on circular letters demanding loans—as in the
second year of the reign of James I (1604).

Our example shows part of an interesting proclamation of the thirty-fifth
year of Elizabeth's reign (1593) printed in Secretary No 1.   [122]

*   *   *

Secretary No 2, larger in face and more upright is 'not known from any type
specimen, either English or foreign' writes Mr Johnson. It is found on circular
letters issued in the third year of the reign of James I (1605) and was used on
other ephemera (licences and notices). Some school books of the day show a
specimen of the hand, e.g. Edmund Coote's *The English Schoolmaster*—in the
later editions of 1636, 1662 and 1673.

1. Script types have often been used with music. Our example is from John
   Barnard's *The First Book of Selected Church Musick* (Collected out of divers
   approved authors) printed by Edward Griffin in 1641. Barnard was a canon
   of St. Paul's Cathedral. Mr Johnson, writing of this work said 'There is still a
   third fount of secretary, of a still larger size and of more handsome design.
   This was used for the words in a music book of 1641 . . . The type appears in
   no other book from the same press of those preserved in the British Museum,
   nor have I found it anywhere else. Barnard's book is a handsome (folio) production decorated with some fine calligraphic initials and tailpieces'. Very few,
   if any, complete sets (six parts) of Barnard's work are extant because of de-
   struction or mutilation by Cromwell's men.   [123]

2. In England, in addition to the secretary hands there was another gothic script
   of considerable antiquity, a legal, upright script called court hand, the design
   of which says Mr Johnson 'remained uniform for several centuries, and in the
   writing books of the calligraphers of the seventeenth century there are a number of fine specimens of the script. . which appears to be confined to England'.
   Though it was used in legal documents as a written hand or printed from engraved plates it does not appear to have been often used in type form. When
   the use of the court hand for legal documents was abolished in 1733 its place
   was taken by a script known as engrossing. Our specimen shows two sizes of
   court hand in type form from the Sale Catalogue of the James Foundry, June

1782, whence they had come from the Grover Foundry (established about 1674 by James and Thomas Grover). [124]

73. From *A Specimen of Printing Types* by Tho. Cottrell, Letter Founder, London, undated. This fine specimen of engrossing, which Mr Johnson has called our last English gothic script was cut *circa* 1765 for William Richardson, a law printer who issued a specimen of the 'New Printing Type in Imitation of the Law Hand'. Like the German Kanzleischrift (see illustration 66 page 118) and the contemporary French ronde, Cottrell's legal script is partially romanized, many of the capitals, and the lower-case h and r having the roman forms.

Students will note the extraordinary examples of word division in this Cottrell page. [125]

Notes on the illustrations
of Latin or Renaissance scripts

74 Our examples are facing pages (printed from wood blocks) from the beautiful
& writing manual of the Venetian master, Vespasiano Amphiareo (born at
75. Ferrara in 1501), a teacher of calligraphy for thirty years. Printed by Gabriel
Giolito & published in Venice in the year 1554, this work, the only one which
Amphiareo appears to have completed, went into many editions. He claimed
the invention of the Cancelleresca bastarda hand: from it the second group
of scripts—the latin or renaissance—are derived. A comparison with illustrations 26, 27 and 28 show that the hand is a less formal and rounder style of
writing than that of Arrighi. [126,128]

76. Lines from a four page specimen *Caractères d'écriture Gravés Imprimés* par
Firmin Didot, Paris 1809. This script is 'a descendant of civilité which is largely
gothic . . . (and) is frequently found as a decorative type in French books of
the first half of the nineteenth century'. [130]

77. From Fournier le jeune's *Modèles des Caractères*, Paris 1742. This script was
also called financière because it was employed in the (French) Ministry of
Finance. See text, page 127. We show the *Lettres Ornées* specimen because it is
not included in all copies of the *Modèles*. It is in the form of a slip measuring
3⅛″ × 4¾″ pasted to the edge of the *Caractere de Finance* specimen, which is itself
printed on a short page, i.e. a page measuring only 7½″ in width. [132,133]

78 From *La Belle Esclave* by Claude de l'Estoille printed by Pierre Moreau, Paris
& 1643. Moreau, a Parisian writing-master, began printing books from engrav-
79. ed plates but later turned his attention to typefounding. He cut the bâtarde
ordinaire or italienne scripts shown in our examples (based on the style of
contemporary handwriting) designing them for use in bookwork. Fournier
says that Moreau dedicated the first proofs of his new types to Louis XIII in
1642, who gave him the post of Printer in Ordinary to the King by way of
encouragement. In the six years from 1643 Moreau printed about a dozen
books set in three sizes of his bâtarde italienne. On page 101 of *La Belle Esclave*
appears another script used as a heading to an extract from the Royal Privilege
which Mr Johnson describes as 'an upright script descended from civilité,
based on the hand known as Ronde'. Besides designing script types Mr D. B.
Updike records that Moreau 'has the distinction of having designed raised

245

letters for the use of the blind, but his plans are said to have failed through lack of money to develop them'.

After passing through several hands Moreau's types were sold in 1787 to the Imprimerie Royale and made their last appearance, apart from specimen books, on paper money in 1792.

In order to give Moreau's title-page the space it needs it is shown out of order, i.e. following, instead of preceding, the page headed *Epistre*.

[135,136,137]

80. Though some of Pierre Moreau's books are fairly well known, seventeenth century Latin scripts in England are a rarity. 'It must be admitted', writes Mr Morison in his article on script types in *The Fleuron* 'that though English script types were decidedly inferior in design to those made abroad, they were nevertheless early in use. Here I may not delay to discuss the use of English secretary hands which are to be found very early in type. The first script other than these that I have been able to discover in use in England . . . is . . . of the same general character as Moreau's, & there can scarcely have been in England at that time a craftsman capable of cutting so fine a character. As far as my information goes it was first used in the certificates granted to Nonconformist preachers under the First Declaration of Indulgence by Charles II in 1672'. Mr Morison says that he does not know the name of the printer of these licences but thinks that they may have been handled by Moses Pitt, a notable London bookseller of the day. [138]

81. Part of a page of an Ichabod Dawks's News-Letter, January 3, 1698, printed in the English No 2 size of the Grover cursorials. This type was not changed throughout the life of the newsletter (which was published every other day, Sunday excepted), the first issue appearing about June 1696. None are known after December 1716. Rowe Mores described these cursorials as flimsy types imitating a pseudo Italian handwriting. They are in fact says Mr Johnson, based on an inferior Italian hand, showing some gothic survivals. He thinks it probable that 'these first cursorials were cut at the instigation of Dawks and for the purpose of reproducing more or less in facsimile the manuscript newsletter which was handed about in the coffee-houses'—and records the use of these cursorials by other printers. See illustration 85, page 146.

The Grover foundry possessed six sizes of these cursorials. In that confusing compilation, the sale catalogue of the (John) James foundry of June 1782 five of them are shown: Double Pica, English, English No 2, Pica, and Small Pica under the heading SCRIPTORIAL. The design varies, often considerably, with the changes in body size. [139]

32.'When we reach the generation of Fournier and Luce, Fleischman and Rosart, the Latin scripts of the continental countries appear in great numbers' writes Mr Johnson.'Even German type-cutters were influenced by this flood of scripts and Latin scripts began to appear in Teutonic specimens . . . . and (in Italy) . . . that prolific type designer G. B. Bodoni . . . naturally copied the French & produced a score of scripts, of no great merit and with bewildering titles'.

But in England no Latin scripts were designed for over seventy years after the cutting of the Grover cursorials (neither William Caslon I, his son, nor John Baskerville produced a Latin script). It was not until about 1774 that Thomas Cottrell, a pupil of William Caslon I, who had started his own foundry in 1757 introduced a new fashion in script types. Mr Johnson says that Cottrell 'was influenced partly by the French, but introduced an innovation which was in turn copied by the continental founders. He attempted to produce the illusion of actual script by fitting his letters with exactness (our example is of his Double Pica Script). This excess of ingenuity was particularly associated with the English founders, and the type was called Anglaise by its imitators in France, the Didots and others'.   [141]

33. English founders followed Cottrell and designed close fitting scripts in his style. These were still in part based on the true Italian hand, but eventually scripts of this kind were influenced by the 'modern' cult in type design. They began to show greater differentiations in modelling, or in the gradation from thick to thin, and, Mr Johnson observes, 'increased ingenuity in imitating a current round hand. Then we get the typical Anglaise, admired and copied by the Didots, the script of the nineteenth century'. Our example of Firmin Didot's Anglaise is from *Caractères d'écriture, Gravés, Imprimés* par Firmin Didot, Paris 1809.   [142]

84. The custom of starting a new chapter or section of a book with a decorated letter in one or more colours and often with the addition of gold was begun by the scribes. In the early period some of these often beautiful, often extremely elaborate initial letters were made to occupy the whole of a page. But by the fourteenth & fifteenth centuries they had become simpler. It was for this kind of initial letter that the early printers left blank spaces in their books for the rubricator to fill in, later marking such spaces with small printed letters (directors) to indicate which letters had to be drawn in in colour & so avoid mistakes on the part of a too hasty scribe.

Initial letters *printed* with the text were first used in the 1450's 'The Psalters of Fust and Schöffer of the years 1457 and 1459' wrote Dr Konrad Haebler in *The Story of Incunabula* 'show extraordinarily artistic ornamental letters in many colours and in three different sizes . . They belong to the most beautiful and best achievements which the early decoration of books accomplished . .'

The art of drawing these initial letters & then of cutting them on wood or engraving them on metal has been called an anonymous one. Which of the two methods was used for producing particular initials is a subject on which the authorities are chary of making pronouncements. It is thought that initials with a very great amount of fine detail and those with outline borders, the borders of which have been bent are likely to have been engraved on metal rather than cut on wood. Dr Haebler says that the initials on a dotted ground (fond criblé) which originated with Parisian printers 'were probably executed on metal rather than on wood, and attempts to imitate the dotted ground on the wood-block met with less happy results.'

The superb example of a decorated initial letter shown on page 144 is one of the very few reproductions in this book not in facsimile: in the original the body of the initial measures 240 millimetres deep. It is used most effectively as an opening in both folio volumes of *La mer des hystoires*. Pierre Le Rouge, Paris 1488. Paris and Lyons were two of the centres where the art of the initial flourished.

Other examples of decorated initial letters will be found on pages 11, 13, 16, 25, 33, 34, 37, 46, 56, 122 and 123 of this book.   [144]

85. One of the earliest of all decorated types, the Union Pearl of the Grover foundry, may be regarded as the first English decorated letter. Edward Rowe Mores in his *A Dissertation upon English Typographical Founders and Founderies*,

1778, describes the type as 'a letter of fancy... it receives the name from the pearls which grow in couples, to which the nodules in the letter were conceived to bear some resemblance... though it has been said that the name of this letter is *Union* only, and that it was so named because it was cut for a poem to be inscribed to Queen Anne at the time of the union of England and Scotland'. Mores dismisses the latter idea for the poem never appeared.

Mr Johnson has found no example of its contemporary use except for the one word setting in the notice from a London news sheet, THE OBSERVATOR dated February 7, 1708. This notice, inserted by the printer, H. Meere, is set in the pica size of the Grover cursorials. We show this notice and the specimen of the type as it appeared in the James Sale Catalogue of 1782.   [146]

86. Three pages from the second volume of Fournier's *Manuel Typographique* published in Paris in 1766, showing some of his lovely decorated and shaded types and some of his decorated initial letters. In the notes to illustration 38 on page 225 there is a reference to some of the many activities which Fournier crowded into a comparatively short life—and by which he immensely enriched the art of typography. Of the more than eighty types he cut nine were decorated or shaded letters (the first by about 1749 and the rest before 1766) ranging in body size from nonpareille upwards. His largest shaded letters are of approximately 84 point and 108 point body size and were intended for use on posters and bills.

If we accept the definition of outline or open letters given on page 191, then Fournier does not appear to have cut any types of that kind. His decorated & shaded letters were copied by other French founders & in the Netherlands by J. F. Rosart for the Enschedé foundry. Bodoni's ornamented types and ornaments were also modelled on those of Fournier, as were the decorated capitals of Joaquin Ibarra of Madrid. Mr Morison has written that 'soon all Europe was using one kind or another of such decorated capitals or "titlings" as they were known to English printers... But there can be no doubt that it was in France that they were used to greatest extent and greatest advantage'

Of Fournier le jeune's work Mr Updike wrote 'The emblems, ornamental letters, and be-garlanded borders which Fournier made popular in printing were inspired chiefly by the work of men like Cochin, Eisen, St. Aubin, and other French vignettists of the eighteenth century. Seeing what had been done for the book by the engraver and etcher, he attempted to transmute their designs into material for printers. Such typographic ornaments were not new—an immense repertoire of them already existed. Fournier merely adapted them to the fashion of his day, but he did so with great taste and unity of

T

effect...Of his ornaments and ornamented initials one may say that he touched nothing that he did not adorn'. [149]

87. Our examples are from the *Specimen de Caractères Typographiques Anciens* issued by Joh. Enschedé et Fils, Haarlem 1870. We have already noted that J. F. Rosart (born at Namur in 1714) modelled his decorated letters on those of Fournier. In the preface to the Enschedé specimen issued in 1768, Johannes Enschedé wrote 'Mr Rosart cut nearly all the large Roman, Italic and Shaded Capitals; the great and small Canons; the Paragon; and most of the Flowers and Borders'.

For the following facts about the two decorated letters we show the writer is greatly indebted to Dr B. Frans Enschedé: 'The Deux Points de Cicero Romain Orné, No 1 was cut by Matthais Rosart (the son of Jacques François Rosart) and bought from him by Johannes Enschedé on the 28th September 1768. He paid for the 39 strikes 58½ guilders....The Deux Points de Cicero Romain Orné, No 2 is to be found in the specimen of the Widow Decellier at Brussels, issued after 1779. In this year she bought the foundry of J. F. Rosart who died in 1777. Though this type does not appear in any of the Rosart specimens which are referred to at page xxv of Dr Enschedé's book (Fonderies de caractères et leur matériel dans les Pays Bas du XVe au XIXe siècle), it can be safely derived from its appearance in the Decellier specimen that it was cut by Jacques François Rosart. The Enschedé typefoundry acquired matrices of these capitals in 1799, when the typefoundry of Ploos van Amstel was bought'. [150]

88. From the 1780's the first shaded and decorated letters were cut, or procured for use, in England. Sir Francis Stephenson thinks that some of the early examples of decorated types in this country were cast from matrices bought by our founders from Holland.

In the book issued by William Caslon III (born 1754—died 1833) in 1786 he shows specimens of Cast Ornaments which include (white) transitional-style roman capitals on shaded backgrounds & what might be called shaded roman capitals drawn with a double outline. The interiors of these double outline letters are shaded with lines running diagonally.

The Eight lines Pica Ornamented letters are from the specimen of S. and C. Stephenson, London, 1796. The beautiful Fry Ornamented letters are presumed to have been cut by Richard Austin (who started business as a punchcutter about 1786) in 1796 & the line of Canon Ornamented capitals is from the William Caslon III specimen of 1816. Another example of ornamented

Decorated

capitals is shown on page 176 of this book. It is from the 1833 specimen book of Vincent Figgins where it appears at the foot of a page of Two-line Letters in Shade. [151]

89. The illustrious family of the Didots has been mentioned in the notes to illustration 46, page 229. In our example we show two early nineteenth century alphabets of decorated modern capitals by P. Didot l'ainé (1761-1853) reproduced by permission of Dr Frans Enschedé. [152,153]

Notes on the illustrations of shaded types

90. Another page from the second volume of Fournier's *Manuel Typographique*, 1766, showing two sizes of roman and two sizes of italic shaded capitals. Fournier, in the first volume of the *Manuel* (1764) refers on pages 170, 171 to shaded letters. He wrote 'shaded letters are so called because the main strokes are made in two parts, so that the stems appear as one thick and one thin line. The hollow between them is cut with a graver either on the punch or on the type after it is cast'.

'The agreeable shaded letters produced by Fournier' wrote Mr D.B. Updike 'may be looked at for the amusing and ingenious manner in which serifs on the shaded italic and roman capitals in large sizes have, by a few strokes of the graver, been made to end in a kind of "spray". This is an example of a delightful effect achieved by the simplest means. They are not to be confounded with his decorated capital letters, which are, as ornamental type-letters go, simple, and, if sparingly used, most attractive. Both had considerable vogue at that day and have been revived in ours. They were inspired by the lettering of engraved title-pages'.

We have already noted that Fournier cut nine decorated and shaded letters (page 145) and that the largest of the latter were of approximately 84 point and 108 point body sizes. These he cut 'expressly for posters and bills'. [154]

91. Joseph Fry, an eminent Bristolian, born in 1728, and William Pine, a printer, started a foundry in that city in 1764. It was known as Fry and Pine's. Later their manager Isaac Moore was admitted to the partnership. In 1768 the foundry was moved to London. Joseph Fry had two sons, Edmund and Henry, whom he admitted to the foundry in 1782. Reed refers to Edmund as probably the most learned letter-founder of his day. Like his father he had been educated for the medical profession, and had taken his degree but deafness prevented him from pursuing that calling. When it became necessary to move the foundry a second time in London and to divorce it from the printing side of the business new premises were built which became known as the Type Street Foundry. Among the many activities of the Fry's and their partners were the reproductions of the types of William Caslon I & John Baskerville. According to Reed, Dr Edmund Fry was one of the few founders 'who witnessed the then (*circa* 1800) entire abandonment of the time-honoured and graceful characters of the first Caslon' with regret.

In his specimen of 1788 Edmund Fry shows two pages of titlings headed
Ornamented Two-line letters ranging from five-line pica to two-line brevier
which are not ornamented but are shaded letters. These pages are repeated
in the Fry and Steele specimen of 1795. In the same founders' specimen of
Metal Cast Ornaments curiously adjusted to paper, of 1794, only *one* decorated
capital is shown.   [156]

92. In 1794 Edmund Fry took Isaac Steele into partnership and in the following
year issued the specimen from which our example is taken. It is typical of
many title-pages of the period 1770-1810 not only in its arrangement but
in its use of shaded types for the important lines.

For an account of the Fry's and in particular of Dr Edmund Fry—of his
great learning; his important philological work *Pantographia*; his rich collection of punches and matrices of 'learned' languages; his excellence as a cutter
of oriental punches; his design of a raised type for the blind, among his many
other activities—the reader should refer to Talbot Baines Reed, in the new,
revised and enlarged edition.

In 1824 Fry changed the name of his business appropriately to the Polyglot
Foundry. In 1828, after 46 years' continuous labour he sold the entire contents
to William Thorowgood of Fann Street, to which foundry all the material
was removed in 1829.   [158]

93. Both the Canon Italic Open and the Two-lines English Open are from the
1816 specimen book of William Caslon III. Both types are bold modern-face
letters with the addition of shading & are typical of the work of many founders
of that period.   [159]

Notes on the illustrations of fat faces

94. From one of the two undated specimen books issued by Tho. Cottrell, Letter Founder, London, *circa* 1765. These letters are referred to on page 161 where, it will be noted, Nicolette Gray regards them as the forerunners of the Fat faces. But Mr Johnson writes that the lottery handbills of the early nineteenth century illustrate the development of the design from the Bold faces, that is, the thickened versions of the normal book types.

    Cottrell was apprenticed to the first Caslon, later working in the foundry at Chiswell Street as a dresser. During his time with William Caslon I he made himself expert not only in his own department but in all those appertaining to typefounding—even the operation of punch-cutting which was practised secretly by his master and his master's son.

    In 1757, after a dispute with their employer, Cottrell and Joseph Jackson, another workman of Caslon's, were dismissed from the foundry. At first the two worked in partnership but in 1759 Jackson left the business. Reed wrote: 'Cottrell's first fount was an English roman, which, though it will compare neither with the performance of his late master, nor with the then new faces of Baskerville, was yet a production of considerable merit for a self-trained hand'. After Jackson's departure Cottrell pressed on with a series of romans, the smallest a Brevier. He cut the Engrossing which Rowe Mores refers to as Base Secretary. The same writer mentions his poster letters (four-line to twelve-line), probably cast in sand, saying that Cottrell was the first to produce such letters. His other founts include romans and italics based on those of Caslon I; a Domesday; a Latin script and 29 varieties of printer's flowers (Small Pica).

    For some reason Cottrell's specimens—at least, those that survive—are undated. He died in 1785. Nine years later his foundry became the property of Robert Thorne. What happened to the business from 1785 to 1794 remains a mystery. [160]

95. The decorated and shaded types of the eighteenth century were intended for use in books. Large letters were used towards the end of that century, and according to Rowe Mores, Thomas Cottrell was the first to produce such types—'some uncommon founts of proscription, or posting letter of great bulk and dimensions . . .' But apart from Cottrell little material of this kind was produced until the nineteenth century. From its first decade, types were

produced designed specifically for use on posters and bills, that is, for the purposes of advertisement.

The first of these advertising types were the fat faces, which the writers of the day referred to contemptuously. Hansard, for example, wrote of them as 'typographical monstrosities' and of the 'folly of fat-faced preposterous disproportions'. Mr Johnson has said that 'In the early years of the nineteenth century, the State lotteries were highly popular, and the bills issued by the various contractors who organized the sale of tickets are interesting documents for the history of jobbing types. From the year 1806 onwards, especially on the bills of one of the chief contractors, T. Bish, fat faces are generally used'. He refers also to the use of fat face types on the bills of Drury Lane Theatre from 1807 and continues 'Whatever the intentions of the original founder, the smaller sizes of the fat faces soon came into use for display in books . . . . The publishers of the more sensational books, such as reports of murder trials or political trials . . . . found these exaggerated letters suited to their purpose'.

Continental founders soon followed England's lead and the Imprimerie Nationale in Paris, writes Mr Johnson 'even took the—for them—unprecedented step of commissioning Thorne, a foreigner, in 1818, to cut some fat faces for their use as a new form of display type'. Our example, showing both roman and italic fat face, is, in the original, printed in black on yellow paper.

[162]

96. Double Pica No 2, roman and italic fat face from William Thorowgood's *New Specimen of Printing Types*, late R. Thorne's No 2, Fann Street, Aldersgate Street, London 1821. Reed, writing of this specimen of Thorowgood's said 'His first specimen-book was issued a few months after the purchase (of Thorne's foundry in 1820), and a second followed in January 1821, which may be taken as representing the contents of the foundry pretty much as Thorne left it; although even in this short space of time some additions are apparent, which formed no part of his predecessor's stock'.

Both Vincent Figgins (1815) & the Fry's (1816) show fat faces among their specimens.

[164]

97 Two pages from William Thorowgood's specimen issued on the 1st January
& 1821. This book contained the contents of Thorne's foundry much as he had
98. left it but the types on the pages we show are presumably some of Thorowgood's additions to the Thorne range. For an obvious reason it would be most

unlikely of Thorne to issue a specimen such as the six lines Pica No 1—our illustration No 97. In this example it will be noted that the serifs in the name THORN (*sic*) are all bracketed but a variant is shown on the page following our specimen, a six-lines Pica No 2 in which the serifs of the capitals in the same name (THORN, *sic*) are unbracketed, if we except the N. Although on the same body the No 2 size is a considerably heavier letter in the upper-case, a fraction larger in face and showing in the O and R considerably reduced counters. It is only slightly wider in the upper-case than the No 1.

The twelve-line Pica roman No 2 (our illustration No 98) is by no means the largest fat face in the volume. Two folding plates show 14 Line Pica roman and italic specimens headed 'Cast in mould and matrixes', and the largest fat face shown in the book is one of 24 lines Pica. Note in the 12-line pica example that the lower-case m is wider than the capital above it!   [165,166]

Notes on the illustrations
of antique or egyptian types

99. Our example, the first of what we call Egyptian types, appeared in Vincent Figgins's *Specimen of Printing Types*, 1815, under the title ANTIQUE, a name which remains an alternative today for these slab-seriffed faces. Mr Johnson thinks that Egyptian was the original name, and Antique the copy. From the evidence available it cannot be proved that Robert Thorne was the inventor of egyptian faces but the name is first used in connection with types from his foundry. Mr Johnson refers to the Figgins Antique capitals of our specimen and says that in 1820 other founders had shown the letter 'so that Thorne's priority is not beyond dispute'. A reference to lettering in the phrase 'Fashionable Egyptian Sign-Boards' appeared in 1806 (see page 169) but no Egyptian type is known in that year.

   The face was in regular use by 1817 on the bills of lottery contractors; it was used by the bookseller William Hone in 1819 and from 1821 on the bills of Drury Lane Theatre. From 1821 it was also used as a heading type in books. One of the earliest continental specimens to show the design was that of Andreae of Frankfurt in 1830. In Vincent Figgins's specimen of 1833 he shows a 20-line Pica Antique! [168]

100. Robert Thorne died in 1820 and in June of that year his foundry was put up to auction and sold complete to William Thorowgood who is said to have bought the business with the proceeds of a draw in one of the State Lotteries! In the catalogue of the sale are listed six sets of matrices in the sizes two-line Great Primer to Brevier, under the heading *Egyptian*.

   Thorowgood's first specimen book was issued in 1820 soon after the purchase and in it appear the six Egyptians. Our examples, two line Great Primer Egyptian and two line English Egyptian are taken from his second specimen book—*New Specimen of Printing Types*, late R.Thorne's, No 2, Fann Street, Aldersgate Street, London—which appeared in January 1821. The specimens shown in this book represented the stock of Thorne's foundry much as he had left it. (It is interesting to note that 132 pages of composed specimens were left in type at the time of Thorne's death). Thorowgood proceeded to organize the affairs of his new business 'with great energy' says Reed 'and no small success' despite the fact that he was neither founder nor printer. In 1822 he was sworn Letter-Founder to His Majesty and issued in that year a Greek fount. The foundry evidently prospered for Thorowgood issued specimen books in 1822, 1824, 1825, 1827, 1828 and 1829. By 1825 three sizes of Fraktur, two of Greek, one of Hebrew, and four of Russian, are part of his stock. The Frakturs & two of the Russian founts were obtained by him from Germany.

In 1828, on the retirement of Dr Edmund Fry, Thorowgood bought up the Polyglot (formerly Type Street) foundry and thus acquired a great collection of oriental and 'learned' founts, book founts, blacks, titlings and flowers. The foundry continued to expand and Thorowgood took into partnership (about 1838) one of his travellers, Robert Besley (born 1794) and the firm became Thorowgood & Besley until Thorowgood retired in 1849. The firm was then re-named Robert Besley & Co. [170]

101. From Thorowgood's *New Specimen of Printing Types*, late R. Thorne's, No 2, Fann Street, Aldersgate Street, London, 1821. This specimen book, as has been noted, represented the contents of Thorne's foundry pretty much as he left it; 'although even in this short space of time some additions are apparent, which formed no part of his predecessor's stock'. Reed refers here to the short time which elapsed between Thorowgood's purchase of Thorne's foundry in 1820 and the issue of this second specimen book in January 1821. The six-line Pica Egyptian of our example is, despite the fact that it shouts the name of the original owner of the Fann Street foundry at us, one of these additions—that is, a type cut after Thorne's death in 1820. [172]

102. Egyptian types were in regular use by 1817 on lottery bills in the style of our example. In this bill the mixture of fat face & slab-seriffed face is to be noted. [173]

Notes on the illustrations
of shadowed or three-dimensional types

103. From the *Specimen of Printing Types* by Vincent Figgins, Letter Founder, West Street, West Smithfield, London 1815. These shadowed or three-dimensional types first appeared *circa* 1815. The earliest examples were fat face outline letters with heavy black shadows. Nicolette Gray writes 'Here... the founders seem to be providing compensation for the thin stems and hair serifs of the fat face; they seem to have been very conscious of its inadequacy'. [174]

104. From *Specimen of Printing Types*, Vincent Figgins, 1833. Seven sizes of two-line letters in shade, or as we call them, shadowed or three-dimensional letters, in sizes from Great Primer to Pearl, the latter being an italic. The appearance of the first shadowed face approximately eighteen years before this specimen book was issued was a signal the other foundries did not ignore. 'The introduction' writes Mrs Gray 'was immediately enormously popular. Every founder came out in a wide range of sizes, many with italic. The variation in the width of the shadow is considerable. A significant point is the introduction of quite small sizes, and it is remarkable how the letter changes with its size. The big letter is very full and bulky, very near to its parent fat face. The small letter is almost elegant, far nearer to the succeeding outline types'. [176]

Notes on the illustrations of sans serif types

105. Our example shows the first sans serif type, a single line of titling which appeared under the name of Two lines English Egyptian in the specimen issued by W. Caslon, Junior in 1816 (the last to be issued by the firm). This forerunner of a new group of jobbing faces seems to have competed for the name given to the group of advertising faces, named by Robert Thorne, the Egyptians, which had appeared the year previously in the specimen of Vincent Figgins under the name Antique. Mr Johnson writes that 'the type itself seems to have been an unsuccessful experiment on the part of Caslon, and we hear nothing more of it until 1832. In that year Vincent Figgins displayed it under the name

sans serif (see the illustration No 106, page 180) and William Thorowgood, successor to Thorne, under the name grotesque'.

On the retirement of his father, William Caslon III, from the business in 1807, his son, also William, changed the name of the firm from W. Caslon & Son to W. Caslon, Junior. When his father died in 1833, William Caslon IV inherited the foundry, enlarging it, 'especially', remarks Reed, 'by the addition of the new-fashioned fat-faced types'. He also introduced special, built-up matrices in 1810 for the casting of large types previously produced in sand moulds. Nine years later he sold his foundry to Blake, Garnett & Co and the stock was removed to that company's premises in Sheffield. Between 1820 and 1830 the firm's name was changed to Blake and Stephenson and in 1841 became Stephenson, Blake & Co.   [178]

106. A page from *Specimen of Printing Types* by Vincent Figgins, Letter Founder, West Street, West Smithfield, London 1832. From the time of the appearance of W. Caslon Junior's single line of titling in 1816 no more was seen of the sans serif design until black, clumsy versions appeared under their correct name in this specimen of 1832. In the same 8vo book he shows ugly, rudely cut, two-line pearl sans serif capitals, & a tremendously black, eight-line pica titling: in his specimen of the following year 20-line pica sans serif letters are shown! Though sans serif appeared in the Thorowgood supplement of 1832 it is probable that Vincent Figgins was the founder who revived it.   [180]

Notes on the illustrations of reversed or cameo types

107. Lines from *A Specimen of Printing Types* in the Fann-Street Letter Foundery, London 1828. Thorowgood (W) & Co. Two lines of reversed Egyptian italic & a line of Tuscan Reversed are shown in our example from this 8vo. specimen. A note on the invention of the Tuscan face is given in a footnote on page 183 and a specimen of Brevier Tuscan is shown on page 192.   [182]

108. From the *Specimen of Printing Types* by G. W. Bower (late Bower & Bacon), Sheffield 1837, one of the minor foundries which started in Sheffield as Bower, Bacon, and Bower, *circa* 1810. While William Thorowgood in his specimen

of 1828 refers to white letters on a black ground as REVERSED types, G.W.
Bower labels similar types in his specimen, WHITE.   [184]

Notes on the illustrations of ionic types

109 The name Ionic appears to have been used for the first time in the specimen
& of Blake and Stephenson of *circa* 1833 where it is used to title an outline letter.
110. It was also used by the early Victorian typefounders as an alternative name for
Egyptian types and Nicolette Gray has described the early Ionic face as 'an
Egyptian with the slab serif bracketed and a definite differentiation between
the thick and thin strokes'.

The examples shown from the *Specimen of Printing Types* by Henry Caslon
(IV), Letter-Founder, Chiswell Street, London, *circa* 1844, are of bold types
quite unlike the Ionics of today, which are almost exclusively used as newspaper and jobbing text faces.   [186, 188]

Notes on the illustrations of outline or open types

111. A page from the *Specimen of Printing Types* issued by Vincent Figgins, London
1833. Notice that all the types are small. An even smaller size is shown on the
page following our specimen—a nonpareil outline. Outline letters had been
used years before these first types appeared—on engravings and etchings.

Vincent Figgins, born in 1766, was apprenticed to Joseph Jackson in 1782
(Jackson, born in 1733 was apprenticed to William Caslon I) and remained
with his master until the latter's death in 1792. For the last three years of his
master's life Figgins had managed the foundry for him entirely. Notwithstanding this he failed to succeed to the business and it was purchased by
William Caslon III. Figgins decided to start on his own.

The opportunity which enabled him to establish his reputation occurred
almost immediately. He was commissioned by the printer Thomas Bensley
to cut a two-line English roman to correspond with the beautiful fount previously cut by Jackson for Bensley. Figgins completed this task with distinction. Then he completed Jackson's unfinished fount of Double Pica and issued
his first single leaf specimen in 1792, following this with his first specimen-

book (five leaves) the year later. By 1798 he had a Pica Greek to his credit. A range of learned and foreign founts followed—Persian, English Telegu, a Syriac, Hebrew in 1817 (the smallest Hebrew with points, in its day, in England), a Small Pica Irish, a German Text and a Saxon, among others.

Figgins suffered, as did other founders of the time, by the complete revolution of public taste in favour of modern-face types. He had founts of the new design ready by 1815 and shows in the same specimen book examples of a new style of jobbing face, the Antiques (i.e. Egyptians).

Reed should be consulted for an account of this founder's work and that of his sons, Vincent Figgins II and James Figgins, to whom he relinquished his foundry in 1836, eight years before his death. They traded as V. & J. Figgins.

[190]

112. Two further designs in outline. They are from the *Specimen of Printing Types* by Blake and Stephenson (successors to Mr W. Caslon, of London) Letter-Founders, Sheffield, *circa* 1833. The W. Caslon referred to on the title page of this specimen was William Caslon IV to whom reference is made in the descriptive notes to illustration No 105, page 260. [192]

Notes on the illustrations of clarendon types

113 The type called Clarendon was shown in the Fann Street Letter Foundry's
& *A General Specimen of Printing Types*. London. W. Thorowgood & Co. 1848.
114. About ten years previously Thorowgood had taken into partnership one of his travellers named Robert Besley and the firm became known as Thorowgood & Co, or Thorowgood and Besley. In 1845 the foundry registered a design called Clarendon, an Egyptian with bracketed serifs attributed to Besley and cut by a skilful punch-cutter, Benjamin Fox. Immediately the copyright period of three years had elapsed the type was widely copied much to the chagrin of its originators. Further notes on this face will be found on page 195.

Thorowgood retired in 1849 and the foundry became known as Robert Besley & Co. Our examples are taken from the latter's specimen book of 1854 where the pages from the 1848 W. Thorowgood & Co. specimen are repeated. In the case of showings of founders material this use of existing settings was a common thing, the same formes being used for printing more than one edition of a specimen book. [194, 196]

Notes on the illustrations of broad-nibbed pen writing

115 The only writing sheet designed, written, and completed for her pupils by
&   the scribe, Mrs Irene Wellington, who was one of Edward Johnston's best
116. students. In a letter to the writer Mrs Wellington said 'I have not found time
     ever to do that chart as I would like, nor to finish a new one which is planned'.
     But despite Mrs Wellington's misgivings and her criticism of the 'unequal
     & horrid tails to the y' the sheet demonstrates excellently many points about
     writing with a quill or reed which students of typography, who have not as
     yet had an opportunity to handle either instrument, should know.

     In order to keep the sheet as nearly as possible same size (the original meas-
     ures 9$\frac{15}{16}$" or 252 millimetres over the line beginning with the small numeral 1
     and ending with the skeleton lower-case m) we have printed it on three pages
     despite the fact that the *Footnote concerning the diagrams* occupies only part of
     a third page.   *   *   *   [198, 200, 201]

     The examples of calligraphy on page 64 are from the hand of that 'unparalleled
     genius as a scribe', Edward Johnston. This description of Johnston appears
     in Sir Sydney Cockerell's *Foreword* to Priscilla Johnston's book on her father
     published by Faber and Faber in 1959. The three words appear on a letter
     dated 31 Jan 1913 written from Ditchling to the Reverend J. Clare Hudson
     of Horncastle in reply to a request from the latter for broad-nibbed pens cut
     ready for writing. Johnston sent a turkey's quill pen and a bamboo pen and
     wrote that certain types of steel nibs 'are v. fair but no steel pen can compare
     with a sharply cut cane or quill (tho' the steel pens will do if a person cannot
     cut his own with a true and sharp nib)'.

Notes on the illustrations
of miscellaneous display types

117. The first example of a miscellaneous display face is Bifur from the Deberny
     & Peignot foundry. It was designed by A. M. Cassandre. The second speci-
     men was cut by the Klingspor foundry which, alas, no longer exists: it is
     Rudolf Koch's Neuland. Both are titlings. The last showing is Ludwig and
     Mayer's Koloss designed by Professor J. Erbar. All are of the 1920's. [206]

APPENDIX I
Stress or Shading

In typography letters based on the circle or part circle are usually described as having either oblique or vertical stress, or shading.

OBLIQUE STRESS

If we borrow from the terminology of the compass, letters with oblique stress may be described as having the thickest parts of the strokes at points approximately North-East and South-West. The 60 point Bembo characters shown below will make this point clear and figure (b) on page 200 shows how such round forms are made with a broad-nibbed pen.

BbCeOoPpR

We use the term *approximately* because the position of the thickest parts of the strokes in these round letters with oblique stress will vary not only from type to type but may do so within the range of a single lower-case alphabet. For instance, while the lower-case e may conform perfectly to our description of a letter with oblique stress and therefore NE/SW shading, the o from the same alphabet may be very nearly vertical in stress. To illustrate this we print below examples of the original 60 point Caslon Old Face (Founders).

eo

Again while certain lower-case characters conform to the definition of letters having oblique stress or shading the capitals of the same fount may be letters having an almost vertical stress.

VERTICAL STRESS

Letters with vertical stress or shading have the thickest parts of the strokes due East & West. The letters shown below are set in 60 point Bodoni (Monotype

264

Series 135). Figure (a) on page 200 shows how letters with vertical shading are formed with a broad-nibbed pen.

BbCeOoPpR

We have used the terms *oblique* and *vertical* in describing stress or shading. For the former some writers use the term biassed (French *biais* meaning oblique), others the term *diagonal*, and yet others refer to such letters as an obliquely shaded o as a letter having a *tilted axis*. The latter, when referring to a letter with vertical stress or shading speak of it as having a *vertical axis*.

U

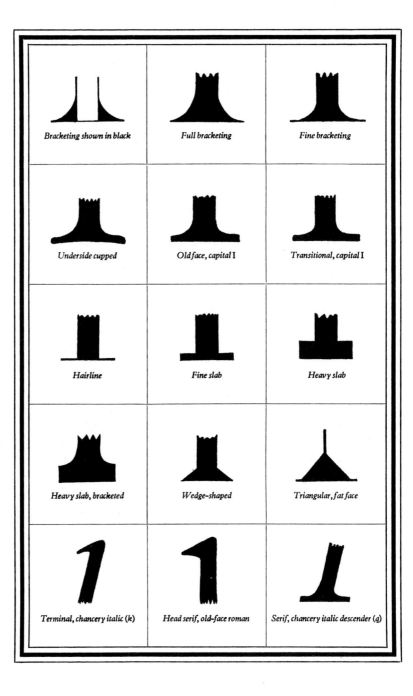

Bracketing shown in black	Full bracketing	Fine bracketing
Underside cupped	Old face, capital I	Transitional, capital I
Hairline	Fine slab	Heavy slab
Heavy slab, bracketed	Wedge-shaped	Triangular, fat face
Terminal, chancery italic (k)	Head serif, old-face roman	Serif, chancery italic descender (q)

APPENDIX II
Serifs

Francis Thibaudeau's system for the classification of type faces published in the early 1920's in Paris was based on the varying shapes of the serifs, and any complete description of a type face will, of course, include notes on the serifs, unless the face happens to be one of the large category of *sans* serifs!

The term *serifs* is used to describe the cross-strokes which finish the stems or arms of letters. They are usually drawn at right angles or obliquely to these stems or arms and may extend on both sides or only on one side. The stem of a letter may be the straight or oblique stroke of a capital or lower-case letter and the arms may belong, for example to a capital E or a lower-case k.

These finishing strokes will vary very considerably in shape and size. Some may be bracketed—our first diagram on the opposite page shows exactly what is meant by this term—or unbracketed, wedge-shaped or triangular (forms met respectively in types like Wide Latin and as terminals of the thin strokes in the fat faces). They may be cupped, hairline, fine slab, or heavy slab with or without bracketing.

All serifs are not flat on their undersides. Some are cupped or curved as in the American Type Founders Cloister, Monotype 'Garamond' Series 156, and Monotype Poliphilus. The diagrams on the opposite page will help to make these brief notes clear. Students who wish to delve deeply into the subjects of stress, of serifs, and of the nomenclature of letter forms should read Mr Joseph Thorp's TOWARDS A NOMENCLATURE OF LETTER FORMS which appeared in *The Monotype Recorder*. Volume 30. April/May 1931, & the other excellent articles by the same author which appeared in subsequent issues of the same publication.

Bibliography

Printing Types, Their History, Forms, and Use
D. B. Updike. Harvard University Press, Cambridge (Mass.) Second
Edition 1937

Type Designs. Their History and Development. A. F. Johnson. Grafton & Co,
London. Second Edition 1959

One Hundred Title-Pages. 1500–1800. A. F. Johnson. John Lane, London 1928

Four Centuries of Fine Printing. Stanley Morison. Ernest Benn Ltd, London
1924

German Incunabula in the British Museum. Stanley Morison. Gollancz,
London 1928

A History of the Old English Letter Foundries. Talbot Baines Reed.
First published in 1887 and republished in a new edition revised and
enlarged by A. F. Johnson. Faber and Faber Ltd, 1952

The Typographic Arts. Stanley Morison. Sylvan Press, London 1949

Type Designs of the Past and Present. Stanley Morison. The Fleuron Ltd,
London 1926

Ichabod Dawks and his Newsletter. Stanley Morison. Cambridge University
Press 1931

The Study of Incunabula. Dr Konrad Haebler. The Grolier Club.
New York 1933

A Survey of the MSS of Tours. E. K. Rand. The Mediaeval Academy
of America, Cambridge, Massachusetts 1929

A Dissertation upon English Typographical Founders and Founderies.
Edward Rowe Mores. London 1778

Early Type Specimen Books of England, Holland, France, Italy & Germany.
William Blades. London 1875

The Encyclopædia of Type Faces. W. Turner Berry, A. F. Johnson,
W. P. Jaspert. Blandford Press, London 1958

Early Woodcut Initials. Oscar Jennings MD. Methuen & Co. London 1908

Initials from French Incunabula. Dr Abraham Horodisch. With an introduction by Dr Hellmut Lehmann-Haupt. New York 1948

Five Hundred Years of Printing. S. H. Steinberg. Penguin Books 1955

A Book of Scripts. Alfred Fairbank. Penguin Books 1949

On Designing and Devising Type. J. van Krimpen. The Sylvan Press, London 1957

Nineteenth Century Ornamented Types and Title Pages. Nicolette Gray. Faber & Faber, London 1938

A Guide to the Processes and Schools of Engraving. The British Museum 1933

THE CHANCERY TYPES OF ITALY AND FRANCE. A. F. Johnson and Stanley Morison. *The Fleuron* No 3. London 1924

ON SCRIPT TYPES. Stanley Morison. *The Fleuron* No 4. London 1925

TOWARDS AN IDEAL ITALIC. Stanley Morison. *The Fleuron* No 5. Cambridge University Press 1926

THE 'GARAMOND' TYPES. Paul Beaujon (Mrs Beatrice Warde). *The Fleuron* No 5

THE CLASSIFICATION OF GOTHIC TYPES. A. F. Johnson. *The Library.* Vol 9. No 4. March 1929

THE EVOLUTION OF THE MODERN-FACE ROMAN. A. F. Johnson. *The Library.* Vol 11. No 3. December 1930

EARLY HUMANISTIC SCRIPT AND THE FIRST ROMAN TYPE. Stanley Morison. *The Library.* Vol. 24. Nos 1, 2. June-September 1943

A GUIDE TO PRESENT-DAY TYPES. A. F. Johnson *Paper & Print.* Nos 1-9 March 1932—Spring 1934

ON 18TH CENTURY FRENCH TYPOGRAPHY AND FOURNIER LE JEUNE. Paul Beaujon. *The Monotype Recorder.* March-April/May-June 1926

THE ITALIC TYPES OF ANTONIO BLADO AND LUDOVICO ARRIGHI. Stanley Morison. *The Monotype Recorder.* January-February 1927

THE ROMAN AND ITALIC OF JOHN BASKERVILLE. Paul Beaujon. *The Monotype Recorder.* September-October 1927

Bibliography

TOWARDS A NOMENCLATURE FOR LETTER FORMS. Joseph Thorp. *The Monotype Recorder*. April–May 1931

EXPERIMENTAL APPLICATION OF A NOMENCLATURE FOR LETTER FORMS. Joseph Thorp. *The Monotype Recorder*. July–August 1932 and Spring 1933

FAT FACES: THEIR HISTORY, FORMS AND USE. A. F. Johnson. *Alphabet & Image*. No 5. 1947

A CATALOGUE OF ITALIAN WRITING-BOOKS OF THE SIXTEENTH CENTURY. *Signature*. New Series. No 10, 1950

*   *   *

Readers will find a selected list of the writings of A. F. Johnson, compiled by Sheila Jones in *Signature*, New Series, No 13, 1951 and in the second edition of his own book, *Type Designs* pp. 167-178 a 'List of Authorities' of which Mr Johnson writes 'It is hoped that the list will be useful as a select bibliography of the subject'.

A hand list of the writings of Stanley Morison 1950-1959 compiled by P. M. Handover has recently been published. It appeared in *Motif*, No 3. September 1959.

Index

Charlemagne, and perfection of a
book-hand, 19
Chinese, printing from movable metal
types in eleventh century, 3
Chiswick Press, revival of use of
William Caslon I's types at, 97
Civilité types, Robert Granjon's, 115,
242
Clarendon types, 195; notes on
illustrations of, 262
Classification of type faces, xxii, 207
Cockerell, Sir Sydney Carlyle, 263
Colonna, Francesco, 31
Coote, Edmund, 243
Cottrell, Thomas, type designer, 117,
131, 161, 230, 254
Court Hand, 115, 117, 243
Cursive or chancery hands and the
development of italic types, 43
Cursorials, 129, 131, 246

DAWKS, Ichabod, 246
Day, John, 53
Decorated types, 110, 111, 145, 147;
notes on illustrations of, 248
Didot, Firmin, 175, 229, 230, 235
Didot, François Ambroise, 76, 110,
147, 229
Didot, Pierre, 229, 235
Dijck, Christoffel van, 32
Directors, small letters printed as
guides for scribes, 248
Display types, the, 109, 207, 263
Duerer, Albrecht, 215
Durandus type, 212

EGENOLFF-BERNER foundry,
Frankfurt, 55, 220
Egyptian types, 169; notes on
illustrations of, 257
Emblem books, 223
Engrossing, 117, 243, 244
Enschedé foundry, Haarlem, 61,
224, 249, 250

Erbar, Professor J, 263
Estienne, Robert, 220

FAT FACE types, 161, 167; notes on
illustrations of, 254
Fere-humanistica or gotico-antiqua, 5,
211
Feyerabend, Sigismund, 215
Figgins, Vincent, 65, 169, 179, 191,
260, 261
Financière, 127
Fleischman, Johann Michel, 61, 224,
228
Fournier, Pierre Simon (le jeune) 61,
76, 89, 110, 145, 225, 226, 249
Fox, Benjamin, punch-cutter, 262
Fraktur, 7, 213, 215
French Antique, 171
Fry, Edmund, typefounder, 253
Fry, Joseph, typefounder, 252

GARAMOND, Claude, 32, 59, 75
Gill, Eric, 237
Gillé, J. G, 147, 175
Giolito, Gabriel, 245
Gold, printing in, in fifteenth
century, 219
Gothic or black-letter types, 5, 17;
notes on illustrations of, 211
Gothic or mediæval script types, 113;
note on availability of, 117; notes
on illustrations of, 240
Gotico-antiqua, see *Fere-humanistica*
Grandjean, Philippe, 61, 75, 87, 224,
228, 233
Granjon, Robert, 53, 115, 221, 223,
242
Greek type, first book used in, 218
Griffo, Francesco, type designer, 220
Gryphius, Sebastien, 223
Gutenberg, Johann, 3, 5, 211

March 10/08